KU-470-483

Dedicated with respect and admiration
to the memory of two remarkable people:

Cary Lu
and
Arlene Myers

TABLE OF CONTENTS

Acknowledgments

This book, more than most, owes a debt of gratitude to a large number of people—from the product managers who gave permission to provide you with Microsoft software to the two teams that worked to produce not only the paper you hold in your hand but the CD bound into the back. Individual and collective thanks belong to all, but especially to the following core contributors:

At Microsoft Press, Editorial: Steven Guty, acquisitions director and project instigator; Ron Lamb, project editor and shepherd of both the book and the Goodies on your CD; Jim Fuchs, technical editor extraordinaire, capturer of screen illustrations, and gatherer of those same Goodies; Joel Panchot, artist and creator of the drawings in this book; Peggy Herman and Richard Carter, compositors and builders of the printed page; Cheryl Penner and other members of the Proof department, trackers of grammatical sins and other errors no longer to be seen.

At Microsoft Press, Interactive: William Pardi, program manager, liaison, and patient supplier of test "builds"; Michael Bronsdon, product planner and visionary; Josephine Lowry, project editor and overseer of CD lesson content; and Jacki Bricker, lead tester and guardian of product "goof-proofing."

In addition, special thanks to Henry Cooper, singer/guitarist, and Kim Field, multitalented editorial director of Microsoft Press, for permission to include the upbeat sound clips from their recording, "Baby Please," and to Travis Beaven for volunteering the time needed to film and produce the videotaped waterfall on your CD.

And finally, very personal thanks to Mark, Kate, and Eileen...just because.

01110100...
00010110011...
01101000110011...
☺0001011001110...
01101000110☺101011001...
0111010011001☺101011001...
1001011001☺10101011001...

Introduction

You would like to curl up on the couch and watch TV or read the latest best-seller from your favorite thriller/romance/science fiction writer. Instead, you're about to start wading into a book about computers. :-(

That frowning face made out of punctuation marks is called an "emoticon" (ee-mow-tick-on). It's used a lot in email and is just one of those fun things people do with computers—in this case, to add some human feeling. Here are some others. This :-) is a smile, this :-o is surprise or amazement, and this ;-) is a wink.

Your preference for *Seinfeld,* a novel, a video, or a ball game is certainly reasonable, because just about everyone else would make the same choice. But…sometime recently you decided the time was right to invest many hundreds to possibly several thousands of dollars in that computer on your desk or dining-room table, and now you'd like to get your money's worth.

Sadly, technology hasn't yet advanced to the point where you can learn such topics in your sleep, but if you're willing to provide a little patience and a little effort, this book and its companion CD will do their best to help you learn to use your PC not only competently but with confidence— even (or especially) if you broke out in hives when you saw the high-tech terms in the "specs" (technical specifications) for the machine at the computer store. ("16 MB Sync DRAM, expandable to 64 MB." "512 K internal pipeline burst cache." Yippee…)

The book will not, of course, take you from beginner to computing grand-master. Reaching such an exalted level takes years of practice, keen interest, and more time than most people want to spend learning about something that's supposed to make life easier. But you *will* find yourself easing into the information age, even if you've never touched a CD, not to mention a whole computer, in your life.

About You

In leading you into the (truly) fascinating world of computers, neither the book nor the CD will assume more about you than that:

- You have a Windows computer plugged together according to the manufacturer's instructions, and you and it are ready to get to know each other.

- You're going to work through the book from beginning to end. This sounds silly, but like most things, learning to use a computer means you start with simple tasks and build on what you know.

- You're going to use the CD as you work through the book. This one is particularly important because the CD and the book are designed to work together to help you learn.

About the Book

The first few—very few—pages are devoted to explaining what that machine is and why it does what it does. Soon enough, however, you'll flip the On switch, put your hands on the keyboard, and start to learn by doing. You'll begin with startup, and then you'll learn how to set up and use the CD. From there, you'll poke and prod your way to knowing how to use your computer to your advantage. As you work through the book:

- You'll periodically be directed to recorded lessons on the CD. At first, the lessons will be animated overviews and question/answer sessions dealing with a topic such as using the mouse. As you become more experienced, the lessons will turn into interactive sessions that guide you through some aspect of using your PC.

- The text of the book will describe computing as a whole in the kind of detail you'll need in order to begin developing the "intuition" that guides more experienced users. The descriptions won't be technical, so don't worry that you'll be wading into a lot of computerese here. You'll see computer terms, sure, but only because they're useful. After all, "mouse" is much easier on the eyes than "the hand-sized plastic thing with the skinny cable at one end."

- Along with the CD-based lessons and the text descriptions, the book will also expand on the topic at hand wherever possible by walking you through step-by-step sessions that help you apply what you've learned to take control of your own computer. These sessions are designed to take off the training wheels and put you in charge. Through them, you'll take your first independent steps onto "the road ahead," "the bridge to the 21st century," the...oh, you know.

Here's hoping you enjoy the journey.

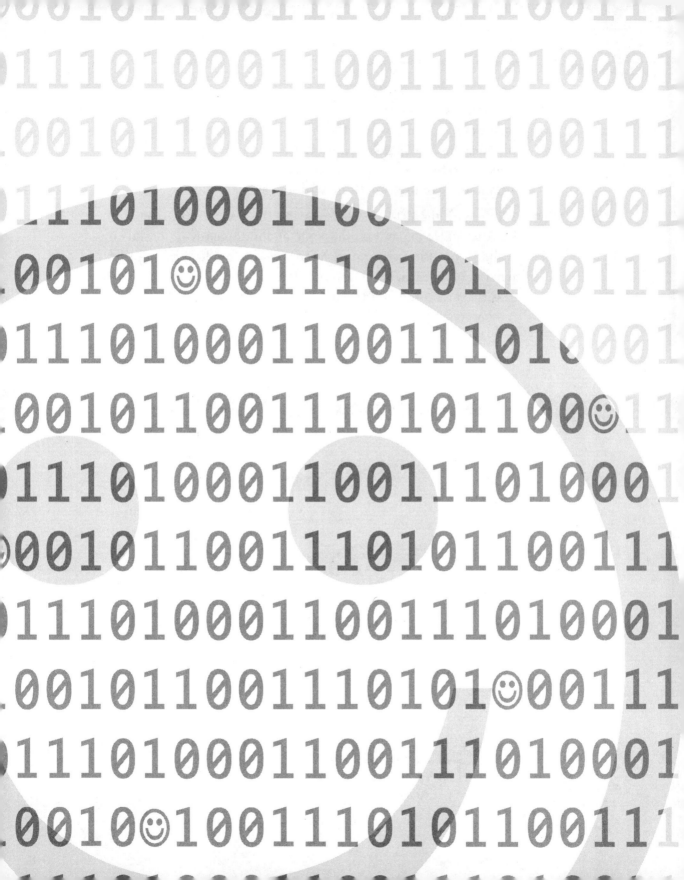

Up Close and Personal

When people set about learning to use computers, they often—perhaps usually—prefer to learn the how-to's and skip the what-for's. But even though learning what to do without figuring out why you do it *is* faster and *can* be all you need in most situations, relying on ritual alone won't really give you a feeling for the computer and its software. The result, just as in memorizing only one way to reach a destination, can leave you high, dry, and lost when you make a wrong turn somewhere along the way. But life with a PC doesn't have to be that way.

The first step in becoming comfortable with a computer is figuring out what this machine is all about. A computer is a little different from a TV, a stereo, or a VCR. Why?

A Most Adaptable Tool

To start with, remember that your telephone doesn't type, your toaster doesn't add, and your calculator doesn't draw. Your computer, on the other hand, can help you type, add, draw, balance the budget, and even play games. Unlike other machines, it is an electronic jack-of-all-trades that can adapt to performing many different jobs, and the reason it can do all this is because of two features that distinguish all computers.

- First, as you know, a computer relies on *programs* that tell it what to do. In other words, a computer is *programmable,* so it can be told how to do this and that even if "this" is as different from "that" as writing the Great American Novel is different from blasting aliens back to Zonkland.

- Second, a computer is *interactive*. Thanks to its programs, your computer responds to every action on your part with an appropriate reaction on its part. This is how it interacts with you to accept the words you type and display the documents you want to see.

Programs and interactivity are what your computer is all about.

A PC Is Both Hardware and Software

Whether it's a home PC, a laptop, or even a small handheld computer that fits comfortably in your pocket, every working computer is a mix of both *hardware* and *software*. Hardware is the catchall term for the entire mass of electronics that came home with you from the store in one or two boxes labeled *This End Up* and *Handle With Care*. Software, as you already know, is just a fancy word for programs—programs that run the gamut from games to word processors to spreadsheets, electronic checkbooks, and more.

While hardware is always visible, software is normally invisible. That is, you don't see the actual *code* that makes up a program. Instead, you see the *medium,* such as a floppy disk or a CD-ROM, that the code is stored on, and when the program is running, you see the *interface* it presents to you on the screen.

You don't, however, just slap hardware and software together and get instant computing. Something has to make that happen.

Three Easy Pieces

To understand what a computer does, no matter how complex its work happens to be, just remember that a computer always computes in the same three stages, known as *input, processing,* and *output,* as shown in Figure 1-1.

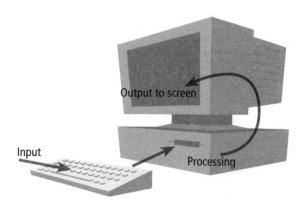

Figure 1-1.   *What a computer does when it computes.*

■ Input, whether it represents a drawing, a recipe, or a joystick movement, is whatever information or commands you enter into the computer.

■ Processing is what the computer does when it uses a program to churn your input around. Processing is the part of computing that often used to be called "number crunching," though truth to tell, arithmetic represents a small portion of what computers are now used for.

■ Output, of course, is the result of processing input.

Three Basic Pieces of Hardware

Although computers come in a wide variety of shapes and sizes, they are all characterized by a few pieces that neatly match the three things a computer does. They are:

■ The keyboard and mouse. Pretty hard to miss or misinterpret, these are your main ways to provide input. They are, in geek-speak, your *primary input devices.*

■ The "box," or system unit. This is the heart of your setup, where the processing takes place. It contains the computer's processor and memory, its disk drives, and probably a modem and a CD-ROM drive.

■ The monitor. The TV-like part of your PC, the monitor displays the results of whatever processing, including just plain typing, has gone through the box. The monitor is, to switch again to geek-speak, your *primary output device.*

In addition, you can add assorted hardware known as *peripherals* to your PC. Peripherals, which some people think of as expensive add-ons and others consider must-have toys, attach to the box via cables that plug into those odd-looking connectors (called *ports*) on the back of the system. Some peripherals, like joysticks and scanners, are input devices; some, such as speakers and printers, are output devices; some, such as external modems (which send *and* receive information), are both. What type of device a peripheral happens to be depends entirely on what it's designed to do.

Figure 1-2 shows a typical desktop computer setup with a standard set of peripherals.

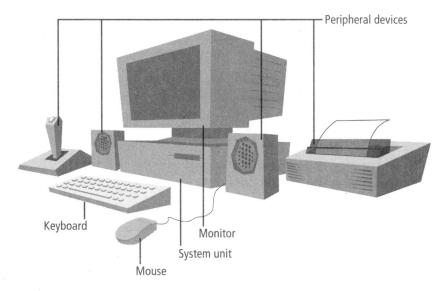

Figure 1-2.   *A typical computer system with the usual add-ons.*

First, You "Boot" It

If you're a little nervous about using a PC, don't be. Your PC doesn't bark, can't bite, and won't ever call you dumb unless you learn to program and teach it how. It won't break if you press the wrong key, either, so don't worry about hurting it.

Knowing what a computer is and what it does still doesn't make it anything more than a large ornament on your desktop. You have to use it. That's the good part, and that's what this book is all about, so…it's time to make your computer compute. The first things to learn (assuming you haven't done them already) are how to start it and how to stop it. Both are simple.

Startup

Sometime, somewhere, you'll probably hear someone talk about "booting the computer." *Booting* is the techie term for starting the machine. Although the saying might make you picture someone drop-kicking a PC across the room, the expression actually comes from "pull yourself up by your boot-straps." A PC, of course, has no boots and therefore no straps to pull, but it does haul itself up in the sense that once the electricity starts to flow, the computer wakes itself and gets ready to work without help from anyone, including you.

To boot the computer:

1. If this is your first startup, you might want to make a quick check of the cables and plugs to be sure that all connections fit snugly. (Also, read the box on the next page titled "Getting to Know You" because you'll have a small bit of setting up to do. It's not difficult. In fact, explaining it takes longer than doing it.)

2. Check the floppy-disk drive to be sure it's empty.

 OTE If there's a disk in your floppy drive at startup, your PC displays a rather unfriendly message about a "non-system disk or disk error." Don't be dismayed if you see that message sometime. The situation is neither serious nor anything to get depressed about. Just open the drive door or remove the floppy and press the Spacebar or one of the alphabet keys. Off you'll go.

---

3. Turn on the computer and, if necessary, the monitor.

Whenever you start the computer, remember the monitor. People have been known to forget about the monitor switch—or even leave the monitor unplugged—and then spend ages agonizing over a "broken" display. The result: a blush and a classic Homer Simpson "doh!" moment when they figure out the problem.

Getting to Know You

The very first time—and only the first time—you start a new PC, you see a series of questions before you boot into Microsoft Windows proper. The electronic equivalent of filling out a warranty card, these questions simply ask for a little information (your name, for instance) and for the number (similar to a product serial number) on the Certificate of Authenticity attached to the copy of Windows included with your PC. The numbers are on the certificate after the words "Product ID," and they take this form: xxxxx-OEM-xxxxxxx-xxxxx (where the x's stand for numbers). Just type the numbers in, using the number keys at the top of the keyboard, when Windows requests them. Although the spaces you type into are little boxes, you don't even have to press the Tab key to move from box to box. Windows does that for you. When you finish with each question, slide the mouse on your desktop until the arrow-shaped pointer is on top of the appropriate onscreen button, and then quickly press and release the left-hand mouse button. Before you know it, you'll be done.

What Goes On in There

Whenever you start your PC, you hear the machine begin to hum, you see various lights blink on, and you probably hear a beep. All this is normal; the computer is checking itself and the equipment attached to it somewhat in the way you stretch, yawn, and look at the clock when you wake up. At about the same time, you also see some technical-looking messages begin to appear (the actual term is *scroll*) on the screen. All this is normal too, the computer's equivalent of muttering to itself as it wakes up.

After your PC has gone through its basic routines, it ends startup by handing control over to a master program known as the *operating system* or, as

---

OTE Although the text simply refers to Windows, you should know that Windows, as a product, has been around since the late 1980s. Just as a 1998 car is different from (and better than) its 1980s predecessors, so too is your Windows different (and better than) its ancestors. Whereas cars are known by model years, however, Windows and other computer programs are known by versions. This book is for Windows 95 or a later version. It does not cover earlier versions, such as the one known as Windows 3.1.

---

cyber-smarties like to call it, the *OS* ("oh-ess"). There are a number of different operating systems, including the Mac OS, which runs on the Apple Macintosh, and yours, which is Microsoft Windows.

Figure 1-3 shows what Windows typically looks like at startup.

IP Don't worry if your screen doesn't match the illustration exactly. Words like My Computer, for instance, might not be underlined. (They will be shortly, and you'll be the one to make it happen—painlessly, and that's a promise.) At any rate, such variations aren't important for now. What *is* important is that you see all or most of the items in the illustration—in particular, the long gray bar (known as the taskbar) across the bottom and the pictures (icons) labeled My Computer, Inbox, and Recycle Bin.

In case you're wondering...the background for the illustrations in this book has been deliberately lightened from the normal black— just to make the pages look a little nicer for you. Don't worry about the difference. Everything else is the same.

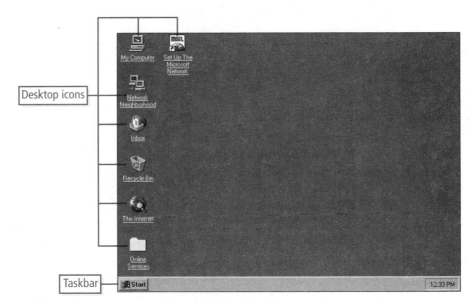

Figure 1-3.   *Windows at startup.*

It Doesn't Look Like That At All!
If your screen looks completely different, it could be that the manufacturer has set it up to show a customized startup for you. In that case, you should be able to find a "return to Windows" or a "quit and go to Windows" option on the screen that will take you to the view shown in the illustration. If you can't find such an option, check the documentation for your computer.

The Gooey Desktop

After startup, what you always see on the screen—what you're looking at now—is the Windows *desktop*. Like the physical desktop on which your computer sits, the Windows desktop is home base. It's where Windows starts you off at the beginning of every session with your computer.

Technically, this desktop represents the visual side of Windows known as its *graphical user interface,* or *GUI* ("gooey"), a fancy name that simply tells you Windows is *graphical* because it uses icons instead of complicated lines of computer text to communicate with the *user* (that's you) through a shared onscreen *interface* you both can understand.

Now, on to actually doing something—in this case, a necessary something if you want to use the CD in the back of the book.

A First Look at Your CD

The CD is *very* easy to use, but it is unlike a music CD in that it needs to be *installed* on your computer. Why is this? Because a computer is really stupid. It can't do anything unless it's given extremely detailed instructions—the kind that are sooo simple (the term computer people use is *atomic,* after atoms) that even this literal-minded machine can't possibly misinterpret them. For instance:

- Remember the number 1.
- Remember the number 2.

- Add the number 1 to the number 2.

- Remember the result.

- Show the result on the screen.

- Et cetera, et cetera, et cetera.

(Actually, the instructions are more detailed than that, but you get the general idea.)

It's said that someone once mistook the CD-ROM drive for a cup holder, and it broke. Urban legend? Maybe. Regardless, if you're wondering why the text goes into such excruciating detail here, it's to make sure that your first use of a CD-ROM drive is as pleasant as possible.

At any rate, instructions like these are in the programs on your CD, and in order for you to use any of the lessons on the CD, the programs that make it all happen must first be installed on your computer. This process, often known as *setup,* is simple, but it *can* take a few minutes, during which you might wonder what's going on and whether you've done everything right.

That's understandable. Installing a program might seem kind of a technical thing to jump into if you've never touched a computer before, but don't worry. The following steps explain the entire process, beginning to end. In addition, the process itself has been made as painless as possible *because* the CD was designed especially for computing newcomers, and its creators are a wise and thoughtful bunch.

Just follow the instructions, taking as long as you feel you need, and you'll be fine. Like the lessons and everything else in the book, the instructions here have been tested a number of times to be sure they work correctly.

Inserting the CD

The first step is, of course, to put the CD into your CD-ROM drive. How you do this depends on the type of drive you have. Some drives open when you press a button; others open when you flip the drive "door" down. In addition, some drives allow you to simply place the CD in the drive; others ask you to place the CD in a *caddy* like the one shown in Figure 1-4 on the next page.

- If you do not need a caddy, open the CD-ROM drive, place the CD in it (printed side up), and gently close the drive door.

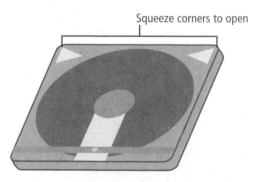

Squeeze corners to open

Figure 1-4.   *A CD-ROM caddy.*

■ If you do need a caddy, open the caddy by squeezing the corners labeled in the illustration and place the CD in it, printed side up. Close the caddy and turn it so that the arrow (also shown in the illustration) is facing away from you, and then slide the caddy into the drive. If necessary, close the drive door.

From here on, the CD takes over the job for you.

Installing the CD

The CD has been designed with a feature called *autoplay,* which means it begins running soon after you insert the disc in your CD-ROM drive. Actual installation of the CD, however, will take either a few seconds or about 10 minutes or so. Why the big difference? Because the lessons on the CD rely on Microsoft Internet Explorer, and if Internet Explorer, or IE ("eye-ee") as it's often called, has not yet been set up to run on your computer, the CD installs IE for you. This is the part that takes a little time, because IE is a substantial program and requires several minutes to move from the CD to your hard disk, which is the place it must call home. Because the process can be either very short or rather long, the following list explains what goes on, step by step:

1. A small gray box appears for a short time to tell you that it is preparing a program called the InstallShield Wizard, which will guide you through the rest of the setup process. This is one of the features that make installation so easy.

2. Your screen changes to a simple graphic display with the words *PCs for Beginners* in the upper left corner and setup continues.

If IE has been set up on your computer, installation ends here and the CD launches directly into its first screen, so you can skip ahead to the next section, titled "What You're Looking at Now."

On the other hand, if you see the message shown in Figure 1-5, the setup program on the CD has determined that Internet Explorer has not been installed on your computer. It is asking permission to install it for you. If you choose not to install Internet Explorer, setup stops and you will not be able to use the lessons on the CD.

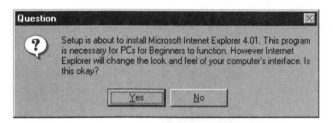

Figure 1-5.   *You might need to install Internet Explorer 4.01.*

NOTE   The Internet Explorer you install here is the same program you can use to explore the Internet itself. If you're wondering whether you can install IE now and use a different Internet *browser* later on, the answer is yes, you can. As you'll see in Chapter 9, you can easily install more than one Internet browser and choose whichever one you want, when you want.

To install Internet Explorer, press the Enter key on your keyboard. At this point, the PCs for Beginners setup program passes the ball to the Internet Explorer setup program, which looks like the screen shown in Figure 1-6 on the next page.

This is the part of installation that's going to take a few minutes. You don't have to do anything, however, so just sit back and relax. Oh, and during setup, don't worry if:

■ You hear your hard disk chunking away. That's IE moving from the CD to your hard disk.

■ Things slow down or even seem to stop for a few seconds. It can happen.

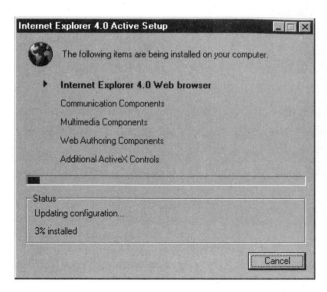

Figure 1-6.   *Installing Internet Explorer is painless.*

- Your screen flickers or even goes blank for a short time. That's OK too.

- You see messages like *extracting DirectAnimation* in the Status area. Modern-day programs usually consist of many different pieces. Setup knows what to install and when.

When IE's setup program finishes, it might *restart* your computer for you. Again, this is to be expected, so don't worry.

After your computer restarts, you go to the first screenful of information on the CD.

You're done, and congratulations. Although you probably didn't mean to when you started this chapter, you've just installed your first computer program.

What You're Looking at Now

The first screenful of information the lesson CD offers you looks like Figure 1-7.

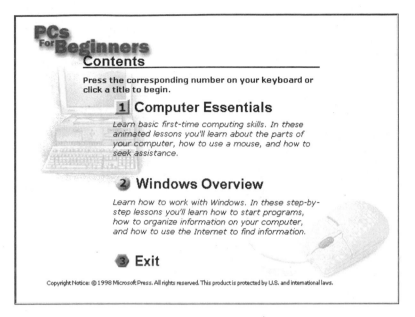

Figure 1-7. *A first look at the CD.*

The first two items on this screen—Computer Essentials and Windows Overview—take you to two different sets of lessons:

- Computer Essentials consists of 7 "goof-proof" animated lessons that introduce you to the basics of using a computer.

- Windows Overview consists of an additional 13 lessons that have you interact with your computer to perform tasks related to using and managing Windows.

If you wish, you can run through all the lessons in one go. Or, you can skip the lessons and work through the examples in the book. Or, you can go through the lessons as the book refers you to them. If you take this last (ahem, preferred) course, the book will refer you to every lesson on the CD as you need it. Each reference to a lesson will be in a box titled "Try It."

Since you've gone to the trouble of installing the CD and now have it on your screen, try taking it for a spin. Here's your first "Try It" box.

Try It

The logical first lesson to try on the CD is one that reviews computer basics. Here's how to start the lesson:

- If you're comfortable using a mouse, slide it on your desktop until a "pointer" shaped like a hand is on the number 1, and then *click* the left mouse button by quickly pressing and releasing the button.

- If you prefer to use the keyboard, press the 1 key at the top of your keyboard.

Either action takes you to the introduction to "Computer Essentials." From this point on, just follow the instructions that tell you to press the left or right arrow keys. When your screen looks like Figure 1-8, press the 1 key at the top of your keyboard.

When you reach the point shown in Figure 1-9, just leave the CD running for a few seconds. You'll be coming back to it in the very next section.

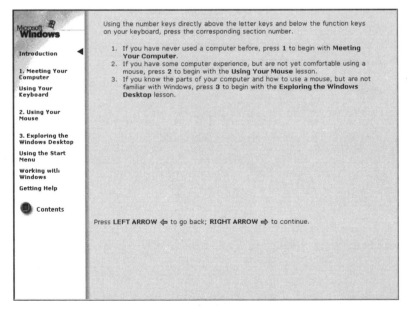

Figure 1-8.   *The last PCs for Beginners introduction screen.*

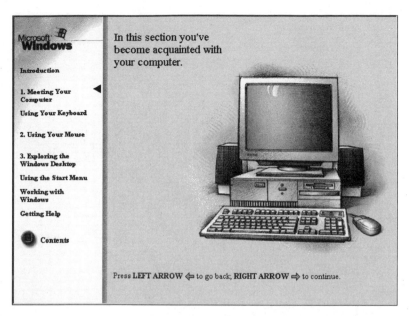

Figure 1-9.   *Leave the CD running when you see this screen.*

And now, back to getting to know your PC.

A Closer Look at the Desktop

As you learned earlier in the chapter, the Windows desktop is the place from which you start working with your PC. It's home base. It's control central. It's the *virtual* (meaning not real, but *like* something in the real world) representation of your wood or metal desktop. It's also a highly customizable place that you can fiddle with, to make it just the launching pad you want for the programs you use and the documents you work on.

As you saw in the lesson, and as you can see on your own screen, every Windows desktop comes with a *taskbar* across the bottom, and every task-bar comes with a big *Start* button at the left that helps you tell your computer what to do. Each desktop also comes decorated with a group of icons.

Try It

Unlike the image on a TV screen, the Windows desktop is made up of a number of different parts that respond to your mouse. For an overview of the main pieces of the Windows desktop, try the lesson titled "Exploring the Windows Desktop." You should be looking at the final screen of the lesson "Meeting Your Computer." Here's how to get to the one you want:

1. Slide the mouse on your desktop to move the arrow-shaped pointer on the screen.

2. Move the pointer to the title of lesson 3, "Exploring the Windows Desktop."

3. When the pointer becomes a hand shape, keep it on the lesson title and click the mouse by quickly pressing and releasing the left mouse button.

As before, follow the instructions on your screen. When you finish the lesson, you'll need to quit the CD so that you can do a little practicing with Windows itself, outside the lesson environment. To exit the CD, press the Esc key (upper left corner of the keyboard). When a message appears asking if you're sure you want to quit, press the Enter key.

(Quitting, by the way, means you're just leaving temporarily. You can easily go back to the CD anytime, as you'll soon see.)

As you begin to customize your own desktop, you'll add other icons to it and get rid of icons you no longer want, but when you start off with a new system, you typically begin with a group of *default* (put there for you) icons. The basic ones are labeled in Figure 1-10.

■ My Computer is your way to see everything on your system, from your disk drives to your documents. My Computer is not the only way to see what you have, but it's a handy one that's always in front of you at startup.

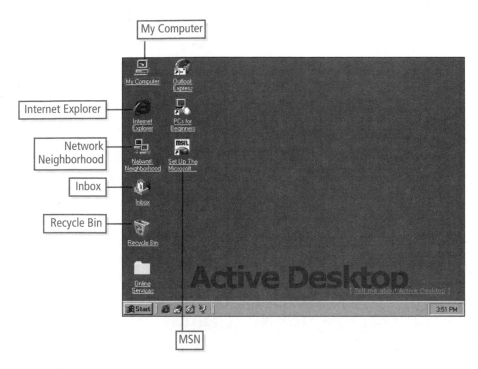

Figure 1-10.   *The basic Windows 95 icons.*

- The Inbox is your electronic message center, the place from which you send and receive email, either to and from the office or over the Internet (which many people are finding invaluable for keeping in touch).

- The Recycle Bin is your politically correct trash container, the place where you toss unwanted documents. Like a real recycle bin, it lets you salvage documents you throw away by mistake—at least until you empty it.

- The Internet Explorer icon gives you access to the Internet, the global network everyone's talking about. Chances are it won't be long till you're "surfing" the 'Net just like millions of others, from kids to grandmas. To do so, however, you need an *Internet Service Provider,* or *ISP* ("eye-ess-pea"), which is an organization that provides the underpinnings needed for Internet connections. (No, you can't just "call up" the Internet.) There are many ISPs, but just in case you want to take the easy way, Microsoft provides...

■ The MSN icon, which enables you to subscribe to—and later connect with—the Microsoft Network, an online service that offers both Internet access and certain members-only features ranging from news and entertainment to a live Internet Gaming Zone (your kids will thank you), travel services, and ways to research and buy airline tickets or your next car.

Depending on how your manufacturer set up your computer, you might also have a folder icon labeled Online Services, or you might have icons for other online services, such as CompuServe or America Online. In addition, you might see icons for various preinstalled programs and for Netscape Navigator, an Internet browser comparable to Microsoft's Internet Explorer, which is part of Windows. These icons, like those mentioned in the text, give you access to the programs or services they represent.

Calling It Quits (Until Next Time)

You've spent a fair amount of time with your PC at this point, and you've done quite a bit by installing the CD and trying a few lessons. If you're ready for a break, you probably want to shut the machine down for a while. Don't, however, just turn it off.

Once upon a time, when computers were simpler and less powerful, you actually could save your work, quit your programs, and turn off the computer. But these days, everything is more sophisticated and more "bulletproof," as well as being a lot friendlier and easier to use. In keeping with all this sophistication, Windows asks you not to just turn the computer off when you finish using it but to give it a chance to put its electronic house in order and generally prepare itself to run properly the next time you start up. This is good.

Here, then, is the correct way to shut down. If you haven't done this before, you might want to try it now, even if you plan to continue on to Chapter 2 and the lessons on the CD. Because you might not yet be comfortable using a mouse, the following sets of steps tell you how to shut down with either the mouse or the keyboard.

What Happens If I Leave It On?

Some people leave their office computers running all or most of the time. If you're taking a short break of maybe a few minutes to an hour or so, you can leave your computer running too—*provided* it's a nice day outside and the power company isn't working on the lines to your house. Otherwise, it's much wiser to shut down a home computer when you're not going to be using it for some time. Not only does shutting down save energy (admittedly not *that* much, but some) but, much more importantly, it prevents possible damage to the computer's circuitry if your power flickers or goes out.

Oh…why can an office computer be left on then? Because office buildings, at least those that are heavily computerized, are generally equipped with backup power sources that maintain a steady flow of electricity to the machines. Only rarely does their power get cut off abruptly. Of course, if it does, the computers go out like the proverbial lightbulb. Sometimes, the machines are damaged. Always, any work on them that hasn't been recently saved goes bye-bye. Such occurrences have been known to cause a fair amount of impolite language.

Mouse Steps

To shut down with the mouse:

1. Move the mouse until the arrow-shaped mouse *pointer* is resting on the Start button at the left edge of the taskbar.

2. Hold the mouse still, and *click* by quickly pressing and releasing the left mouse button, which is highlighted in Figure 1-11.

Figure 1-11. *Press and release the left mouse button to click.*

Clicking makes a *menu* of commands slide up from the Start button.

3. Move the mouse so that the mouse pointer moves to the last command (Shut Down) on the menu. You know you're there when a dark highlight covers the command name.

4. Click the left button again while the command is highlighted. Now you'll see a small *dialog box* offering several options:

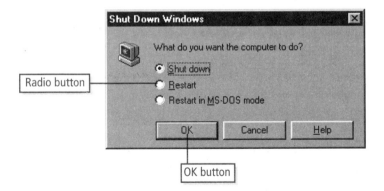

Notice that a dark dot is in the small circle (called a *radio button*) to the left of the Shut Down option. This dot shows you which option Windows will carry out if you continue.

5. To shut down, then, place the mouse pointer on the big rectangular OK button (labeled in the illustration) and click the left mouse

button. Now wait a few seconds while Windows puts its house in order. When it's through, you see the message *It's now safe to turn off your computer.*

6. Now you can turn off the power to your computer. Don't forget the monitor too, if necessary.

Keyboard Steps

If you decide to use the keyboard to shut down, use the keys shown in Figure 1-12.

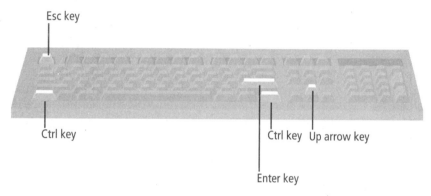

Esc key

Ctrl key

Ctrl key Up arrow key

Enter key

Figure 1-12. *The keys you need to shut down with the keyboard.*

To shut down:

1. Hold down the key labeled Ctrl. Still holding the key down, press the key labeled Esc.

2. These keys make a *menu* of commands slide up from the Start button at the left edge of the taskbar.

3. Press the up arrow key, and a dark highlight covers the last command (Shut Down) on the menu. This is what you want, so...

4. Press the Enter key to tell Windows to activate the Shut Down command. Now you see the following dialog box and radio button described in the steps for shutting down with the mouse.

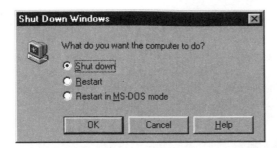

5. When you just want to turn off the computer and quit for a while, you want the Shut Down option—the one with the dark dot in the round *radio button.*

6. Windows chooses the Shut Down option by default, so everything is A-OK for shutdown. Press the Enter key. As described earlier, Windows puts itself to bed and tells you when it's done with the message *It's now safe to turn off your computer.*

7. Turn off the computer and the monitor, if necessary. You're done.

What About Those Other Choices?

As you saw, the Shut Down dialog box offers more than a simple "turn it off" option. What are those other choices, and when do you use them? To be honest, probably not all that often. When you get deeper into computing, however, you might need them once in a while. For future reference, here's what those options mean and when you're most likely to use them:

■ Restart. This option restarts Windows without turning off the computer. To choose it, click the radio button to the left of Restart and then click OK. You don't need to restart, or *reboot,* very often—usually only when a program causes problems. (By the way, these instructions are mouse-only because when and if you need this option, you'll be an experienced "mouser.")

■ Restart in MS-DOS mode. This option also restarts the computer without turning it off, but instead of taking you to Windows, it sets up the computer to work with an older operating system called MS-DOS, which is now part of Windows. To choose Restart in MS-DOS mode, click the radio button to the left of this option and then click OK. Try this option if you have a non-Windows game that is not running correctly.

And as for those other buttons in the Shut Down dialog box:

- Click the Cancel button if you change your mind about quitting.

- Click the Help button if you want Windows itself to display information about the different shutdown options.

That's it for now. Next stop: getting to know your mouse and keyboard.

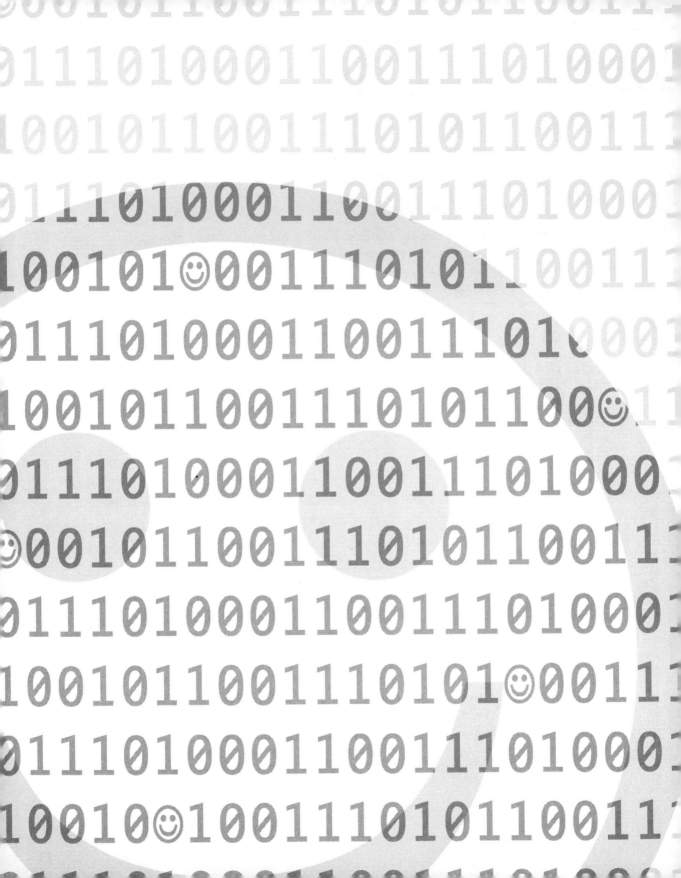

The Mouse and Keyboard

As you know, the mouse and the keyboard are your primary input devices—the main tools you use to communicate your wants and needs to Microsoft Windows and to your applications. Each of these devices has its strengths, and each is necessary for using a computer effortlessly and well:

- Because Windows is so graphical, your mouse provides by far a better way than the keyboard to choose items on the screen, start programs, arrange your desktop, and so on.

- The keyboard is not only preferable but essential for entering data and performing tasks that require more than a simple "do this" command.

The Mouse

As you probably know, you roll the mouse around on your (physical) desktop. As you roll it, an arrow-shaped pointer moves on the screen, matching direction and relative distances traveled, as shown in Figure 2-1 on the next page.

This pointer is what you use to, well, *point* to items on the screen so that you can *select* the one you want your PC to concentrate on.

Figure 2-1. *The mouse and its pointer match speed and direction.*

Mouse trivia. The plural of mouse is mice, not mouses or meece. And this one's fun: You move in footsteps, mice move in mickeys—so many mickeys forward, back, or to the side. Technically, one mickey is defined as the smallest mouse movement a computer can detect. (And yes, a famous mouse in red pants had something to do with this.)

Although a mouse is easy to use, a few commonsense tips will help you use it well:

- Use a mouse pad. If you don't have one, use a pad of paper, a book, or another smooth, slightly textured surface. Moving a mouse on a rough or uneven surface can cause the pointer to jerk or stall on the screen whenever the little ball (shown below) underneath the mouse stops rolling.

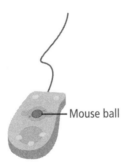

Mouse ball

- If you move the mouse to the edge of the pad and want the pointer to move farther in the same direction on the screen, lift the mouse, bring it back, and continue rolling. (Sometimes people think they must keep going, and going, and going, even over the edge of the desk. Not so.)

If you still feel a little awkward using a mouse, try the following lesson on the CD for some practice.

Try It

In the Computer Essentials section of the CD is a lesson titled "Using Your Mouse." Some of the information reviews things you probably already know and can do, but the lesson is both fun and useful, so give it a try. Here's how to get to it:

1. If necessary, place the CD in the CD-ROM drive; it will start running automatically and take you to the screen from which you go to select the lesson you want. If you exited the lesson CD earlier, but the CD is still in the drive, point to the PCs For Beginners icon on your desktop. Hold the mouse still, and click by quickly pressing and releasing the left mouse button.

2. When the opening screen appears, click option 1 or press the 1 key on your keyboard.

3. Click lesson 2, "Using Your Mouse," or press the 2 key on your keyboard.

4. Follow the instructions in the lesson. When you reach the screen with text that begins *You use these mouse actions...*, press the Esc key and then the Enter key to quit the program and return to the Windows desktop.

Atten...shun

A mouse is just about the most obvious (computer folk like the term *intuitive*) thing in the world to use, except for maybe a beach bucket on a sandpile. But just because it's easy to use doesn't mean it's a dumb little piece of hardware. When combined with the Windows feature known as Active Desktop (the one that Microsoft Internet Explorer might already have turned on for you), the mouse becomes a surprisingly versatile tool that makes onscreen items sit up and pay attention with little or no effort from you.

As the lesson showed, you can *select, click, double-click,* or *drag* with the mouse. To make you comfortable, the lesson used a colored circle for practice. In real life, you select, click, double-click, and drag for different reasons, as you're about to see.

Active Desktop, Reporting for Duty

Before you move on to mousing in general, take a moment to look at the icons on your screen. If the labels under the icons are not underlined, you can—actually, need to—get in a little real-life, real-Windows practice with your mouse. What you'll be doing is setting up your desktop so that Active Desktop is turned on. That way, you'll know that the settings on your computer will match those assumed by the book and the CD from this point on.

(If the labels on your screen are already underlined, you can skip this and go directly to the section titled "Selecting.")

What with instal-ling Internet Explorer and turning on Active Desktop, you might be wondering (with good reason) if using a computer is always going to be so... complicated. Actually, it's not. What you're doing here is the equiva-lent of polishing your shoes and pressing your clothes: a little tedious, perhaps, but once it's done, it's done.

If you need to turn on Active Desktop, these are the steps involved. Don't worry about understanding them at this point. Understanding will come —maybe quickly, maybe a little more slowly. It doesn't matter. The impor-tant thing here is to "just do it" so that you can continue with the CD and the book. The steps viewed as a whole might seem daunting, but they're really not. Just take them one at a time. Ready? Then:

1. Move the mouse pointer to a blank part of the desktop. Hold the pointer still, and press the *right* mouse button.

2. When a short *menu* pops up, slide the mouse so that the pointer is on the words *Active Desktop*. An even shorter menu will slide out to the side. If you don't see a check mark to the left of the words *View As Web Page*, slide the mouse to the side until the dark high-light covers *View As Web Page*. Click the left mouse button.

3. That wasn't difficult, and now you're halfway there. Place the pointer on a blank part of the desktop again.

4. Press the right mouse button to open the same menu, and highlight the words *Active Desktop* again.

5. This time, when the little menu slides out, move the mouse until the highlight covers the words *Customize My Desktop*. Click the left mouse button again. Now, you'll see a dialog box similar to the one shown here.

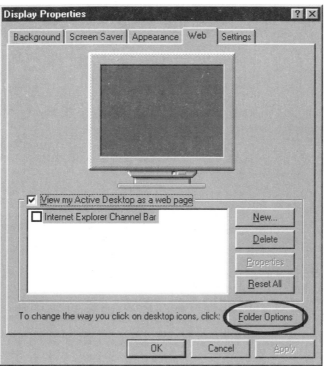

6. Move the mouse until the pointer is on the Folder Options button circled in the preceding illustration, and click the left button. Now you see this message:

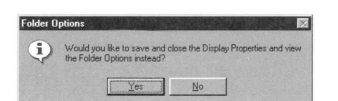

7. Move the mouse pointer to the button labeled *Yes*, and click the left mouse button. The dialog box shown on the next page appears.

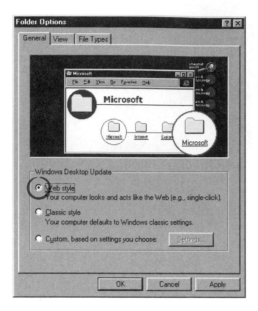

8. Move the mouse until the pointer is on the small circle (circled in the preceding illustration) to the left of the words *Web style*, and click the left button so that a dark dot appears as in the figure.

9. Move the mouse until the pointer is on the button labeled *OK*, and click the left mouse button.

That's it. You're done. You did some significant mousing here, but work your way through the next sections anyway. They fill you in on some of the whys and wherefores of using the mouse.

Selecting

If you point to an underlined item and it doesn't turn dark, your computer's not misbehaving. Just click the little desktop blotter icon (third from the Start button) on the taskbar. All will be well again.

To select any underlined item on the screen, the Active Desktop includes a cool new way of working known as *hover select,* which requires you to do nothing more than point at the item you want and hold the mouse still for a second or two. Hover select might seem—actually is—pretty obvious, but prior versions of Windows required you to point and then click to perform the same action. Where old-timers now have something new to get used to, you don't have anything to unlearn, so you're ahead of the crowd on this one.

1. Move the mouse until the pointer is on the My Computer icon.

2. Hold the mouse still for a second or two, and the icon turns dark. That's hover select in action.

3. Leave the mouse pointer on the icon for a minute. You won't hurt anything.

By the way, an explanatory box like the one that popped up for a short time when you selected My Computer appears whenever you select one of the default icons on your desktop. It's just another way Windows and Active Desktop provide a little extra assistance.

Single-clicking

Other than pointing to select, single-clicking is the easiest mouse action and probably the one you'll use most often. As you saw on the CD, all you do to click is quickly press and release the mouse button. You've already noticed, however, that your mouse doesn't have just one button. So which one do you click? That depends on what you want to do:

■ To *open* an item, you move the pointer to it and click the left button. That's left-clicking, or just plain clicking. When you see "click" in this book, always assume that means "click the left button."

One Click or Two?

If the only computer you ever use is the one you're practicing with now, everything you learn here about using the mouse will soon become instinctive. However, if you shift from this computer to one that has not been set up for Active Desktop, mouse actions are slightly different. Basically, you add one more click when you're working with an "inActive" Desktop item. For example, a single click opens an item on the Active Desktop, but a double-click is needed on an "inActive" Desktop. The difference isn't hard to remember, but you might have to stop and think for a second or two if you frequently shift from one type of desktop to the other—or if you're trying to re-open a document from within an application, such as a word processor. (More about applications later in the book.)

■ To see an extremely useful *shortcut menu* of commands, you move the pointer to an item and click the right mouse button. This is right-clicking. When you need to right-click, the book will tell you so.

 IP Whenever you're not sure what something on the screen does or what command(s) you can use, right-click. At worst, nothing will happen. At best, a menu will pop up to show you the commands most often used on that item. Right-clicking can, in fact, be very helpful in learning your way around Windows. You'll be surprised at how much "hidden" information comes to light when you click that right mouse button.

Give both actions a try on your own computer. You'll quickly see the difference between the two:

1. My Computer should still be selected, so put your hand back on the mouse and, without moving the pointer, click the left button. (If you accidentally jiggle the mouse and the pointer moves away from My Computer, just move the pointer back to the icon and click.)

As soon as you click, a *window* appears, showing you what My Computer contains:

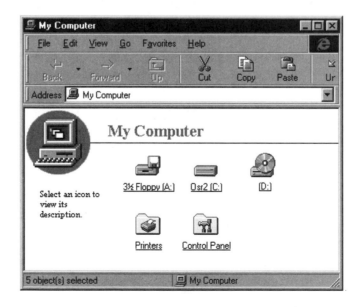

As simply as that, you've *opened* a window. That's something you'll do a lot.

2. Now try right-clicking, which gives you another way to open a window. Move the mouse pointer to your Recycle Bin icon. When the icon is selected, hold the mouse pointer still and click the *right* mouse button. This time, you see a menu of commands:

To use a menu, you slide the pointer until the command you want is highlighted by a dark bar. Try sliding the pointer (and the highlight) up and down the menu.

3. Now to actually choose a command, slide the highlight to Open and click (left button this time). Windows quickly opens a window to your Recycle Bin because that's what you just told it to do.

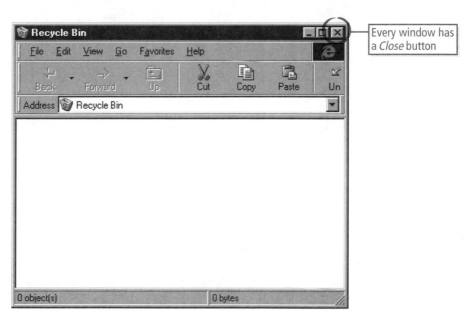

Every window has a *Close* button

4. Obviously, if you can open a window, you can close it too. To close both the My Computer and Recycle Bin windows, click the *Close* button (marked with an X and labeled in the preceding illustration) in the upper right corner of each window.

Double-clicking

While single-clicking is all you need to open icons on the Active Desktop, there will be times you double-click to open an item. Just like riding a bicycle, double-clicking can take a little getting used to, but once you've got it, you don't forget. The main thing to remember is that you must click fairly rapidly, as in click-click rather than click...pause...click. Also, hold the mouse still for both clicks—some people fall into a click-jerk-click habit when trying to double-click and end up frustrating themselves unnecessarily.

To see double-clicking in action, try this:

1. Place the mouse pointer on the "clock" showing the time at the far right end of the taskbar at the bottom of the screen:

2. Double-click. If you've done it right, a window titled Date/Time Properties opens up on the desktop. If the window didn't open up, try double-clicking a little faster—and remember, hold the mouse still.

   If you're not feeling terribly adventurous, feel free to stop after the next step.

3. To end the exercise at this point, click the Close button (marked with an X) in the upper right corner of the Date/Time Properties window, and go on to the section titled "Dragging."

On the other hand, if you want to see a little more, leave the Date/Time Properties window open and continue on.

The Date/Time *properties sheet* you're looking at is one of numerous small programs called *utilities* that are built into Windows. This particular utility is what you use if you ever need to set or change the time and date. This is how it works:

1. Click the downward-pointing triangle to the right of the box that shows the current month. As soon as you do, a list of months drops down.

2. To change the month, all you do is slide your mouse until the highlight is on the month you want and then click. Try changing the month to December. The calendar beneath the month and year changes to the new month.

3. Just for fun, suppose you also want to change the date. That's easy: you just move the pointer to the date you want and click. To try, point to the 31st and click. As easily as that, you've changed the current date (at least the one your computer would think of as "today") to New Year's Eve.

A Cancel button appears in many windows. It's always your way of telling your PC, "Hey, I was just fooling around" or, "I messed up big time. Forget what I did, and keep the original setting, OK?"

4. Of course, you don't really want to change the date, so put the mouse pointer on the button labeled *Cancel*—*not* the one labeled OK—at the bottom of the window and click.

Dragging

In addition to clicking and double-clicking, you can also use the mouse to *drag* items around the screen.

To drag, all you do is select the item, hold down the left button, and move the mouse.

Practice dragging and at the same time see how you can control the way your desktop looks:

1. Select My Computer and click to open the window again. Now place the mouse pointer on the dark *title bar* at the top of the My Computer window, as shown on the next page.

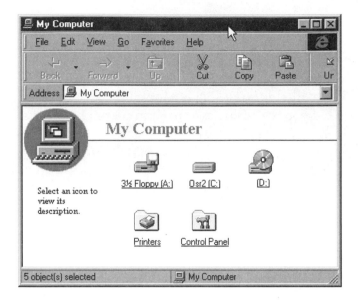

2. Hold down the left button as you move the mouse forward, backward, left, or right, moving in whatever direction you want. As you move the mouse, the window tags along.

3. When you tire of dragging the window around, release the mouse button. The window will stay put where you dropped it.

4. To close the window, click the Close button as you did earlier.

Although dragging a single window around the screen isn't exactly thrilling, remember how you did this. You can open two, three, four, five, or more windows at the same time, and dragging one or the other out of the way can be as handy as arranging papers on your real desktop. When you drag a window, just remember to "grab" it by the title bar—it's the only part that works for dragging.

The Keyboard

If you're a typist, even of the hunt-and-peck variety, you already know most of what you need to use a computer keyboard. The only possible puzzlement might come from the assortment of additional keys surrounding the standard ABCs. These extra keys make a computer keyboard considerably larger than a typewriter keyboard, and they have the effect of making it look somewhat intimidating, especially because some of them

There's a sentence that's famous in computer books and documentation: "Press any key." If you see this, remember that you can press any key you choose: A, B, C, the Spacebar, whatever suits your fancy. Don't search the keyboard for the "any" key. There isn't one.

Try It

For a visual introduction to the different sections of the keyboard, try the following lesson on the CD. You're an experienced mouser now, so you can forgo the earlier can't-miss instructions and just get to the lessons quickly:

1. Make your way to the Computer Essentials/Windows Overview screen either by inserting the CD and letting autoplay take over or by clicking the PCs For Beginners icon on your desktop.

2. Click the "Computer Essentials" section.

3. In the list of lessons on the lefthand side of the screen, click the lesson "Using Your Keyboard."

As usual, follow the instructions in the lesson. When you reach the screen beginning *The more you work with your computer...,* leave the lesson program running and return to the book for a short while.

---

have peculiar names like Ctrl, Alt, and—yikes—Break (which doesn't actually break anything). All the keys are easy to use, however. For an overview, refer to the following section, titled "Keyboard Highlights." Don't bother memorizing any of that stuff, though; it all comes naturally over time.

Keyboard Highlights

The keys highlighted in Figure 2-2 are the keys you'll use most often—other than the letters and numbers, of course:

- *F1* through *F12.* These *function* keys are programmed by software creators to give you quick ways to give your programs often-used commands, such as "Save that document," "I want to quit now," or even "Help!" The actual function assigned to a particular key varies, depending on the program you're using, but once you know what these keys do in a given program, you quickly get used to pressing the ones you need most. In fact, you do it without a second thought.

- *Esc* is your "oops" key. If you change your mind about doing something, you can usually press this key to *escape* and not go any further.

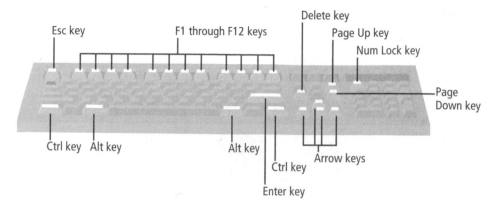

Esc key   F1 through F12 keys   Delete key   Page Up key   Num Lock key   Page Down key

Ctrl key Alt key   Alt key   Ctrl key   Arrow keys   Enter key

Figure 2-2.   *The specialty keys you'll use most often.*

■ The *numeric keypad* gives you a calculator-style set of keys for entering numbers. To use these keys, you press...

■ *NumLock,* which switches the numeric keypad between calculator-style mode and a navigation-type mode in which all but the 5 key can be used to move around in a document.

■ The *arrow keys,* both on the numeric keypad and on the lower part of the keyboard, move the blinking cursor that tells you where your typing will appear.

■ *Page Up* (*PgUp*) and *Page Down* (*PgDn*) move—scroll—through a document a screenful at a time.

■ *Ctrl* and *Alt* don't do anything by themselves, but when you press them in combination with certain other, predefined keys, they give those other keys new meaning. Pressing Ctrl and the I key at the same time, for instance, creates *italic* characters in some programs.

■ *Delete* (or *Del*) deletes the current character.

> **OTE** *Ctrl, Alt,* and *Del* together form a powerful trio. When you press all three at the same time, you send Windows a "shut it down" signal. You can use this three-key combo (generally shown in books as Ctrl-Alt-Del or Ctrl+Alt+Del) to quit a misbehaving program that *hangs* and won't respond no matter what you try. You can also, but only if necessary, use Ctrl-Alt-Del to shut down Windows itself. This is *not* recommended; you should always use the Shut Down command on the Start menu.

A Side Trip to the Start Button

In order to experiment with the keyboard and your own computer, you'll have to start a program or two so that you have a place to type something. Just as you don't write on your real desktop, you don't write on the Windows one either. To start a program, you begin with the appropriately named Start button on the taskbar.

Try It

Clicking the Start button tells Windows you want to see its *Start* menu. For a first look at this menu and how to use it:

1. You should still be inside the CD lesson program, so click the big blue button labeled *Contents* in the lower left portion of the screen.

2. On the contents screen, click the section "Computer Essentials."

3. In the list of lessons on the next screen, click the lesson "Using the Start Menu."

4. When you finish this lesson, try the next one, too.

Now for a trial run with the Start button before you work through the more detailed example in the book:

1. Once again, click the Contents button.

2. On the contents screen, click the section "Windows Overview." (Aha, something new!)

The lessons in the "Windows Overview" section are different from the ones in "Computer Essentials" because the overview lessons actually have you interact with the program on the CD.

1. Watch the overview introduction to see how the lessons work. (The introduction begins after a few seconds.)

2. When the "Windows Overview" list of lessons appears, highlight the lesson "Starting a Program" and click the left button.

3. When you finish the lesson, press the Esc key and then press Enter to return to Windows.

The Start button is always visible on the taskbar, and until you learn a few shortcuts (in later chapters), it will be stop number one whenever you want to get going with any kind of real work with your computer.

WordPad, Calculator, and a number of other useful programs you see on the Start menu and its submenus actually come with Windows. They're freebies, so to speak.

For the next step-by-step examples, you'll use the Start button and the Start menu to start two programs, one the relatively simple word processor called WordPad that you saw from the CD, the other a nifty little gadget called Calculator.

1. Place the mouse pointer on the Start button, click to open the Start menu, and then work your way through the Programs and Accessories submenus.

2. Start WordPad.

3. Start Calculator in just the same way: Begin with the Start button and work your way through the Programs and Accessories submenus. This time, however, click Calculator, which opens up looking like this:

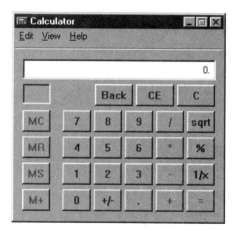

As easily as that, you've gotten two useful programs *running* on your computer. Notice that each sits neatly in its own window, separate from the other but ready to work whenever you are. WordPad, though small for a word processor, is a fairly sophisticated program that easily meets the needs of letter writing and similar tasks. Calculator is an electronic version of the number cruncher on your real desktop and can be just as handy.

The Direction Keys

Except for young—and not so young—children who think joysticks and computer games are the primary reasons computers were invented, most people spend most of their time using these machines as fast, easy, and highly sophisticated typewriters. You have WordPad running, so type away:

1. First, you have to tell Windows which program you want to use. The easiest way, since you can see both the WordPad and Calculator windows, is simply to click the title bar of the window you want, like this:

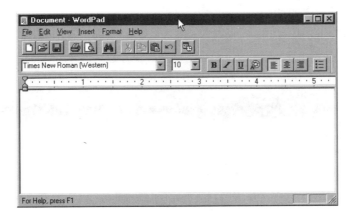

When you click, the WordPad title bar becomes dark. That dark title bar always tells you which of several open programs is the *active window,* the one your next command will affect. If Calculator's window opened on top of WordPad, notice that WordPad's window has now leapfrogged to the front. That's because the active window always lies on top of any other open windows.

2. Now type something. Even if you're not feeling a little creatively challenged at the moment, try the following, pressing the Enter key where you see [Enter]. (Don't type the [symbol or the] symbol; they're just printed here to help you see the key name better.) Press the Shift key, of course, to create CAPITAL letters:

    Roses are red, violets are blue. [Enter]
    I like computers, and so do you. [Enter]

3. The blinking vertical bar at the beginning of the last line is the cursor, which tells you where the next character you type will appear.

Now, just to get some keyboard experience, suppose you didn't like what you typed and wanted to change something. You *could* press the Backspace key, just as you do on a typewriter, to move back one character at a time, but Backspace would also *delete* (erase) each character it passed over. Furthermore, if you wanted to go to the beginning of your typing, you'd press, and press, and press, erasing as you went. Not much of an option.

On a computer, however, there are much easier ways to move around. You can use either the keys on the numeric keypad or the identically named keys, such as Home and End, to the left of the keypad.

 NOTE Although the keys used in this example are standard in word processing types of software, applications can differ and the full-blown word processor you choose to use might be a little different. Bear in mind here that the goal is to see what the keyboard can do, not to learn all about word processors.

Now for some more keyboarding. If you want to use the keypad for these examples, first check the Num Lock light at the top of the keyboard. If the light is on, press the NumLock key to shift the keypad from numeric entry to navigation mode. When you're ready:

1. Press the Up arrow key. The cursor immediately jumps up one line. Press the Up arrow key again, and the cursor is in front of *Roses*.

2. Now press the End key. This time, the cursor jumps to the end of the same line.

3. Press the Home key, and the cursor jumps back. Ahh...such power, such control. But there's more.

4. Remember that the Ctrl and Alt keys change the meanings of certain other keys? Here's an example. Press Ctrl and End at the same time. The cursor jumps to the end of your small document rather than to the end of the current line.

5. Press Ctrl and Home, and the cursor jumps to the beginning of the document.

6. Press the Right arrow key several times. The cursor moves to the right one character with each press. That can be a little slow when you're in a hurry, though. To hustle a bit...

7. Hold down Ctrl and press the Right arrow key. Now you're jumping a word at a time. Try using the Ctrl and the Left arrow keys to move in the other direction, too.

8. No one can tell where you put the cursor after that last step, so you're on your own here: use whatever combination of keys you need to move the cursor back in front of *Roses*.

Next, suppose you want to edit your poem. It *is* a little silly.

1. Move the cursor in front of *violets*. Press Ctrl *and* Shift *and* the Right arrow key at the same time. The highlight now stretches over the entire word.

2. Type *pansies* and add a space with the Spacebar. As simply as that, you've "erased" one word and substituted another.

3. Move the cursor in front of *so* in the second line, and use Ctrl, Shift, and the Right arrow key to cover *so do.* Press the Delete key (Del on the numeric keypad). All gone.

4. But your poem doesn't make much sense anymore. Move the cursor in front of the period at the end of the sentence. Press the Spacebar to make a space, and type *do too*. There.

The Numeric Keypad

Now turn your attention to Calculator. If the WordPad window is covering it up, not to worry:

1. Look at the taskbar:

There are buttons for both WordPad and Calculator. Each time you start a program, Windows creates a taskbar button for it, and that button remains as a way to return to the program whenever you want. The button goes away only when you close the program.

2. Click the button for Calculator. Windows immediately brings Calculator to the front and makes it the active window.

Now that Calculator is the active program, you can try out the numeric keypad.

1. If the Num Lock light is *off*, press the NumLock key to toggle the keypad to numeric-entry mode.

2. Press the following keys: 1, 2, 3, the plus (+) key, 4, 5, 6, and the Enter key on the numeric keypad. Instant addition.

3. To clear the little display window and get ready for a new calculation, press the Escape (Esc) key in the upper left corner of the keyboard. Or, if you prefer, click the Clear button, marked with a big C, on Calculator itself.

In Chapter 3, under the heading "Help! I'm Stuck!" you'll see how to find detailed instructions on using WordPad, Calculator, or any other program. Remember, this section is for getting comfortable with the keyboard, not for becoming a whiz with any particular program.

You can do subtraction, division, multiplication, and a whole lot more, too. Here are a few more examples you can try.

1. To subtract, use the minus (-) key like this: press 3, 6, 9, the minus key, 2, 5, 8, and the Enter key. Press Esc or click the Clear button.

2. To divide, use the division key (/). Try it by pressing 1, 6, the division key, 2, and Enter. Again, press Esc or click the Clear button.

3. To multiply, use the multiplication key (*) like so: press 2, 5, the multiplication key, 8, and the Enter key. And again, press Esc or click the Clear button.

4. You can also do decimals with the decimal-point key, which is marked with both a dot (.) and the letters *Del*. To try decimals, press 1, 2, the decimal key, 5, 0, the plus key, 4, the decimal key, 2, 5, and the Enter key.

For quick figuring, remember Calculator. Although you haven't seen it here, there's even a way to morph this program into a scientific calculator on those numerous occasions you need to figure logarithms, cosines, and exponents. Yeah, sure....

TIP If you want to see Calculator's scientific side, it's easy. Click *View* at the top of the Calculator window, and then click *Scientific*. To turn Calculator back into its simpler form, click *View* again and then click *Standard.*

Cleaning Up

You've done quite a bit of experimenting with the mouse and keyboard, and you might be ready for a break. To clean up the screen, try two different ways of closing a program, one with the keyboard, the other with the mouse:

1. Calculator should be the active window. If it isn't, click its button on the Taskbar.

2. Hold down the Alt key, and press the function key labeled F4. Gone.

3. Now you have WordPad to put away. Point to the word File at the top of the window, and click. This open's WordPad's File menu, which contains all the WordPad commands having to do with whole files (documents).

4. Run the highlight down to the Exit command, and click. Exit is the standard "I'm done" command in Windows programs.

5. Oops. WordPad refuses to go away. That's because you have some unsaved work in the window. WordPad (and other programs) won't exit until you take care of any unsaved work:

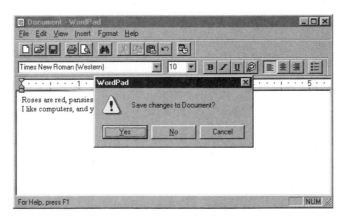

Basically, WordPad is saying, "You're the boss," and it's displaying a *dialog box* asking what you want to do. Such boxes appear in a multitude of sizes, with an equally vast array of questions and options. All, however, represent a program's way of getting information from you—carrying on a dialog, if you will.

6. You don't want to save your WordPad experiment because it would just clutter your hard drive, so point to the No button at the bottom of the dialog box and click. Satisfied now, WordPad goes away.

A Step or Two Farther

If you're eager to continue a little more, the following practice session takes you through some fun and useful exercises with the desktop and your mouse. You'll be moving a little faster here, but just take everything a step at a time and you'll be fine.

First, the desktop:

1. Place the mouse pointer on a blank part of the taskbar at the bottom of your screen.

2. Hold down the left button, and roll the mouse forward, back, and side to side. As you move the mouse, the taskbar jumps to whichever side of the screen the mouse pointer is closest to.

3. Release the button, and the taskbar stays wherever it was when you released the button. Relocating the taskbar like this is called *docking* and is just one way you can arrange the desktop to suit your preferences.

4. If you prefer the taskbar along the bottom of the screen, drag it back and dock it there.

And now the mouse. Here, you'll see how to adjust mouse settings to your own personal preferences:

1. Click the Start button, highlight Settings, and then click Control Panel on the submenu that appears. A window quickly opens to show you the contents of Control Panel (which contains a group of utility programs that help you "control" or customize your PC).

2. Click the mouse icon. This starts the mouse-control program known formally as Mouse Properties.

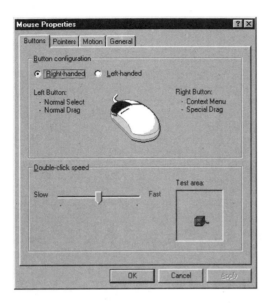

In the lower half of the window, you can see a movable *slider* on the left and an animated jack-in-the-box on the right. The slider allows you to adjust your double-click speed; the jack-in-the-box lets you test the speed you've chosen.

3. Point to the jack-in-the-box and double-click. If you and Windows are in synch, the toy pops open. If you want your double-clicking a little faster or a little slower, drag the slider to the left to leave more time between clicks or drag it to the right to leave less time between clicks. (Hint: if you drag the slider all the way to the right, you'd better be faster than Wyatt Earp with your mouse-clicking finger.)

4. Try out your new setting by double-clicking the jack-in-the-box again. If the box is already open, successful double-clicking will close it. If the box is closed, successful double-clicking will open it.

5. When you've had enough, do either of the following: point to the OK button and click *if* you've made an adjustment you want to keep, *or* point to the Cancel button and click to keep your double-click speed the way it was.

That's your introduction to the mouse and keyboard. Over time, both will become almost like extensions of your body, and you'll use them automatically as you work with your computer. Even if you feel a little slow or a little awkward right now, don't worry about it. Practice makes perfect, as the saying goes, and the more you practice, the more fluid you'll become with both pieces of equipment—in fact, you'll get faster whether you intend to or not.

If you want to quit for a while, remember to do so by clicking the Start button and using the Shut Down command on the Windows Start menu.

Everybody's Favorite Time Waster

The best way known to humanity for becoming adept with a mouse is by playing computer Solitaire. Yes, that's the card game, and it's even better than in real life because your computer does all the shuffling and laying out for you, and you never have to try and keep the cat off the cards or line them up neatly. To play, you just drag cards from one pile to another.

A lot of computers come with Solitaire already installed. If you have it, you should find it under Games on the Accessories submenu (from the Start button, work through Programs and Accessories to Games). If it's there, just click Solitaire to start the game. If you want help on playing the electronic version, click the Help menu, and choose Help Topics.

Doing Windows

Now you know the basics of using a computer: how to boot it and how to shut it down, how to start and stop a program, how to use the keyboard, and how to use the mouse. From this chapter on, you'll begin to dig a little deeper and see some of the many ways you can control the way your PC works with you, starting with those wonderful things called windows.

The Idea of a Window

Like a real-life window, a window on your computer screen has a "frame" called a *border* and a viewing area, appropriately called a *pane*, for displaying content. In these respects, computer windows and real windows are very similar—they let you see something, whether that something is your neighbor's barbecue or the letter you're writing to Aunt Maude. The only real difference between the two kinds of windows is that the one in your house lets you see either in or out, where the computer version only lets you see in.

Although an onscreen window is made up of many pieces that respond to your mouse, the best place to begin is with the basics, shown in Figure 3-1 on the following page.

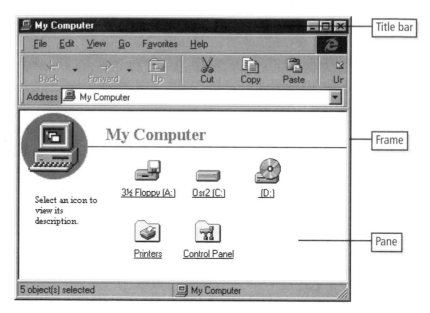

Figure 3-1.   *The basic parts of a window.*

Do I Have To?

Before you go on, here's a brief message from your sponsor…. Maybe you've been wondering whether you have to memorize *everything* you find in this book. (Loud "yecch.") The answer is no, no, no. You absolutely do not have to master or even remember all this stuff.

This book is about opportunity, so it will show you many things that introduce you to the potential of your PC. Some things you might think stupid. Some you might think incredibly great. Regardless, learn only what you want, when you want. The idea is to get you up and running, doing whatever it is you want to do with your PC. And to that end, you should treat this book like an all-you-can-eat buffet: just because it's there doesn't mean you have to swallow it. Take what you need and leave the rest for another day—or even for eternity. You won't hurt anyone's feelings.

Of course, if you do end up wanting to know all the gory details, welcome to the club. The book will help you get set for a few years of fun, during which you won't have to listen to any couch-potato jokes. Nope…you'll have to put up with a few geek remarks instead. :-)

Working with Whole Windows

In the real world, you can install or replace entire windows. Or you can wash them, pane by pane. In the computer world, too, you can work with either entire windows (as you did in the last chapter, when you dragged one around by its title bar), or you can work with only the part of a window you need to get a particular job done (as you did when you clicked the Close button to close a window).

So what else can you do with windows besides open, close, and drag them around? Lots. You can change their shape, their size, and the way they display information. You can make them take up the whole screen, or you can reduce them to buttons on the taskbar. If you have a bunch of windows open, you can spread them out like playing cards, or you can stack them like bricks in a wall. All these choices are yours, and you'll begin to add them to your bag of tricks after this brief fling with your CD.

Try It

For an illustrated overview of windows and a hands-on session introducing some of the things you do with them, turn to your CD and try the following lessons.

For the overview:

1. Start the CD either by inserting it in your CD-ROM drive (in which case it starts running automatically) or by clicking the PCs For Beginners icon on your desktop.

2. When you see the opening screen, click Computer Essentials.

3. In the list of Computer Essentials lessons, click "Working With Windows."

4. When you reach the screen that begins *You can easily move around and between...* click the big blue Contents button.

Now, to see a lesson that covers the way you change active windows with the taskbar, use the mouse to alter the size of a window and, as you did in Chapter 1, close an open window with the Close button.

(continued)

Try It *continued*

1. On the Essentials/Overview screen, click Windows Overview.

2. You've seen the Overview introduction, so you can click the left mouse button to skip it. (Or you can watch it again, if you want.)

3. Whether you clicked the mouse in step 2 or watched the introduction, the CD next takes you to the list of Overview lessons.

4. Click the lesson "Managing Open Windows."

5. When you finish step 15 in the lesson, stop for a moment and read the following explanation without clicking the Next button.

6. Why not click Next at the end of step 15? Because this Next button returns you to the lesson list. You might think you can save a little time by clicking the Close button at the lesson list to quit and return to Windows, but you can't. (You quit the CD at the lesson list by pressing the Esc key and then the Enter key.) It's a little easier to return to Windows from here, so: click the Close button in the step 15 lesson window, and click Yes or press Enter to confirm that you want to quit.

Now, to push a little farther.

Custom Window Shapes and Sizes

When you open a window, it opens at a certain size and shape, but it doesn't have to stay that way. You can easily change a window's shape or size, or both, to suit its contents and your needs. For instance, a list of some kind might be easier to scan in a long, narrow window, whereas a graph or picture might be much better off viewed in a short, wide window. Changing the size or shape of a window is called *resizing*, and all you need is your mouse and its left button.

Figure 3-2 shows the parts of the window you'll work with when you resize a window. Note that the mouse pointer turns into a two-headed arrow when it's resizing a window.

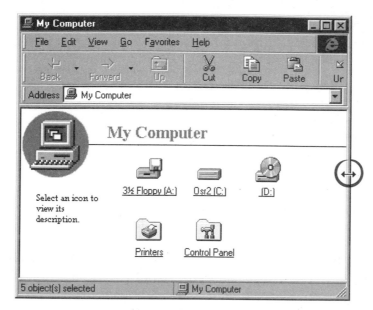

Figure 3-2.   *The mouse pointer changes its shape when you resize a window.*

Shaping the Width

First try changing the width of a window:

1. You need a window to work with, so open My Computer.

2. Place the mouse pointer on the left or right edge of the window—whichever gives you enough room to work.

3. When the pointer becomes a black, two-headed arrow, hold down the left mouse button and drag, both to the left and to the right. The window grows wider or narrower, depending on the direction in which you drag.

Adding a Scroll Bar

While you're at it, use what you just did to see something else about windows: scroll bars. It's easy, because a scroll bar appears whenever a window is so small you can't see all of its contents at one time. Here, give it a try:

1. If necessary, place the mouse pointer on the left or right window border again. When the two-headed arrow appears, drag until the window is so narrow that a scroll bar appears.

2. Widen the window again until the scroll bar goes away. Release the mouse button when the window displays all its contents but not a whole lot of blank space.

 IP Reshaping or resizing a window is an easy way to get rid of scroll bars. Just keep stretching the window until the scroll bar you don't want goes away. There are limits, to this, of course. Some windows need to display so much that you can't see all the contents at one time no matter how hard you try. The screen itself just isn't big enough.

Shaping the Height

Now try making the window longer and shorter:

1. Place the mouse pointer on the top or bottom edge of the window. Wait for the two-headed arrow, press the left button, and drag up or down.

2. Return the window to approximately its former size. (You don't have to be exact here.)

Reshaping the Whole Thing

And suppose you want to change both the height and the width of a window. Do you have to stretch the window one way and then stretch it the other? Of course not. You can change both at the same time:

1. Place the mouse pointer on a corner of the My Computer window (the lower right is usually easiest). The pointer changes to a *diagonal* two-headed arrow, but the procedure is still the same: hold down the left mouse button and drag, this time either down and away or up and in. As you drag, the window grows or shrinks in the direction you're dragging.

2. Drag until the window is once again roughly its former shape and size, and then release the mouse button. Leave My Computer open— you'll be experimenting with it again in a minute.

Windows. Just putty in your hands, aren't they?

Another Look at Maximize, Minimize, and Restore

The ability to customize window shapes and sizes is something you'll probably come to rely on almost without thinking: "Oh, I've got room on the screen. Let's make this window bigger so I can see more." Or you'll want to make an application window just the right size to work in but still leave room on the screen for other often-used tools.

At other times, though, you know that such pinpoint control isn't really all that necessary. An all or nothing approach works just fine. For example, maybe you've been working on a letter and you've decided to take a break by trolling the Internet. Both the letter and your Internet window benefit from a lot of screen real estate, so as you switch from one to the other, all you're really interested in is giving the new window as much room as possible. This is when you turn to the Maximize and Minimize buttons built into the upper right corner of every window. To refresh your memory, these buttons are shown in Figure 3-3 in old faithful, the My Computer window.

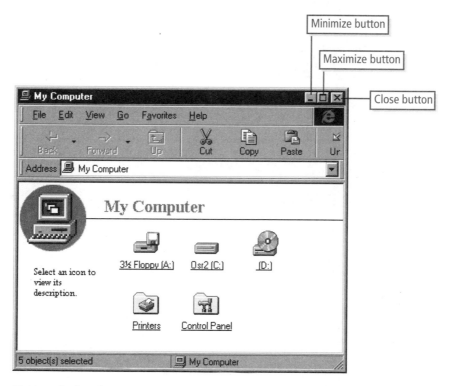

Figure 3-3.   *Every window has a Maximize, Minimize, and Close button.*

Some of this next practice repeats material on the CD, but it's another hands-on look at the buttons in action, along with a little more explanation:

1. Click the Maximize button in the My Computer window. All of a sudden, you've got instant full-screen—and a lot of vacant white pane, to boot, but never mind, some windows have more to display than others.

2. Click the Minimize button, and My Computer not only shrinks, it goes away. If you were watching, you probably saw the window sort of fold in on itself and "float" down to the taskbar. That's where all minimized windows go, to wait until you want them again.

3. And then there's the Restore button. Click the My Computer button on the taskbar to return the window to its earlier, gigantic, size. Notice that the Maximize button has changed slightly, to this:

In this form, the button is now called *Restore*, and it exists basically to "undo" a change in the shape or size of a window.

4. Click the Restore button. The My Computer window shrinks back to its earlier, more practical, form.

Moving from One Window to Another

When one window is maximized, you can't see any others you opened. If you're going to be working in the same window for a long time, that shouldn't bother you at all. After all, whenever you want to view the contents of another window, you can always click the other window's button on the taskbar. Suppose, though, you need to look first at this window and then at that one. There are a couple of easy ways to keep several windows at your beck and call.

Switching Between Windows with the Keyboard

If you like to keep your hands on the keyboard, here's a little trick that helps you easily switch from one open window to another: it's the Alt key and the Tab key.

1. First, you need some windows to switch between. Any will do. My Computer should still be open, so you just need another one or two. Just for a change of scenery, click the Start button, work through Programs and Accessories, and click Paint, to open a nifty drawing program that also comes with Windows. Finally, start WordPad again, to end up with three open windows on your screen.

2. Now hold down the Alt key and press Tab. Windows displays this:

The square around one of the window icons (it doesn't matter which one) tells you which window is currently active.

3. To switch to another window, just press Tab again while still holding down the Alt key.

4. Release Alt, and the new window immediately becomes the active window.

5. If you want, try Alt-Tab a few more times to see how it works. When you're finished, release the keys. The last window you chose remains the active window.

6. Leave all three windows open for the time being.

Remember Alt-Tab. It's fast, neat, effective, and definitely something to make use of.

By the Way, There's This Thing About Windows...

As you'll see over and over, Windows and most Windows applications offer you two, three, or even more ways to accomplish a given task. This multiplicity of options is not meant to confuse you. On the contrary, bear in mind that different people work in different ways, and what's comfortable for one might be awkward for another. To try to make life as easy as possible, these programs support a lot of alternatives and turn you loose to choose the one you like best. True, learning what these alternatives are can take some time, but that's what books and manuals are for. And once you find the methods you like best, you'll thank the programmers who put them there for you.

Arranging Windows with the Mouse

As you work, you'll probably find yourself relying on both the keyboard and the mouse, using whichever tool is best for a particular job. As you become experienced with a computer, this shifting back and forth eventually becomes as unthinking an action as changing your grip when you switch from knife to fork and back again.

Cascading Windows

One area in which the mouse excels is in arranging multiple windows on the screen. For example, you've opened several windows and now have them scattered all over the screen. Here's a way to organize them neatly:

1. Place the mouse pointer on a *blank* part of the taskbar and right-click. Immediately, this menu pops up:

Notice that the second section from the top gives you several options for arranging onscreen windows. You can *cascade* them, or you can *tile* them either horizontally (stacking one above the other) or vertically (placing them side by side).

2. To try arranging windows on your own screen, click Cascade Windows. Like animated playing cards, your open windows line up, one slightly overlapping the other. Why the overlap? So you can see (from the words on the title bar) what each window contains, and so you can easily switch from one to another with the mouse.

3. For instance, click the title bar of the window in the middle of the pile. It jumps to the top of the heap.

4. Using the mouse this way, you can click through cascaded windows at will. If the title bar isn't showing (as it might not be now for the window on the bottom), just click any visible part of the window *except* the Minimize, Maximize, or Close buttons, and the window you click will jump front and center.

Does Anyone Need All Those Windows?

Right now, you have the WordPad, Paint, and My Computer windows open. And you might be wondering if there's really any point, other than practice, to open this or any other combination of windows. After all, don't most people work on one thing at a time? Well, yes and no. There actually is something you could do with these three windows, although you might prefer a full-fledged drawing program and word processor, rather than Paint and WordPad, for any "real" work. However, just so you get an idea of why anyone in their right mind would open window after window…

You could be using WordPad to write a report on efficient government spending. That would be nice and short and well-suited to a smallish word processor. Because you're also an artist, you're going to add some zing to your report with illustrations you've created with Paint. And what of the My Computer window? Well, that one's open because you saved some research documents on a floppy disk (which, if you look, is visible and accessible through My Computer) and you'll be needing those facts and figures to make your document a solid piece of reporting.

So, just as you might turn to a screwdriver, a hammer, and a tape measure to fix your house, you can easily find yourself using several tools to perform a single task on your computer. But this digresses.

Tiling Windows

For whatever reason, sometime in the future you might, indeed, have several open windows on the screen and, further, you might want to be able to see all of them at the same time. Cascading is certainly nice, but it wouldn't do the trick here because the active window, the one on top, would cover up the other(s). In such a situation, here's what to do:

1. Right-click a blank part of the taskbar again and choose either Tile Windows Horizontally or Tile Windows Vertically, whichever you prefer. This is the pack 'em and stack 'em approach to windows.

2. Now, however, none of your windows is the active one, as you can tell by the gray title bars on all of them. To make one active, just click in its window. Again, anywhere but the Close (and Minimize and Maximize) buttons will do.

3. If you tiled your windows horizontally, go back to the taskbar and try tiling vertically so you can see the difference. If you tiled vertically, try tiling horizontally. Most people tend to choose one over the other, so you might as well see what both are like.

4. You've finished here, so close WordPad and Paint by clicking the Close button, by pressing both Alt and the F4 key at the same time, or by choosing the Exit command on each program's File menu for each. Leave My Computer open, because you'll be using it again in the next section.

Using a Scroll Bar

You've seen what a scroll bar looks like, but you haven't yet had the chance to practice using one. As shown on the CD, a scroll bar helps you see content that "disappears" beyond the edges of an open window. If you use a word processor for writing or a spreadsheet program for budgets and other number-related work, you'll see plenty of scroll bars because written documents and budgets can easily become larger than what a single screen can show. Scroll bars are *really* easy to use, so head for some hands-on practice.

To try out scroll bars, you need to open a window onto something that contains so much information the only way to see it all is to scroll. Luckily, there *is* one such item guaranteed to be on your hard disk. It's a *folder* (the electronic version of a...well, a folder) that contains Windows itself. This folder contains some impressively technical-looking stuff, and its contents are not anything you should *ever, ever* fool around with. In this case, however, you're just going to play with the scroll bar, so you'll be fine. Here you go:

1. Click the icon for your hard disk in the My Computer window. The icon looks like this:

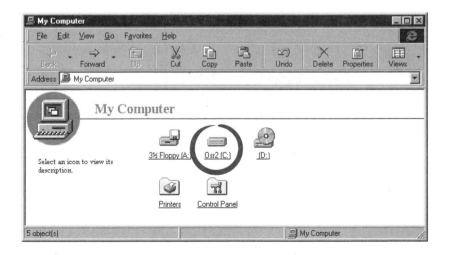

When the contents of the window change to show what's on your hard disk, it looks something like the following.

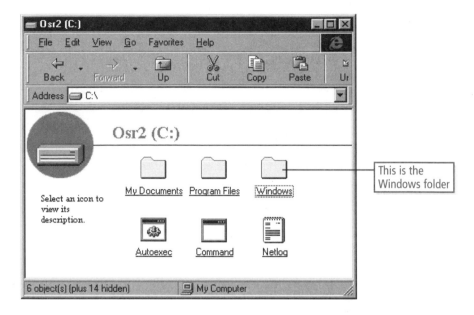

This is the Windows folder

2. Find and click your Windows folder (labeled in the preceding illustration).

3. This window almost certainly contains a scroll bar. If it doesn't, resize the window, making it smaller, until a scroll bar appears. It should look something like this:

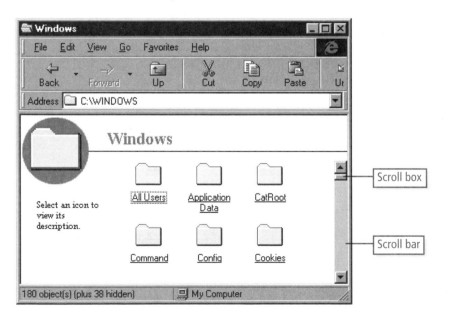

Scroll box

Scroll bar

4. Now place the mouse pointer on the *scroll box* inside the scroll bar. To see more of what this folder contains, just drag the scroll box in the scroll bar. As you drag, the contents of the window scroll to match, bringing previously hidden information into view.

5. There's also a way to jump a screenful at a time: Place the mouse pointer above or below the scroll box and click.

6. Put Windows safely away again by clicking the window's Close button.

That's all there is to using a scroll bar.

 OTE   As you work with different windows, you'll find that the scroll box changes size like Alice did in Wonderland. In one window, the scroll box is big—even big enough to hog most of the scroll bar. In another window, it's quite small. The change isn't due to either temperament or magic. No, the scroll box assumes a certain size in order to tell you how much of that window's contents you're seeing. If the scroll box is big, you're seeing most everything. If the scroll box is small, there's a lot more to look at.

What *Is* All That Stuff?

Just for reference: the Windows operating system consists of millions of lines of instructions called *code*. Those instructions are stored in all those bits and pieces you see in your Windows folder, and they work very closely with one another and with your hardware. That's why you should never mess with Windows. Accidentally removing or changing one of those elements could be the equivalent of "accidentally" pouring sand in your gas tank and then wondering why the dang car won't go. The cleanup headache would be about the same, too.

Controlling the View

You've tried out a number of ways to push, pull, stretch, shape, and arrange windows onscreen. In addition to controlling the size and arrangement of your windows, you can also control the way any given window looks and the way it displays its contents. To do that, you turn to the *menu bar* just below the window's title bar, and to the row or rows of buttons you can display on one or more *toolbars* below the menu bar. Figure 3-4 points out these window pieces, along with the *Views* button you'll be using in the next series of steps.

By the way, the following sessions on views, toolbars, and parts of a window are a little more detailed than the preceding steps. The exercises are not essential, however, so if you want, feel free to skip ahead to the section titled "Help! I'm Stuck!" That's one you *should* work through.

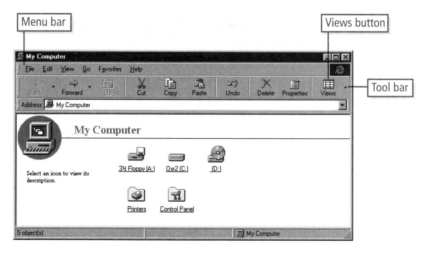

Figure 3-4.   *You can change the view of a window by using the Views button on the toolbar or by using the View menu on the menu bar.*

What's a View and How Many Have You Got?

So far, each time you opened My Computer (or for that matter, the icons for your hard disk and for your Windows folder), you saw what is known as the *default* view—big icons representing folders and drives sitting above some text, such as *3 ½ Floppy (A:)* and *Control Panel*. This view is what Windows calls *Large Icons* view.

Large icons are nice and friendly, but they also take up a lot of space in the window, and they don't really tell you a lot. Windows offers you a choice of three other views, all of which shrink large icons down to what most people consider a more manageable size and, in the process, display a lot more information in the same amount of room:

- *Small Icons* arranges the icons alphabetically from left to right.

- *List* arranges the icons alphabetically from top to bottom.

- *Details* gives additional information about each icon, including what type of information (program, document, graphic, and so on) it represents and when it was created.

Details is the automatic choice of any self-respecting technowizard. On occasion, it will be yours, too—especially when you need to know the date a particular file (document) was created or last worked on.

Switching to a Different View

It's easy to look at—and change—views, no matter which one is in effect at the time. In fact, you can even choose either of two ways to go about changing the view. One way relies on the toolbar, the other on the menu bar at the top of the window. Both methods accomplish the same result, so you can either settle on the one that makes you most comfortable, or you can mix them and match them as the mood takes you. And you can use either method to change views as often as you want. Here's what to do:

1. Open My Computer. Yes, it's getting boring, but it's familiar, so the contents won't distract you. If necessary, widen the window until the Views button appears near the right edge.

2. To try the first, and easier, way to change views, place the mouse pointer smack in the middle of the graphic on the Views button. If you keep the mouse still for a moment, Windows will confirm that you've got the correct button by displaying a small *tooltip* that says *Views*.

3. Click the Views button, and the display in the My Computer window immediately changes to the following view.

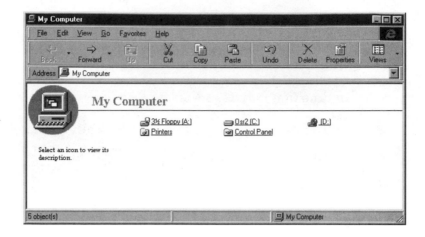

That's the Small Icons view.

4. Click the button again, and the contents realign in List view.

5. Click again, and you get Details view in all its glory.

6. Keep clicking the Views button, and you'll see that you cycle through these views, always in the same order. Stop whenever you want, at whatever view you want.

Giving you a choice of viewing left to right (Small Icons) versus up and down (List) is not quite as nitpicky as it might seem at first. People tend to be more comfortable with one than the other. How do you wash the hood of your car? (In circles... right, be that way.)

If you're someone who likes to get to the point, you probably don't want to click your way to the view you want. You'd rather go straight there. That's easy, too:

1. On the toolbar, click the small, downward-pointing triangle to the right of the graphic on the Views button. Now a list drops down. Notice the black dot to the left of the current view.

2. You use this list just as you use any menu. Run the pointer down the list, highlight a view you like, and click.

Now try the other way to change the view—with the View menu on the menu bar at the top of the window:

1. Point to the name of the menu, *View*, and click. You see a list much like the one on the toolbar, but a tad longer and more sophisticated. Again, however, you see the four different views listed, and again a black dot marks the current view.

2. Highlight a different view and click.

3. If you want to keep your window looking like the illustrations in this book, return the display to the default Large Icons view. You can always change to your preferred view later on.

Displaying and Hiding Toolbars

Changing views is easy, as you've seen. While you're focused on the View menu, however, you can try customizing something else about a window—its toolbars.

1. Open the View menu again.

2. This time, highlight the Toolbars command at the top of the menu. A submenu slides out to the right. As you can see, there's a check mark to the left of Standard Buttons. That check mark corresponds to the buttons currently on display just under the menu names at the top of the window:

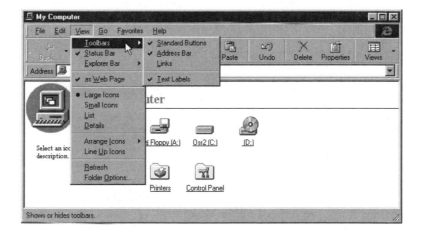

3. If you ever get tired of looking at the standard buttons, you can easily make them go away. Just move the highlight to Standard Buttons and click. Whenever you click a menu option *with* a check mark to its left, you turn that option off.

4. Turning standard buttons off, by the way, doesn't mean the buttons are lost and gone forever. To get them back (which really is preferable because toolbar buttons are so easy to use), open the View menu

What About All Those Other Commands?

This book is concentrating on what you're most likely to want to do, rather than on teaching you everything you never wanted to know about your computer, so you won't try every command on every menu. If you become curious about a command you haven't covered, it's easy to find out what it does. Place the mouse pointer on the command and look at the bottom of the window. A thumbnail description will appear in the area known as the window's *status bar*:

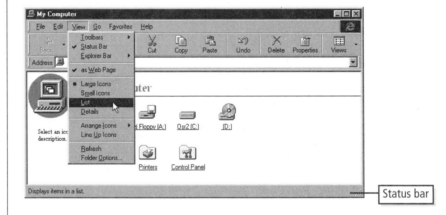

If you like the sound of the command, you can always try it. If you're a little shy, you can consult the program's on-screen help feature, which you'll find out about shortly.

again, open the Toolbar submenu, highlight Standard Buttons, and click again. Clicking a checkable menu option when it *doesn't* show a check mark turns the option back on again.

 IP Not all menu items are accompanied by check marks or dots, but you're unlikely to become confused about which are and which aren't. Here's the rationale: If it's an on/off type of option (such as a toolbar you can display), it gets a check mark; if it's one of several choices offered to you (such as the different icon views), it gets a dot; if it's a command (such as Exit) that simply gets carried out, it gets neither.

And while you're here...

You probably also see a long, narrow bar labeled *Address* below the standard buttons, as you can see in Figure 3-5.

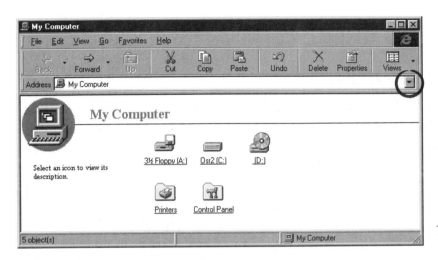

Figure 3-5.   *The Address bar is below the toolbar.*

What *is* this thing? Take a look, and at the same time try one of those "you can do it this way, or this way, or this way" alternatives Windows makes available to you:

1. If you don't see the Address bar, open the Toolbars submenu again and click Address Bar to add a check mark to its left.

2. Click the downward-pointing triangle at the far right of the blank area on the Address bar. Instantly, a list of all the items on your Windows desktop opens up.

3. Click Control Panel in the list, and—bingo. The display in the window changes from My Computer to the contents of Control Panel. As easily as that, the Address bar lets you jump to anything you want to see—including, as you'll see in a later chapter, anyplace you want to visit on the Internet.

4. To finish up this set of steps, go back to My Computer. But this time, instead of opening the list in the Address bar again, place the mouse pointer on the triangle by the large, left-pointing arrow, the *Back* button, at the far left of the Standard toolbar.

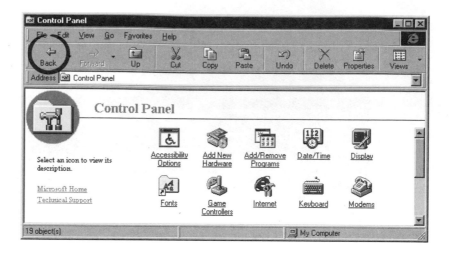

A tooltip appears, telling you that clicking the button will take you back to My Computer.

5. Click the triangle, and a list drops down. Since you've moved only one hop away from My Computer (from My Computer to Control Panel), My Computer is the only place you can go back to.

6. Click My Computer on the list, and back you go.

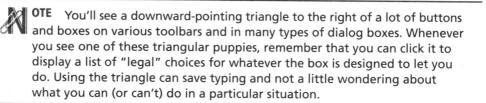

OTE   You'll see a downward-pointing triangle to the right of a lot of buttons and boxes on various toolbars and in many types of dialog boxes. Whenever you see one of these triangular puppies, remember that you can click it to display a list of "legal" choices for whatever the box is designed to let you do. Using the triangle can save typing and not a little wondering about what you can (or can't) do in a particular situation.

Although using the Back button didn't seem all that impressive here, it becomes an extraordinarily useful tool when you've skipped around to many locations because that little Back button "remembers" not only where you've been in that session, but how to get there again. Choose the destination you want from the list, and back you go. No muss, no fuss. The Back button gives you a great way to jump around, all with just one mouse click.

Displaying Labels

To finish experimenting with toolbars, try something that can help you control the amount of space taken up by the Standard buttons at the top of the window: text labels. These labels come in handy while you're learning what the various toolbar buttons do, but you might want to turn them off later:

1. Open the View menu and highlight the Toolbars command again.

2. If you see a check mark to the left of Text Labels (at the bottom of the Toolbars submenu), click to turn off the labels. If you don't see a check mark to the left of Text Labels, click to turn them on. Notice the change in the toolbar buttons.

   As you see, when the labels are off, the buttons are smaller, discreet, and unassuming; when the labels are on, the buttons are nicely descriptive, but they're bigger and more intrusive, too.

3. Leave them on? Turn them off? That's for you to decide, but you might want to keep them turned on, at least for now, to keep your window like the one in the illustrations.

More About Window Panes and Pieces

You've seen how to work with an entire window—frame, pane, and all—and you've seen how you can focus on only the part you need for the job at hand. Are there other, yet unexplored, parts of a window? If so, what do they do? There's an easy way to investigate all the different parts of a window and to have some fun while you're at it. Try the following steps:

1. Right-click anywhere on a blank part of your Windows desktop. This menu appears:

2. Click Properties to open a valuable set of tabbed, index-card-like "sheets" or "dividers" called Display Properties. You should be looking at something like this:

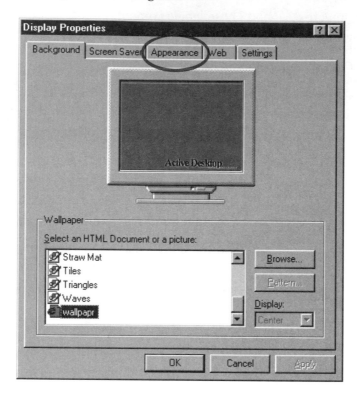

On each of these sheets is a different group of properties—settings—that are related to your display (monitor) and your desktop, and that you can control in much the same way you controlled the double-click speed on your Mouse Properties.

3. You want the Appearance sheet for this set of steps, so click the Appearance tab (circled in the preceding illustration). Now for the fun.

4. To familiarize yourself with the various parts of a window, click on bits and pieces of the windows in the display area (technically, the *preview area*). As you do, you'll see the name of the item you clicked—and its color—appear below, as shown in the following illustration:

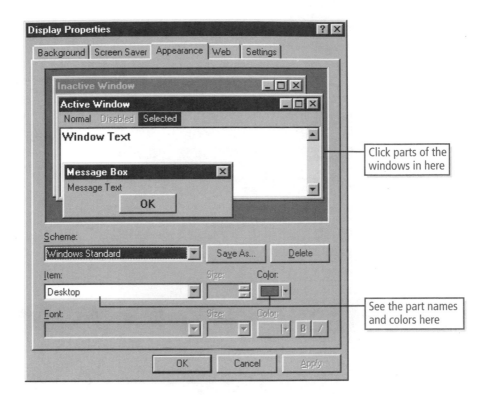

Click title bars, window edges, menu names...whatever you want. Altogether, this is a painless way to learn what the different pieces of a window are called.

5. When you've had enough, click the Cancel button. Or if you're feeling confident and a little adventurous, leave this window open and try the next set of steps.

Take Control with Color

As you saw, the button labeled Color shows you the current color of the window piece you click in the preview area. No doubt, you've already figured out that there must be a way to change some or all of the window colors. Here's how to do it. Feel free to experiment in the next steps. No matter how *ugly* your experiment ends up, you're just going to look at changes in the preview area, so you can scrap it all at will.

1. First, see the effects of an entirely different color scheme for everything, including the desktop. Click the downward-pointing triangle
   at the right of the long, rectangular box labeled *Scheme*, as shown
   here:

As you can see, people with artistic sensibilities have come up with
a number of different color combinations. Some, you'll think are
hideous. Others, you might like a lot. A few, marked "large" or "extra
large" are designed to help people with impaired vision read the
screen more easily.

2. Try out a few color schemes and note how the windows and desktop
   change in the preview area.

3. Now, try changing just selected parts of a window. In the preview
   area, click the part of the window you want to change—say, the title
   bar marked *Active Window*.

4. To change the color, click the button labeled *Color*. When a *palette*
   of colors opens up, click the color you want. Again, you see the result
   in the preview area.

5. If you want, click other window elements in the preview area and change their colors, too.

6. When you're ready to quit, click Cancel to throw away your experiments. (If you want to change screen colors permanently, refer to the boxed text titled "Read Me First...Please" before you try.)

You've come quite a long way now. For everyday tasks, you might not need much more than the Minimize, Maximize, and Close buttons, but if you make use of even half of what you've learned so far, you're well on your way to being not just a capable computer user but quite a knowledgeable one. To close out this chapter, take a look at a special type of window—one that just might save some wear and tear on your teeth and hair sometime.

Read Me First...Please

If you want, feel free to change the color of your title bars and other window elements. Likewise, change to a different color scheme if you want by selecting the color scheme you like and clicking OK on the Display Properties sheet you played with here. If you change color schemes, however, bear in mind that the desktop background color (black) will remain as it is, even if the color scheme is supposed to set it to a different color. That happens because desktop color is closely tied to having Active Desktop, with all its Internet-related abilities, turned on.

For the time being, even though it's natural for you to want to customize your PC with color, leave the desktop background alone. Yes, you can change it, but doing so involves resetting the Active Desktop, and a change like that—here and now—won't guarantee that all the hands-on sessions in the book and on the CD will work for you. At the end of this book, you'll find all the instructions you need. Until then...patience? Thanks.

Help! I'm Stuck!

Sigh. No matter how wise you are, there will be times when you need a little advice. Maybe you can't figure out what to do next, or maybe you don't know how to do whatever it is you want to do, or maybe you're just wondering whether it's possible to do something with a particular program. For whatever reason, don't feel bad because you don't know, and don't feel the problem is yours. Everyone needs a hand once in awhile, even high-level programmers—they just happen to need it at a rather more exotic level than most people.

Well, just as every newspaper comes with its own advice to the *love*lorn, practically every computer program comes with its own advice to the *for*-lorn. It's called, appropriately enough, Help, and it's a good first place to turn when you need a friend.

To see what Help is all about and what it typically looks like, try the following lesson on your CD.

Try It

Here's an overview that shows you several ways to ask for Help:

1. Start the CD either by placing the CD in your CD-ROM drive or by clicking the PCs For Beginners icon on your desktop.
2. On the opening screen, click Computer Essentials.
3. In the list of Essentials lessons, click Getting Help.
4. When you finish the lesson, press Esc and then Enter to quit the CD.

Now take a closer look at what you find in your first and best source of information on using your computer, Windows Help. First up, Help itself and a nifty way to ask for help on Help:

1. Start Windows Help by choosing Help from the Start menu. This is the window that opens up:

2. For help on using this window, click the small question-mark button in the upper right corner, the one circled in the preceding illustration. Notice that the mouse pointer is now accompanied by a question mark. What's this do?

3. Click anywhere inside the large pane that's currently listing Help contents. Immediately, Help displays a message telling you what that area of the window is for.

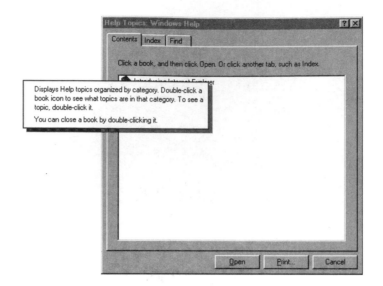

Whenever you see a question-mark button like this one at the top of a window, you can use it to get information about the window itself. Although the example you're looking at now doesn't seem to be that useful, some windows contain many different options, and the question-mark button can be very helpful in figuring out what they all mean.

4. You're going to move on to using Help now, so close the popup message by clicking any part of the window except the Open, Print, and Cancel buttons.

Help Contents

Help gives you two different ways to go about asking for advice:

1. A Contents page organizes Help information by topic, much as chapters organize information in a book. This is the part of Help you should turn to when you're not quite sure what to look for or, as you'll find extremely useful, when you're trying to learn how to use a program.

2. An Index page organizes Help topics alphabetically, just like the index in a book. This is where you turn when you have a question about something very specific, as you'll see in a minute or two.

To familiarize yourself with Help, use Windows Help contents to cruise through the process of getting help on something—in this case, the Calculator accessory you've already seen:

1. If the Help window is not open to the Contents page, as shown in the earlier illustration, click the Contents tab at the top of the window.

2. Here, you see the topics Help is divided into. To "open" a topic, all you do is double-click the book icon to the left of the one you want. To try it, double-click the icon to the left of *Introducing Windows*.

3. Opening the introduction shows you two subtopics, a welcome section and one on using Windows accessories (such as Calculator). Double-click the book icon next to the Accessories topic to see what it contains.

4. Wheels within wheels... This section is even further divided, now into task-related categories:

5. You're getting there. To actually see some help, double-click the book icon next to For General Use, and then double-click the icon showing a page with a question mark that appears next to *Calculator: for making calculations*. Note that book icons open to show you

more items; the question-mark icon takes you to actual Help content:

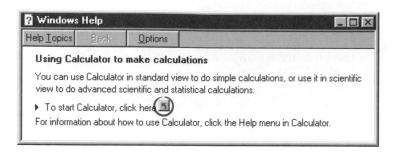

Although this small window doesn't really seem to tell you much, it does briefly describe Calculator. More important right now, notice the small *click here* button circled in the preceding illustration.

6. Click the button, and *voila*—Calculator appears, offering its very own Help on the menu bar.

7. To see Calculator's Help, click the Help menu at the top of the window. Click Help Topics, and you see another Help window, very much like the one you started from the Start menu.

8. Browse through Calculator's Help if you wish. When you're ready to move on, click the Close buttons in both the Help and Calculator windows.

Help Index

And now for the Index. You scan the index of a book to look up the exact term that interests you. You use the Help index in the same way—except you don't have to bother scanning or turning pages. Help does it for you. To give this a try, use the index to find the same Help you found on the Contents page:

1. Start Windows Help again from the Start menu. Click the Index tab to see this page:

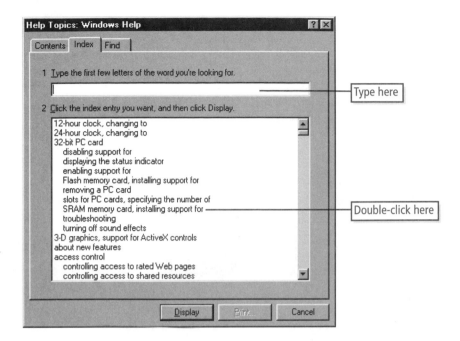

Looks a little different, doesn't it? You can, if you want, scroll through the index in the large pane, but it's a lot easier to type a few letters or maybe a word you want to find and let Help do the work.

2. You should see a blinking vertical bar (the cursor) in the small, rectangular *text box* at the top of the window. If you don't, just click inside the box to make the cursor appear.

Sometimes, you'll find yourself trying several "keywords" before you manage to find the Help topic you actually need in the index. That can be frustrating, but try not to get too hostile. Unfortunately, Help can't read your mind. Keywords are the best that it (and you) can do— at least for now.

3. To try out the index, type the letter *c*. Help jumps to the first *c* entry in its index and highlights the entry.

4. That's not what you're looking for (not in this example, anyway). So add an *a* to your typing. Hmm. *Cables* has both a *c* and an *a*, so the highlight doesn't move.

5. Type an *l* next. Now you've got it.

6. Double-click the entry under Calculator that reads *starting*. There it is. Same Help window, different way of getting there.

The moral of the story, as you can plainly see, is that Help is only a mouse click—and maybe a letter or two—away.

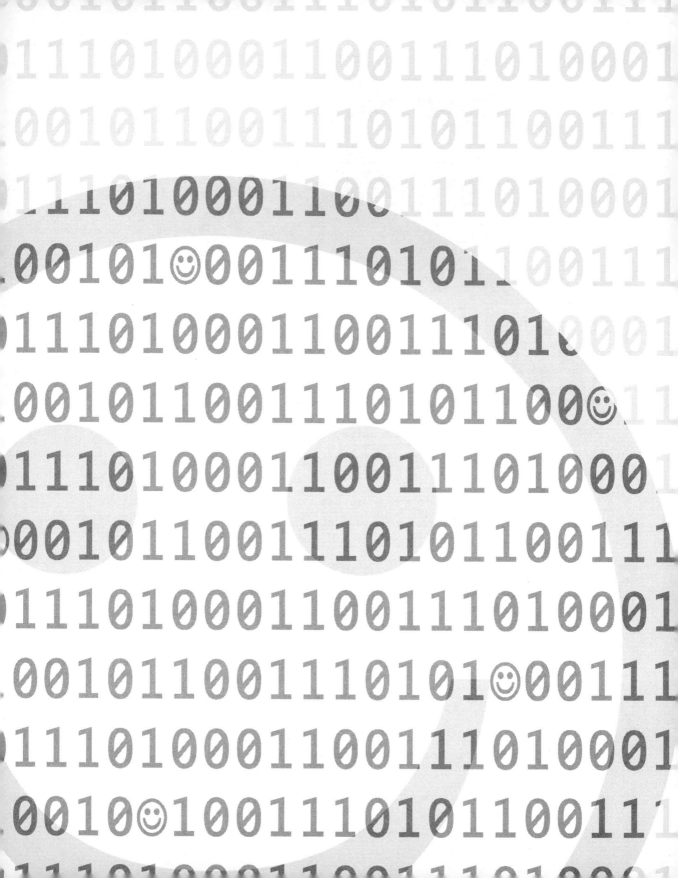

Basics Are Over,
Time for Some Fun

You've spent a fair amount of time learning about Windows and windows, and you know they're as indispensable to the computer as most boys and girls are to each other once they're past the "cootie" stage. But the fact is, you bought your PC to use it and to enjoy it, not to become the world's first Olympic winner in mouse maneuvers.

So how are you going to enjoy this machine? Or, as Microsoft likes to say, "where do you want to go today?" Well, to actually *go* somewhere else in the world—electronically, that is—you need the Internet, and that's for a later chapter. But without ever being connected to anything more than the electrical outlet in the wall, your PC can leave its workhorse duties and join the world of light and sound.

Most people, when they think about the different things a computer can do, tend to think about some or all of the following:

- The Internet
- The "big three" applications: word processing for writing, spreadsheets for financial calculations, and databases for organizing information
- Games

Dinosaur Days

Computers have come a long way since the early 80s, when they first became a force in the world. It's been an amazing journey for so short a time, too. Back then, the ability to display color was still in the future. Graphics and animation were even farther away, and computer sound was an unmusical ding that people generously called a "beep." Even computer text had but one look—something like this:

YOICKS!

Nowadays, a computer named Deep Blue can "think" well enough to push a chess Grandmaster to the wall, and a computer program named EMI ("Emmy") can compose—really compose—music that listeners mistake for pieces by Bach, Beethoven, or Scott Joplin. And even though the average PC isn't very talkative, many companies are working on ways to make computers both speak and respond to speech. Although talking computers won't become common for awhile yet, their potential is enormous in applications as diverse as education and making computers more practical for people with physical disabilities. And even now, today, there's an interactive "talking" Barney (yes, the purple dinosaur) that can use the brains of a PC to chatter away with tots.

Technology marches on...mostly forward.

Seldom do people—at least those still new to computers—first think of applying these machines to sound or video. Yet a computer, at least one equipped with multimedia capabilities (which most are these days) can easily handle these tasks, too.

Since all work and no play makes no fun for anyone, here's a "time out" chapter that shows you around some of the less, er, practical ways you can put your PC to work. The chapter's a short one in relation to the more "serious" parts of the book, but even though its main goal is to give you some rest and relaxation, it will also let you see more about the potential waiting to be used on your PC.

Try It

Along with the sets of lessons you've been so diligently working through, the CD offers a collection of "Goodies," some of which are packaged so that a single mouse click will bring them to life. Later in this chapter, you'll learn how to use your Windows programs to open and run the same goodies, but to sample them now:

1. If necessary, place the lesson CD in your CD-ROM drive. Click Exit when the CD begins to play. (If the CD is already in the drive, skip this step.)

2. Open My Computer, right-click the icon for your CD-ROM drive, and choose Explore.

3. Click the icon (labeled *Goodies*) that looks like a blank page with a large blue *e* on it.

4. Although the free software and game sound intriguing, limit yourself to "clicking here..." for audio and video. In the audio section, feel free to click the icons (one at a time, of course) labeled *track09* and *track12*. In the video section (which includes some teaching videos you'll see later in the book), click the icon labeled *FALLS*.

When you finish, close the windows to your Goodies collection and to your CD-ROM drive.

And now, move on to making such things happen whenever you want, with whatever "goodies" of your own you want to play with.

Egads! That's Me?

Maybe you're like most people, and you cringe when you hear a recording of your voice. If your computer came with a microphone, how about getting in some practice by recording yourself and playing back the result? You can even have fun speeding up the playback and slowing it down. And perhaps, in time, you'll even come to like hearing yourself speak. Here's what to do.

1. From the Start button, work through the Programs, Accessories, and Multimedia submenus. Click Sound Recorder, and this small window appears:

Its control buttons look a lot like the controls on a typical voice recorder, and they work in much the same way.

2. Grab your microphone and think of something to say. When you're ready, click to open the File menu, and then click New to tell Sound Recorder you want to create a new file. (Any kind of information that you save on a computer—words, pictures, sound, video—is always saved as a file.)

3. Click the Record button, the one with a big red circle on it.

4. Speak up, nice and clear, into the microphone.

I Want to, But...

If your computer didn't come with a microphone, that doesn't mean it will never hear its master's voice. Check the Multimedia submenu under Accessories on the Start menu for the Sound Recorder program described here, and check your computer (most likely the back) for a small, round opening with a label (probably MIC) or a picture representing a microphone. If you find both, you can buy and use any microphone, as long as it plugs in via a one-eighth-inch jack.

Also, if you *do* have a microphone, but you *don't* have Sound Recorder, your manufacturer probably included another media program for you. Check your computer's documentation for information and for instructions on how to use the program you have.

5. When you're done, click the Stop button (with the big rectangle on it).

6. To play back your recording, click the Play button, which is marked with a single, right-pointing triangle.

7. If you want to save your recording, open the File menu again and click the Save As command—not the Save command. This dialog box appears:

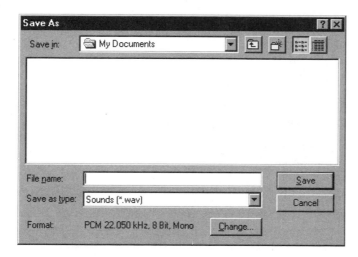

You see and use the Save As command in many Windows programs. It always looks like the one shown here, and it's always used to help you save a file for the first time. The reason you use Save As rather than Save is so that you can give the file a name in the box titled File Name.

8. A blinking cursor should already be in the File Name box, so just type a name for the file. Any name will do, including "My Golden Tones" or even "This is the voice of doom." For your own sake, however, a shorter, more descriptive name is best, especially a name that will later remind you of what you recorded—for example, if all you said was "testing, 1, 2, 3," name the file Test One or something similar.

9. To save the file, click the Save button to the right of the File Name box.

Different Types of Files

By default, sounds are stored on your computer as files ending in the letters *wav* (short for "wave"). These letters, technically known as an extension, identify the type of file to Windows, which is the program that searches out and opens all the files you use. Other types of files have different extensions. Word processed files, for example, are typically saved as *doc* (for document) files; video clips with sound are saved as *avi* (for audio video interleaved) files. Although you'll see extensions frequently, you don't have to either think them up or assign them. Your applications do that for you—thankfully.

That's it. Your voice is now saved for the ages on your hard disk, in an electronic folder named My Documents, which Sound Recorder turns to unless (as you'll see in Chapter 5) you specify a different folder. At any rate, anytime you want to listen to yourself again, here's all you do:

1. Start Sound Recorder again.

2. Open the File menu, and this time choose the Open command. You'll see this dialog box, commonly known as the File Open dialog box:

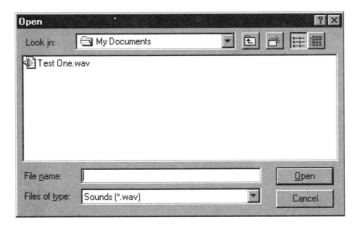

Sound Recorder shows you—by default—the My Documents folder. Since that's where you saved your sound file, you can now...

3. Either type the name of the file in the File Name box and click the Open button, *or* (much easier) find the name of the file in the list in the top of the window and double-click the file name.

4. To play back the sound recording, click the Play button as you did earlier.

5. If you haven't made any changes to the recording—that is, you didn't click the Record button after you opened the file—just click the Close button in the Sound Recorder window to send everything packing.

Fooling Around or Getting Serious

If you enjoyed recording your voice, you'll probably also enjoy making it sound a little different. To play around with your recording, just start Sound Recorder, open the file, click the Effects menu, and choose the Increase Speed or Decrease Speed command (or, if you want, adjust the volume, or add an echo, or even reverse the whole thing).

By the way, these effects are not only for fooling around. Even though you didn't do so here, you can plug a CD player into your computer and record sound that way, too. (Do remember, however, that music you record from a CD is *copyrighted*. That means it doesn't belong to you, and you are *not* free to distribute it.) And you can use the commands described here to "tune up" those recordings, too.

By the way, if you're comfortable with stereo-type electronics, the way you plug a CD player into your PC is by cabling the line-out jack(s) or the headphone jack on the player to the line-in jack or jacks (which should be labeled) on your PC. Depending on the number of jacks on your equipment, the cable you need will probably have either a stereo miniplug (for the CD player) at one end and two RCA phono plugs at the other (for the PC), or it will have two phono plugs at each end.

Rock, Bach, and Video, Too

In addition to Sound Recorder, you probably have some other media-related programs on your Multimedia menu: CD Player, which you use (obviously) to play music CDs; Media Player, which you can actually use to play sound, animation, or video; and Active Movie Control, which you can use to run video clips.

CD Player

It's unlikely that you'll have to do this, but if music doesn't begin to play when you tell it to, check the volume controls on your speakers and on your CD-ROM drive to be sure they're turned up high enough. If that doesn't work, check the connection your speakers are plugged into on your PC. If you see another plug opening near the connection (probably below it), you might have to move the plug to the other opening to play music CDs.

The easiest way to soothe your musical soul is with CD Player, although Media Player (described in the next section) works fine, too. Playing music with CD Player is, in fact, so simple that you probably don't even have to find or start the program, thanks to a feature called *autoplay*. Autoplay detects when you put a CD into your CD-ROM drive and automatically starts the music for you. Here's how to see whether you've got CD Player, and how to try it out with one of your own music CDs:

1. First, although this won't be necessary at other times, click the Start button and work through the Programs, Accessories, and Multimedia submenus to see if CD Player is listed. You're just checking for the program, so when you're done, move the mouse pointer to a blank part of the desktop and click to close the menus.

2. If you have CD Player on your computer, remove the lesson CD from your CD-ROM drive (if necessary) and place a music CD in the drive instead.

3. Sit back. In a few seconds, music should begin to play. If it doesn't, don't worry. You just have to go to plan B, below.

4. If you *do* hear music, skip ahead to the steps starting at the bottom of page 91 telling you how to control what you hear.

Now, here's plan B (which you need only if the Autoplay feature on your PC hasn't been turned on for you):

1. Leaving the music CD in your CD-ROM drive, click the Start button. Work your way to the Multimedia submenu, highlight CD Player, and click.

2. When CD Player appears, it looks like this:

To start the music, click the Play button. A little more effort, but
not much.

Whichever way you start CD Player, there are a number of different ways
to control what you hear and when you hear it. You can, for instance, play
only selected tracks on the CD, or you can play them in random order.
And, of course, you can adjust the volume to anywhere from a whisper to
a shriek, depending on your tastes and overall fortitude. First, though,
take a look at a little technical coolness:

1. If CD Player started automatically, look on the taskbar. You'll see a
    button labeled *CD Player*. If you started CD Player in plan B, click
    the Minimize button to reduce it to a button on the taskbar.

2. Notice that the CD Player button on the taskbar is telling you which
    track is currently playing. This information updates as the tracks
    change. Better yet, though, place the mouse pointer on the button and
    hold it still for a few seconds. You see not only the track number,
    you see the elapsed time changing as you watch.

Ahh, you're not seriously impressed? All right. But these *real-time* updates
really are neat from a technical point of view. At any rate, onward:

1. Click the CD Player button on the taskbar to open the player win-
    dow on the screen.

2. To figure out what all these controls do, just point to them (but don't click), one by one. Hold the mouse on each, and you'll see a tooltip showing the name of the control you're pointing to.

3. Notice, however, there's no volume control? It's there. Click the View menu at the top of the window. Slide the highlight down, and click Volume Control. Something like the following opens (you might see more or fewer pieces on yours):

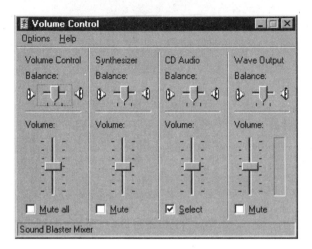

To adjust the volume, the balance between speakers, or both, simply point to the slider on the control you want and drag it one way or the other.

Media Player and Audio CDs

If you don't have CD Player, you probably do have Media Player on your Multimedia submenu. Media Player isn't as sophisticated a music box as CD Player, but like 3-in-1 oil it can be used for other things, too—not only music, but animation and video, as well. Even if you used CD Player in the earlier section, you might want to try Media Player here, too, just to become familiar with it for the sections titled "Media Player and Sound Files" and "Media Player and Video Clips."

To use Media Player:

1. If necessary, remove the lesson CD from your CD-ROM drive and re-place it with a music CD.

2. Click the Start button and work through Programs and Accessories to the Multimedia submenu. Click Media Player, and this window appears:

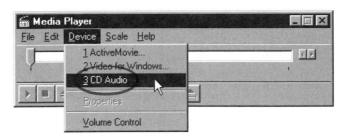

3. Click the Device menu and choose CD Audio (circled in the illustration) from the list of options that opens. Your list might not include the same options shown here, but don't worry about it.

4. Click the Play button, which is marked with a right-pointing triangle, at the far left of the row of controls:

To see what the other controls do, hold the mouse pointer still for a second or two on each one, and a small tooltip will appear to tell you the name of the control.

5. Even though you'll be using Media Player again in the next section, put it away when you're through with your music CD. Doing so will simplify the steps in the next practice session.

Media Player and Sound Files

Now, alas, education rears its ugly little head again. Last time, you chose CD Audio to tell Media Player that you wanted to play sound. But sound, at least where a PC is concerned, doesn't always come on an audio disc.

Sometimes—often, in fact—it comes as a file on a computer disk. Choosing CD Audio to hear such a file won't work, so what do you do? That's what you're about to find out.

You're going to tell Media Player to fetch and play two sound files for you. One of the files is already stored on your hard disk, and the other is in the Goodies collection on your lesson CD. In the process, you'll see how to use a dialog box called File Open, which is a dialog box you'll work with so often in using your PC that the more exposure you get now, the more comfortable you'll be later on. If you're ready, then:

1. Start Media Player by working from the Start button through Programs and Accessories to the Multimedia submenu.

2. To find the sound file on your hard disk, open the Device menu and click Sound. This dialog box appears:

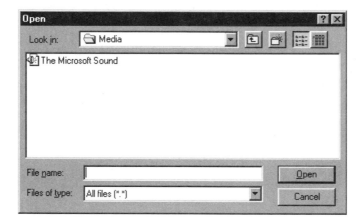

The file you want is called The Microsoft Sound. It's in the Media subfolder of the Windows folder on your hard disk, and you're probably looking at its name right now, in the upper part of the dialog box. (If you don't see The Microsoft Sound, skip it for now. The next steps tell you how to find *any* file, any time, and when you're more experienced with your PC, you'll have no trouble finding this presumably elusive one.)

3. If you see The Microsoft Sound listed, double-click its name. That's the easy way to open any file in any File Open dialog box. To play the sound, click the Play button on Media Player's controls. And yes, the sound is familiar—it's the one you hear when Windows starts up.

4. Next, find the sound file on your lesson CD. (If necessary, replace your music CD with the lesson CD.) Click Exit when the opening lesson screen appears.

5. Click Media Player's File menu and click Open once again. This time, click the downward-pointing triangle to the right of the box labeled *Look in* at the top of the dialog box:

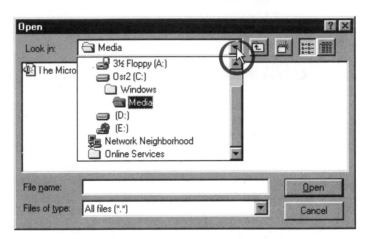

Clicking this triangle opens a list of possible places to look for a file. That list includes not only your hard disk, but your floppy and CD-ROM drives, too.

6. The file you're looking for is on the disc in the CD-ROM drive, so click the name of the drive in the open list, scrolling up or down if necessary.

7. You're going to have to work your way to the file, so first double-click the folder icon named Goodies. When the display changes to show what's in the Goodies folder, double-click the folder icon named Audio. As soon as you "open" the Audio folder, the list of

files near the top of the dialog box changes to show the names of the audio files in the folder.

8. To play the file called *track09*, double-click its name to tell Media Player that's the one you want to open.

9. Click the Play button, and off you go.

10. When the sound file finishes, you can leave Media Player open. You'll be using it again in a moment.

Media Player and Video Clips

Just as a universal remote can control both a television and a VCR, Media Player can "control" not only audio CDs and sound files, but video clips as well. To play a video clip (one of which just happens to be included in the Goodies collection on your lesson CD), all you have to do is tell Media Player what type of file you're interested in. And, of course, push the Play button. Here's how to do it:

1. If necessary, start Media Player (Start button, Programs, Accessories, Multimedia—you know the drill).

2. You want to tell Media Player to turn its attention to video, so click the Device menu and choose Video For Windows from the list that opens. Choosing Video For Windows causes the File Open dialog box to appear.

3. Click the downward-pointing triangle to the right of the Look In box and click your CD-ROM drive in the list that opens. As before, double-click the Goodies folder. This time, however, double-click the Video folder when it appears.

4. Now double-click the icon for the FALLS video clip, and a second window opens near the Media Player window:

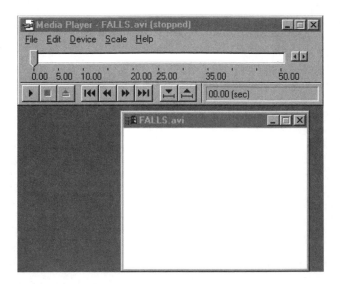

5. There's your "projection screen." To watch the video, click the Play button on Media Player's controls.

6. When the movie's over, click the Close button on Media Player to put everything away.

Active Movie Control

Earlier in the book, you found out that Windows often gives you several ways to do the same thing—here's another example. In addition to Media Player, you can use a program called Active Movie Control to display video clips and play audio files. (Active Movie Control appears on your Multimedia menu when you install the version of Internet Explorer that's on your CD.)

Active Movie Control is newer than Media Player, and it's a little different in that it doesn't offer any menus. In the way it behaves, it acts something like a projector or viewer with two simple buttons: Play and Stop. So how do you use it? Take a look by telling Active Movie Control to replay the video on your lesson CD. You'll find that the window is a little larger, and you might find the resolution clearer with Active Movie Control.

1. Click the Start button and work through Programs, Accessories, and Multimedia. Click Active Movie Control on the Multimedia submenu. Unlike program startups you've seen so far, Active Movie Control opens with its window overlaid by a File Open dialog box, like this:

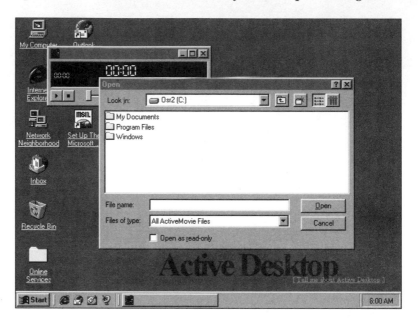

2. To "project" a video, you first choose it, so click the downward-pointing triangle to the right of the Look In box and choose your CD-ROM drive from the list that opens.

3. Double-click the Goodies and Video folders. Double-click FALLS to open the video file. The File Open dialog box disappears, and the Active Movie window expands to display a blank "screen."

4. Click the Run button (not called *Play* this time) in the lower left corner of the window, and the video plays. If you're not keen on reruns, click the Stop button to the right of the Run button.

5. When you're through with this, click the Close button to close the window.

The Many Forms of Movies

As you might have read elsewhere, there are different ways of storing images for use on a computer. Video for Windows is stored in files with the extension *avi*—those three little letters described earlier in the box titled "Different Types of Files." Other formats, supported by both Active Movie Control and Media Player, rely on different methods or standards for compressing and saving video images. One such, specified by MPEG, the Motion Picture Experts Group, can be identified by the extension *mpg* (which seems as if it should stand for *miles per gallon*) at the end of a file.

You don't have to know how these storage formats differ, but it does help to know that they do exist, if for no other reason than that very knowing can help you find a particular video file on a disk. For instance, there might come a time when you want to view a certain video, but the File Open dialog box doesn't list it, even when you choose the disk it's stored on. If that happens, click the downward-pointing triangle to the right of the Files Of Type box at the bottom of the File Open dialog box, and choose the video type from the list that opens up:

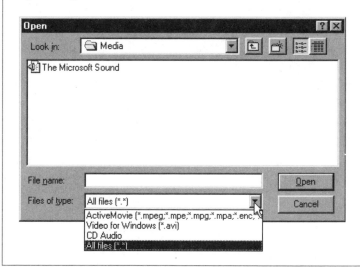

(continued)

The Many Forms of Movies *continued*

Oh. If you don't know the file type to begin with, open My Computer, open a window to the disk the file is on, right-click the file's name, and choose Properties from the menu that pops up. A "properties" sheet will open up, showing you the file's name and its extension. Armed with the extension, you can then go back to the File Open command and choose the correct video type.

This same properties-sheet procedure also works, of course, for other files, too—word processed documents, whatever. The information is presented here, however, just because video comes in so many different formats and because you might find the tip useful in relation to Active Movie Control, Media Player, or both.

Great Ways to Waste Time (While Pretending to Be Busy)

Now you come to one of the best things about using a PC: play. Chances are, your computer came with a few games installed, and chances are even better that you've already tried them out. If you haven't, however, here's an introduction to a few of the standard games you get with Windows and your PC, plus another that you'll find on your lesson CD. In addition to being fun, all of these games are great at helping beginners become comfortable with computers.

Minesweeper

This game is at once enjoyable and infuriating, at least if you're the type of person who hates losing. The idea is to uncover all the squares on the board without uncovering a hidden mine—one of those evil spiked things you see floating toward ships in World War II movies. Winning takes thought, but the game can keep you going for hours. To play Minesweeper:

1. From the Start button, work through Programs and Accessories to the Game submenu. Click Minesweeper; this game board appears:

2. Now you're on your own. Click a square. When you do, you'll un-
    cover a number. That number tells you how many mines are hidden
    in the adjoining squares. (Any square touching the square you
    clicked, including those touching only the corners, counts here.)

3. Try to uncover all the squares except those covering mines, and to
    do so as quickly as possible. Clicking a square with no mines nearby
    can sometimes clear a large part of the board in one move, and that's
    always a kick. If you lose, however, you see:

(This tends to happen more often than you like.)

4. Click the smiley to start a new game.

Freecell

If you like card games, you'll love Freecell. It's a form of solitaire in which all the cards are laid out in eight stacks at the beginning of the game. The object is to shift cards from one stack to another so that they eventually all move up in suits to the top right portion of the window. Freecell is definitely a game you can get hooked on, and it's a great way to take a break when you've been concentrating on other (real) work with your PC. Here's a look at it:

1. From the Start button, work through Programs and Accessories to Games, and click Freecell. In the rather barren window that appears, click Game, and then click New to start a game. The window fills with something like this:

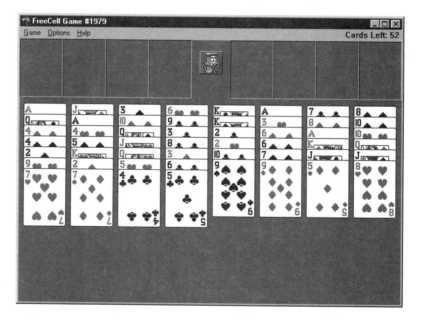

2. To play, arrange the cards just as you do in other forms of solitaire: by placing them in descending order, alternating red and black. To move cards from one column to another, click the card you want to move, point to the column you want to move it to, and click again. As you play, the game will develop like this:

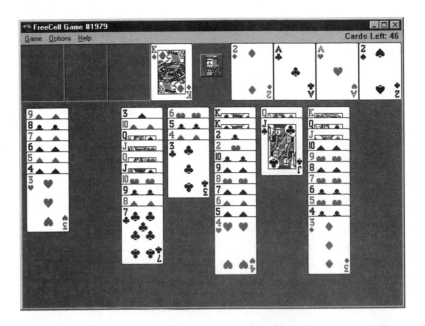

It's believed that every single game of Freecell is winnable. You might want to remind yourself of that when—as will happen—you come across a layout that just doesn't seem doable. If you're the stubborn type, determined to beat a particular game, you can start it over by clicking Restart Game on the Game menu.

If the suits are stacking up (no pun intended) evenly at the top of the window, Freecell will automatically move the next cards in each suit to the top for you. At any time, however, you can move a card up yourself by clicking it, and then clicking the suit to which it belongs. (The card must, of course, be the next one in the suit.)

That's it. Have some fun while you sharpen your skills at pointing and clicking. If you're not sure how to play, remember: advice is sitting under the Help menu at the top of the window.

Well, that's it. Time to head back to work. The next chapter shows you how to begin customizing your PC, so it really does become your *personal* computer. Actually, some of what you'll see there is a lot of fun, too.

Putting the *Personal* in Your Personal Computer

Have you ever wondered why PCs are called *Personal* Computers? Why, for instance, aren't they called *Peewee* Computers, since they're so small compared to the industrial-strength machines that are at the heart of so many large businesses, governments, and universities?

Originally, the "personal" in PC meant the opposite of "group" or "shared" because the 1970s ancestors of your PC were the first computers that individuals could dream of owning all by themselves. Unlike the mainframes and minicomputers that came before them, PCs were not priced in gazillions of dollars. Nor did they have to be shared with anyone if their buyers didn't feel like sharing. They were—still are—primarily personal in the ownership sense, even though hordes of PCs happily work for anyone who needs them in libraries, schools, and small businesses.

But, of course, "personal" in another sense also means "specially for me." That meaning applies to your computer too, and that's actually the topic of this chapter: How to make your PC (which, face it, came off a production line) uniquely yours. Physical differences aside, there are lots of ways to

OTE You'll sometimes see your PC and others like it referred to as "Wintel" machines in news reports and articles. You probably know that *Wintel* is short for *Windows + Intel* and that it refers to the operating system and microprocessor type that drive your PC. But maybe you didn't know that Wintel refers to roughly 80 percent of the PCs in the *world*. 'Tis a popular platform (hardware/software combination) you have there, and that's good because it means the lion's share of available games and applications is made for computers like yours.

customize what you see on the screen and how your PC organizes information. These are, in fact, the ways that eventually come to make your PC reflect your likes, your needs, and your individuality. And it's the combination of all these touches that makes your PC personal in the truest sense.

In keeping with this, most of what you're going to learn in this chapter has to do with the way your computer's desktop looks, but you'll also begin learning how to use electronic folders for storing and organizing the documents you create with your applications. After all, just as your method of filing real papers is uniquely yours, whether they're superorganized and neatly labeled or tossed into a box marked "stuff," so your computer filing system will represent the way you think and the way you organize the work you do on your PC. Your filing system and the documents in it will, in fact, become the ultimate reflection of the "personal" in your PC.

It Starts with a Feeling

Anyone who routinely uses more than one computer will tell you that no two PCs feel the same. Some of the difference has to do with the physical location of the computer—a different desk, a different chair. And some of it is because computers of different makes and models just plain feel different. Their keyboards, for example, aren't quite the same, nor are their monitors and often even their mice. The controls might be in different places, and they might also differ in how they work. The on/off switch on one, for instance, might be a toggle, but it might be a push button on the other. These differences aren't bad; they're just things that make two computers different.

Oddly enough, though, even two computers of the exact same make and model don't feel identical. Each is unique in much the same way a car of the same make, model, year, and even color feels different from the one you drive every day. Sure, you have no trouble driving either one, but still…one is yours and the other is not. Over time, you'll come to feel this way about your PC, too. You'll become so used to the feel of the keyboard, the fingerprints on the monitor, the position of your mouse, and the humming fan that cools the computer's innards that only your PC will truly feel like *your* PC.

Desktop Decorations

One of the most entertaining ways to personalize a computer is by choosing your own desktop color. If you want to take things a step further, you can even "paste" some *wallpaper* onto the background color, or you can overlay the color with any of several patterns ranging from bubbles to bricks. All of this is both simple and fun, as you can see on your lesson CD.

Try It

The Windows Overview section on your CD includes a hands-on lesson that shows you how to change color schemes (as you did in Chapter 3), as well as how to change the desktop color, wallpaper, and pattern. To try it:

1. As usual, place the lesson CD in your CD-ROM drive if it's not already there.

2. On the Contents page, click Windows Overview, and then click to close the Overview introduction.

3. Click the lesson "Customizing Your Desktop Appearance."

4. Quit the CD either by clicking the lesson window's Close button when you complete step 14 or by clicking Contents on the Overview page and Exit on the Contents page.

Now dig a little deeper and take what you learned a step further.

The Desktop Background

The desktop color is the background color on which your desktop icons and open windows sit. When Active Desktop is in effect and you are viewing it as a *Web page* (as you currently are on your computer so that you can work through the lessons on the CD and in the book without problem), you can't easily change the black desktop background to pink, blue, yellow, or any other color. Why is that, and how on earth are you going to play with the desktop color if all you can see is black?

Let's take the "why" first. As you saw in the lesson on your CD, the black background with the words *Active Desktop* at the bottom appears when you apply the *wallpapr* wallpaper to your desktop. (The *wallpapr* spelling is not a misprint, by the way—that's the way you see it in Windows, too.) At any rate, this wallpaper essentially covers the entire screen with a complete *page* of information displayed in the World Wide Web style known as *HTML* (which stands for Hypertext Markup Language and is explained in more detail in Chapter 9). And just as you can't change the color of a book page, you can't easily change the color of this Web-style page.

So how do you gain the flexibility you need for the next sets of steps? You turn *Web view* off temporarily by replacing your Web wallpaper with the pre-Internet Windows *classic* look, which allows you to fiddle with colors to your heart's content. Switching between one look and the other, although it can be confusing to someone who's never used a computer, is easy and should cause you no problems at all, given the amount of knowledge you've gained by now. Here's what to do:

1. Point to a blank part of the desktop, and right-click.

2. When the pop-up menu appears, highlight Active Desktop.

3. Notice that the option View As Web Page is checked on the Active Desktop submenu, to indicate that it's currently turned on.

4. You've done this before: Click View As Web Page to turn it off. Your window quickly changes the Windows Standard color scheme you saw in the lesson on your CD and which is shown in Figure 5-1.

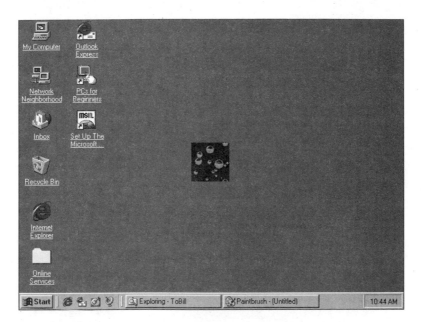

Figure 5-1.   *The Windows Standard color scheme.*

> **NOTE** Although you've turned off View As Web Page here, you're advised to turn it back on when you finish with this section, to be sure your computing environment matches what the CD and the remainder of this book expect. Don't concern yourself about exactly when to do this, though. You'll be reminded, both later in this chapter and whenever necessary in the Try It sections of the book.

And that's all there is to that. Simple, but quite a dramatic change in appearance—a change that you're about to customize even more. To start off, take a closer look at the desktop appearance and, in the process, see how you can even create a custom desktop color if you choose:

1. Right-click on a blank part of the desktop, and choose Properties from the pop-up menu.

2. Click the Appearance tab on the Display Properties sheet that opens.

3. The desktop is always shown by default in the Item box, so all you have to do is select a color you like. You've already done this, too: click the downward-pointing triangle under Color, and then click the Other button at the bottom of the basic *palette* that opens.

4. Clicking Other causes the very colorful Color window to open, as you saw in the CD lesson:

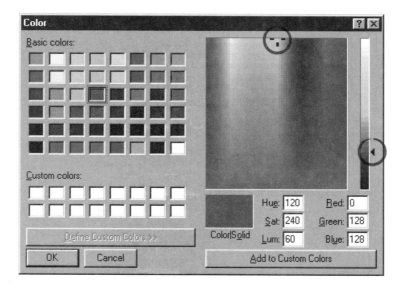

This window contains a number of features that are unique to using color—enough to warrant at least a little explanation, so here are the main parts:

- The Basic Colors at the upper left are, essentially, an extended set of colors you can choose for your desktop.

- The Color/Solid box toward the lower right part of the window lets you preview different shades of a color as you...

■ Use the two rainbow-hued boxes at the upper right of the window to adjust either the color or the amount of white and black mixed in with it to create…

■ A custom color, which you can add to the Custom Colors boxes at the lower left of the window.

Now, try them all. This is better than finger painting—it's not as messy.

5. As you did in the lesson, choose one of the extended set of colors by clicking one that you like, and then clicking OK. The preview window near the top of the main properties sheet shows what the color will look like on the desktop.

6. Now, click the downward-pointing triangle under Color, and then click the Other button again to reopen the Color window.

7. This time, have some fun by inventing your own color. Place your mouse pointer on the triangle (circled in the preceding illustration) to the right of the long, skinny box. Drag the triangle up and down to adjust the amount of white or black in your chosen color. As you drag, you see the left-hand side of the Color/Solid box change to show the result.

8. To change the color itself, point to the daisylike, four-pointed slider (also circled in the illustration) in the rainbow-colored box. This one, you can drag up, down, or to the side. As you drag, both the left and right halves of the Color/Solid box change.

9. When you hit upon a combination you like, click the Add To Custom Colors button at the bottom of the window. Your personalized color will appear in one of the blank boxes under Custom Colors.

10. To see what your custom color looks like on the desktop, click OK.

11. To finish up, click OK, and your custom color shows up on the screen.

Color Schemes

Now, about color schemes. You've seen, both in the book and on the CD, how to choose one that's been created for you. What you're about to do is create one for yourself, simply by selecting different elements in the Display Properties preview window you just used and then applying attributes such as color, *font* (type style), font size (in units called *points*, of which there are roughly 72 to the inch), and bold or italic lettering styles.

 OTE As you're seelng, your PC gives you enormous flexibility in customizing color and color schemes. Because it's just a machine, make sure you take all the credit when visitors compliment you on the way your computer's desktop matches your house. On the flip side, if they run for their sunglasses when they see your customized screen, just put it down to a "temporary glitch" in the display. The truth is out there, but who except you will know what it is?

The title bar of the active window is a good place to start your experimenting. Here's what to do:

1. Right-click on a blank part of the desktop, choose Properties, and click the Appearance tab just as you did before.

2. In the preview window of the Appearance tab, click the title bar labeled Active Window.

3. In the lower part of the Appearance tab, change different aspects of the title bar by:

   ■ Choosing a color as you did earlier. Notice that you can also change the color of the title bar text by using the Color box to the right of the Font box and the Size box.

   ■ Clicking the downward-pointing triangle to the right of the Font box to choose a different type style. (Watch the preview window to see what the font you choose looks like.)

   ■ Clicking the triangles to the right of the Size boxes to change the size of the title bar, the font displayed on the title bar, or both.

   ■ Choosing a color for the title bar text by opening the Color box to the right of the Font box.

■ Clicking the B button to boldface the text, or clicking the / button to make it italic. (If you don't like the result, click the button again to undo the effect.)

4. If you wish, change other elements in the preview window the same way. Not all options are available for each element—only the ones that are most appropriate. You can't, for instance, change the color of your desktop icons, but you can change the font of the text beneath them.

5. When you're satisfied with the results, click the Save As button to the right of the Scheme box, and this little dialog box will appear:

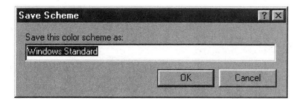

Type a name for your new color scheme. Use any name you want— *Mushroom*, for instance, or *Carnival*, or *North Woods* or, for that matter, *Dog Food*.

6. Click OK, and your new color scheme is added to the list in the Scheme box. To see how it looks on the desktop, click OK in the Display Properties window.

From now on, you can apply your custom color scheme whenever you want just by choosing it from the list and clicking OK. Windows treats it no differently from any of its own built-in color schemes.

Wallpaper

Interior decorators and magazines are forever telling you that one easy way to jazz up a "tired" room is by applying paint or wallpaper. And so it goes for your PC's desktop, too. You saw on the CD how to choose both wallpapers and desktop patterns. There's also a little more you can do.

OTE   What's the difference between the Apply button and the OK button? Actually, they both do the same thing in terms of changing your desktop. The big difference, and one you'll note here, is that Apply assumes you want to do more, while OK assumes you're done. Thus, Apply changes the desktop but does not close the window; OK both changes the desktop and closes the window.

1. Right-click a blank part of the desktop, and choose Properties again.

2. If you changed to your own color scheme in the preceding steps, you might want to switch back to Windows Standard for awhile by clicking the Appearance tab, selecting Windows Standard from the Scheme list, and clicking the Apply button.

You won't hurt anything by leaving your color scheme on while experimenting with wallpaper and patterns, but a little of what you're about to do goes a long way. Be kind to yourself and your eyesight. You're going to get a little aquatic here, and your desktop is going to get a little busy to look at.

To try out wallpapers, you need the Background tab:

1. Click the Background tab to display this:

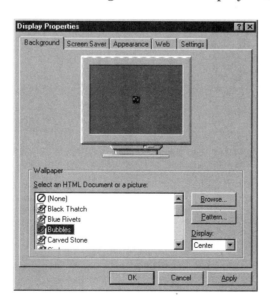

2. The CD lesson showed you how to apply a wallpaper, so verify that Bubbles is selected. Check to see that the Display option specifies Center, and click Apply if necessary.

3. Now you're going to create a desktop pattern of your own. The Background tab you see will be one of the following:

   ▪ If your Background tab looks like this:

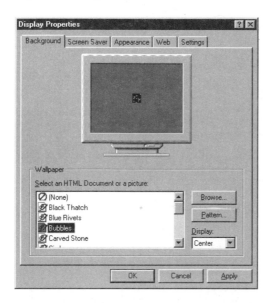

   click the Pattern button on the Background tab to display this dialog box:

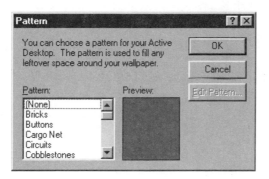

■ If your Background tab looks like this, just go on to the next step.

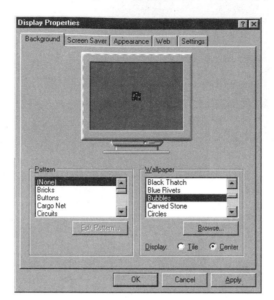

4. You're going to choose an existing pattern, erase it, and create a new one, so click any pattern you want in the Pattern list—Daisies is good—and then click the Edit Pattern button. Now, this dialog box opens:

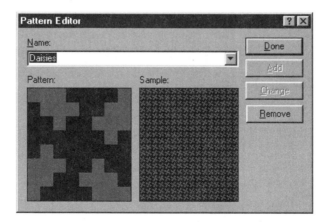

5. The Pattern box is where you edit a blown-up version of the pattern you chose. The Sample box shows how the pattern you're editing will look when many such squares are "quilted" together on your desktop.

6. Since you're going to create a new pattern by editing this one, start off with a clean slate by holding down the left mouse button and dragging the mouse pointer over each of the colored squares. This dragging is really just a fast way to click each square, changing it from colored to black and "erasing" the old pattern. (And, no, you won't be eliminating the original; it will remain just as it was.)

7. Now, start clicking squares to create a new pattern. You're free to make one of your own, or you can follow this diagram:

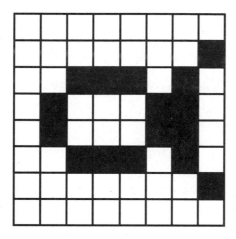

If a highlight does not cover a name or other text you want to change, just click at the beginning or end of the displayed text and drag to highlight the whole thing. Then, just type. Your typing will replace the text you highlighted. This holds true for any dialog box or window.

Although the pattern you edit is made up of an 8 by 8 grid of large colored and black squares, you'll be interested to know that each of those squares actually represents a single dot, called a *pixel,* on your screen. Every image on your monitor is made up of pixels (short for picture elements) in different colors. In a very limited sense, editing a pattern means you're "programming" your computer—at least in the sense of telling it to do something new, just for you.

When you finish your pattern, save it (and your original pattern) by giving the new one a name. The pattern's old name should be highlighted in the Name box at the top of the window, so just type a name for it—in this case, Fish would be nice. (Yes, that's what it is; wait, you'll see.)

8. Click the Done button, and this dialog box appears:

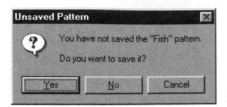

9. Click Yes to save your changes under the new name.

10. To preview your new pattern, click the Pattern dialog box to make it active, and then click OK. To actually put it on your desktop, click the Apply button in the Display Properties window.

11. Drag the Display Properties window out of the way if need be, so you can see both your Bubbles wallpaper and your Fish pattern. Told you it would be busy....

12. To return to Windows Standard, click the Pattern button on the Background tab again. In the Pattern dialog box, click (None) in the Pattern list, and then click OK. To get rid of Bubbles, click (None) in the Wallpaper list on the Background tab, and then click OK. Back to normal.

Paint

You don't use anywhere near the capabilities of Paint in this small exercise, and you might end up wondering what all those tools do. When you're ready for something more substantial, remember Paint's own Help. It offers a lot of information about the tools and how to use them.

Now you're about to see a way to create not just a pattern, but a custom wallpaper that you can either center on the desktop or tile so that it covers the whole thing just as your Fish pattern did. To create your wallpaper, you'll use the electronic canvas, brushes, and colors offered by the Paint accessory. For this example, you'll keep everything nice, simple, and fast because launching into creating a replica of the Sistine Chapel would take a lot of time. Besides, creating art with Paint is a skill that depends first on your own talents and second on a level of comfort with the program that most people need time to develop.

That said, here's the procedure. It includes quite a few steps, but as you'll see, none is difficult, although some might take a little practice because Paint is new to you:

1. Click the Start button, and work through Programs and Accessories. Click Paint, and this window opens:

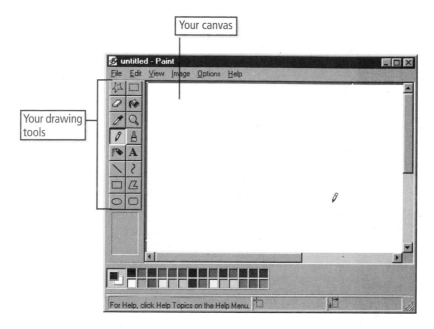

- The two columns of buttons down the left represent your *toolbox*—the kit full of tools you use to draw and paint. To find out what they do, point to each one and hold the mouse still. A tooltip will pop up, giving the name of the tool.

- The palette at the bottom of the window gives you a choice of colors for drawing lines as well as for filling in shapes and backgrounds.

- The large blank area with the pencil-shaped mouse pointer is your canvas.

    The pointer, by the way, works just as it does in Windows. In Paint, it just takes on different shapes, depending on the tool you're using.

2. Because freehand drawing with the default pencil tool can be a tad frustrating if you're not an artist, you're going to take the easy way out and draw something like the following (which is *supposed* to be a bunch of balloons).

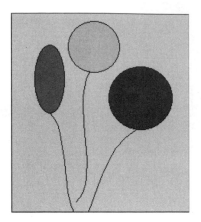

3. To start, click the Ellipse tool (the bottom left-hand tool in the toolbox) and move the mouse pointer to the drawing area. When you do, the pointer becomes a compasslike device with a small circle in the center. That circle is the *hot spot* that pinpoints your exact location on the screen.

4. To draw with any tool, you hold down the left mouse button and drag, so place the pointer about two inches from the top and left edges of the drawing area, and drag to create a vertical ellipse about an inch and a half long.

5. Now, use the same tool to draw a circle. You can make it like the middle one in the illustration or, if you're more creative than that, place it anywhere you want. Paint offers you an easy way to draw perfect circles: just hold down the Shift key as you drag the Ellipse tool.

6. Use the Shift key and the Ellipse tool to make a third circle.

7. Now for the strings. Click the Curve tool (third from the bottom in the right column of your toolkit). Place the pointer at the bottom center of one of your shapes and drag down to create a reasonably straight line. Don't worry if it doesn't look that great:

8. To make the curves, place the pointer somewhere on the line and drag to the left or right. When you have a curve you like, click to make it stick. To make the line even more graceful, point to another place on the same line and drag again to curve the line in another direction:

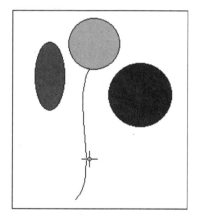

If you don't like the effect, click the Edit menu, and then click Undo to "erase" your attempt.

9. Use the Curve tool to make two more balloon strings. When you're satisfied with the whole thing, you're ready to color it.

10. Click the Fill With Color tool—the paint can that's second from the top in the right column of the toolbox. Click a color you like in the palette at the bottom of the window.

11. Place the pointer, now shaped like the paint can, inside one of your balloons and click. Instant fill, instant color.

12. Do the same to fill the other balloons with color. Again, if you don't like the effect, choose Undo from the Edit menu to erase it so that you can try again.

13. Almost there. To "frame" this work of art, click the Rectangle tool, which is just above the Ellipse tool in the toolbox. Place the pointer at an imaginary upper left corner above your drawing, and then drag down and to the right to create a square or rectangle around the whole image. Click the paint can again, and fill the background with color, too.

14. To turn this into wallpaper, click the Select tool, the dotted rectangle at the top in the right column of the toolbox. Place the mouse pointer slightly *inside* the upper left corner of the frame around your picture, and then drag down and to the right, almost to the lower right corner. This *selects* your image and background color, at the same time ensuring that you don't accidentally catch some of the white background, too.

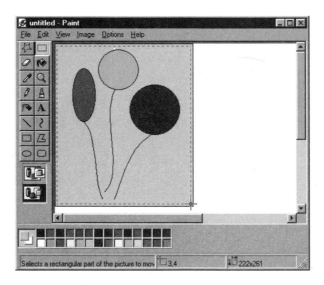

15. With your image selected, choose Copy To from the Edit menu. When the Copy To dialog box appears, type a name for your image—*Balloons* is fine—and then click the Save button.

16. Now click the File menu, and choose the Open command. When the File Open dialog box appears, double-click the name you just gave your image. When Paint asks if you want to "save changes to untitled," click No.

17. Now, your clipped and finished image appears in Paint. To turn it into wallpaper, open the File menu and choose Set As Wallpaper (Centered). Drag the Paint window out of the way if necessary, and you'll see your drawing proudly displayed in the center of the desktop.

18. To turn it into tiled wallpaper, open the File menu again, and choose Set As Wallpaper (Tiled).

19. And here's one final item: Close Paint, right-click anywhere on the desktop other than an icon, and choose Properties. There's your wallpaper in the preview window on the Background tab. Not only that, your PC has been smart enough to add your wallpaper to the list under Wallpaper. Clever, no?

20. To get rid of this rather colorful wallpaper, just scroll to the top of the Wallpaper list, choose (None), and click OK.

Pictures

Custom-designed patterns and wallpapers aren't the only things you can use to decorate your desktop. Just as you can place a photograph of your family on your real desktop, you can place a photograph of your choosing on your PC desktop.

You can, if you choose, add a scanner or a digital camera to your own computer, but both are on the expensive side. A less costly alternative is to take a photograph you like to a camera store or film developer who has the equipment needed to digitize the photo for you. Whichever method you choose, making the photograph part of your desktop is a simple matter of opening it in Paint and using the Set As Wallpaper command again.

IP In addition to personal photos of your own, once you begin cruising the Internet you'll find a wealth of images available for downloading. One especially interesting location—and one where the photographs are freely available for you to download—is the NASA Web site. Even if you're not an astronomer or a science junkie, the space photographs posted there are both compelling and beautiful. If nothing else, they are an amazing tribute to that all-too-human drive to push a little harder and see a little farther into the universe.

Even though you don't have a photograph of your favorite person, pet, or baseball player on the lesson CD, there's still a way you can see how to put a picture on your desktop. All you need is the movie clip on your CD and Active Movie Control (if you have it) or Media Player (if you don't). Both work; there's just one step that will be a little different. Here's what to do:

1. Click the Start button, work through Programs, Accessories, and Multimedia, and click either Active Movie Control or Media Player. (Unless otherwise noted, the following instructions assume that you're using Active Movie Control. Follow a similar procedure for Media Player.)

2. Find and open the movie clip on your CD. If you're not quite sure how you did it, remember you click the downward-pointing triangle to the right of the Look In box in the File Open dialog box. Choose your CD-ROM drive from the list that opens. Double-click the Goodies folder, double-click the Video folder, and finally double-click FALLS to open the video file.

3. You might want to read through the next instruction before trying it so that you'll know what to expect.

4. When you're ready, start the movie by clicking the Run button (in Active Movie Control) or the Play button (in Media Player). Click the Stop button to freeze the movie at a point you like. If you're using Media Player, click the window with the movie in it to make that window, rather than the Media Player controls, the active window.

Whenever you want to take a picture of the screen, press the Print Screen key to get a picture of the entire desktop, or press Alt and Print Screen at the same time to take a picture of the active window and then paste the picture into Paint. That's how the illustrations in this book were created.

5. Now, Press the Alt and Print Screen (or Print Scrn) keys at the same time to capture the "still" image from the movie. (Alt and Print Screen temporarily store information in your PC's memory.)

6. To move the photograph from your movie into a usable file, start Paint again. Press the Ctrl and V keys (the keyboard shortcut for *pasting* information from memory into an application program). Click any tool to "stick" the pasted image onto the Paint canvas.

7. The rest is straightforward. Click the Select tool you used when you created your own wallpaper, and carefully outline the movie image so that you can trim it away from the rest of the image you pasted into Paint.

8. Open Paint's Edit menu, choose Copy To, and assign a name for the file to which you want to copy the clipped image.

9. Open the File menu, choose the Open command, and double-click the name you just assigned to the photograph you took from the movie. When Paint asks whether to save the changes to "untitled," click No.

10. You know what to do next. Open the File menu again, and choose either Set As Wallpaper (Tiled) or Set As Wallpaper (Centered). There's your photograph, right on the desktop.

Turning a video frame into wallpaper shows you just one way in which you can turn your PC to tasks no one ever planned for. Here, by applying what your computer can do to the materials (and programs) you have on hand, you turned a video that was just meant to be watched into wallpaper for your desktop. As you become more experienced with your computer, let your imagination roam. The satisfaction of coming up with a new "recipe" for success is gratifying, to say the least.

Screen Savers with Personal-ity

Now, turn your attention away from what you look at while you're working to what you—and others—might see when you're not working but your computer is still on: screen savers.

Many computers automatically suspend activity and blank the screen when they have been idle for a certain period of time. And current monitors are not as vulnerable as those of yesteryear to "burn in," a condition that can occur when the same image remains on the screen for a long time. Still, it doesn't hurt to provide for a screen saver to kick in whenever your computer is idle, and besides, screen savers are fun and often entertaining, even mesmerizing, to look at. All of them work by displaying a constantly changing, usually colorful image on the screen.

Many screen savers are available commercially, and they range from definitely PG to those that appeal to a more adult audience. All you need do to find some is browse through the software section of your favorite computer store. In addition to—or perhaps as placeholders for—those that you can buy are a number of screen savers that come with Windows itself. At least some of these, and possibly some provided by your computer's manufacturer too, are probably sitting right there on your hard disk, ready to be put to work. The next set of instructions tells you how to choose a screen saver. After that, you'll find two sets of instructions that tell you how to have some real fun with either or both of two especially entertaining screen savers you might have.

First, to choose a screen saver:

1. Right-click on a blank part of the desktop, and choose Properties (yes, again—Display Properties covers a host of display-related functions).

2. Click the Screen Saver tab to display this:

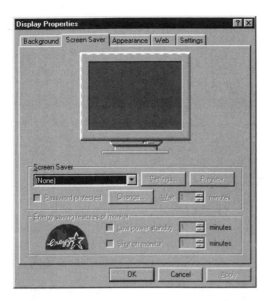

As usual, there's a preview window at the top and various options below.

3. To choose a screen saver, simply click the downward-pointing triangle to the right of the box under Screen Saver.

4. Scroll through the list, and click one that sounds interesting. You'll see what it looks like in the preview window. Preview as many screen savers as you want.

5. To see what the screen saver you're previewing looks like on the entire screen, click the Preview button and hold the mouse still. The Display Properties sheet and your desktop will be replaced by the screen saver.

6. To return to the desktop, just move the mouse—that's the screen saver's cue to get lost for awhile.

7. Before you go on, also note the Wait option under the Settings and Preview buttons. This is where you can tell your computer how many minutes to wait before activating the screen saver. To adjust the amount of time, click the *spinner* buttons (the upward-pointing

and downward-pointing triangles) to the right of the number displayed in the Wait box.

Regrettably, there's no way to guarantee that you have either or both of these screen savers. It's to be hoped that you do, but if not, remember that your PC offers a wealth of other options. Screen savers, though fun, are far from the most important.

8. To make your selection the screen saver that goes on when your computer is idle, click OK.

While most screen savers display an ever-changing pattern or image on the screen, two that come with Windows let you have a lot more say in what they display—literally. They are the screen savers called 3D Text and Scrolling Marquee. Both are fun, and either or both are probably in your list of screen savers. To see what they can do, start with 3D Text, which is a screen saver that uses a software-based display technology called OpenGL to generate its images. OpenGL is a pretty impressive technology, as you'll see from the speed and smoothness of the display, the three-dimensional look of the image, and the way the color, light, and shade are constantly changing. Not too long ago, this kind of graphic display was nonexistent on PCs. To see and work with 3D Text:

1. Right-click the desktop, choose Properties, and click the Screen Saver tab again.

2. Scroll through the list of screen savers, if necessary, and click 3D Text. (If you don't have this screen saver, check for Scrolling Marquee and skip ahead to the next hands-on practice.)

3. If you have 3D Text, you're watching it run in your preview window. Note that the text it displays reads *OpenGL* (pronounced "open-gee-ell"). Although the technology is impressive, the text itself isn't exactly thrilling for most people. Change it.

4. Click the Settings button to display this dialog box:

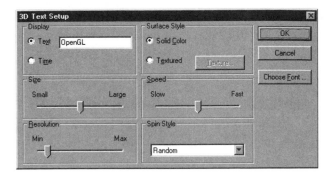

As you can see, there's quite a lot you can do to customize 3D Text, including change the size of the text, speed it up, slow it down, or even change the surface from solid to textured. The most entertaining of these options, though, is in the upper left corner, in the area marked Display.

5. Notice that the words *OpenGL* are displayed in the box to the right of the Text option. Hah! You can change it, and here's how: Place the mouse pointer in the text box, to the right of *OpenGL*. When the pointer becomes an I-beam (a vertical bar with two short crosspieces), hold down the left button and drag across the text to highlight it.

6. Now type your own text. You can type anything you want, up to a maximum of 16 letters.

7. If you want, click the Choose Font button to display this additional dialog box:

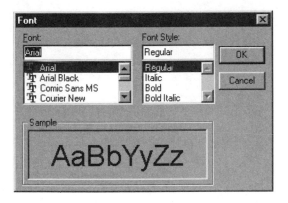

Scroll through the font list, trying out different type styles. A sample of each one you click will appear in the Sample box, in the lower half of the dialog box. Choose the one you want, and while you're at it change the lettering from regular to italic, bold, or a combination of the two—again, if you want. Remember, you don't *have* to do any of this.

8. If you changed the font but prefer the original, click Cancel in the Font dialog box. To make a font change, click OK.

9. In the 3D Text Setup dialog box, click OK. On the Screen Saver tab, click the Preview button to preview your customized screen saver. If you want, adjust the wait in minutes (5 to 10 minutes keeps the screen saver at bay long enough to keep it from popping into view even when you're just taking a minute to think).

10. If you like the change and want to keep it, click OK. When your screen saver kicks in, you'll see something like this:

And what about Scrolling Marquee? It's an older screen saver that's been with Windows through several versions, and it's a lot like 3D Text, although without the 3D effect and with less graphic quality. However,

Scrolling Marquee is just as much fun, and unlike 3D Text, it allows you to control not only the font, but the color.

Now, to customize Scrolling Marquee and make it uniquely your own:

1. If necessary, right-click the desktop, choose Properties, and click the Screen Saver tab on Display Properties.

2. Click the downward-pointing triangle under Screen Saver to open the Screen Saver list, and click Scrolling Marquee.

3. Click the Settings button on the Screen Saver tab to open this dialog box:

Now the fun begins.

4. Click to the right of the text in the Text box, and drag to the left to highlight the text.

5. Type some text of your own. You can use up to 43 characters, essentially filling the entire Text box, like this:

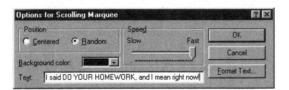

6. If black isn't really your style, click the downward-pointing triangle at the right of the Background color box and choose a new background color.

7. To change the type style and color of your text, click the Format Text button to open the following dialog box.

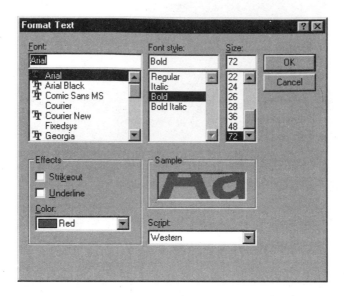

Choose from the list of fonts, font styles, and sizes (in points) until you like the preview you see in the Sample box.

8. Click the downward-pointing triangle to the right of the Color box to pick a new color for your text. (Warning: some combinations of background color and text color can be 60s psychedelic—just try Lime lettering on a Fuchsia background.)

9. When you're satisfied, click OK in the Format Text dialog box, and then click OK in the Options For Scrolling Marquee dialog box. Your message appears in the preview window on the Screen Saver tab.

10. To preview the screen saver on your desktop, click the Preview button. If you want, adjust the time to wait by clicking the spinner buttons at the right of the Wait box.

11. When you're ready, click OK to make the screen saver the one your PC will use whenever it hasn't been busy for the number of minutes you specified.

That's about it for the entertainment side of putting the *personal* in your PC. Wind up this chapter with a look at some other, more serious but useful, ways to customize.

The Display Itself

In addition to giving you the ability to change your screen saver, as well as your desktop color, wallpaper, and pattern, the Display Properties sheet enables you to change the number of colors and the *resolution* (very roughly, size) of your display itself. To do this, you use the Settings tab on the Display Properties sheet:

1. If necessary, right-click the desktop and choose Properties. Click the Settings tab to display this:

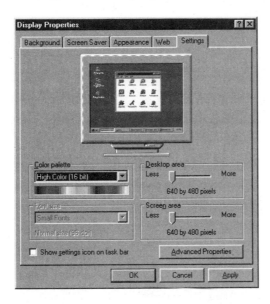

The Color Palette area is where you choose the number of colors to display. The slider under Desktop area is where you choose the resolution you want on your screen.

2. The option displayed in the Color Palette box is the color setting your computer is currently using. To see other options available to you, click the downward-pointing triangle at the right of the Color Palette box. To choose another option, you could simply highlight it and click the OK button. Don't do it now, however, because in order for the new setting to take effect, you might need to restart your computer.

3. The Desktop area setting, however, is one you can play with right now. The settings, described in pixels, tell you how many pixels (dots) across and how many pixels down make up your current display, which is probably 800 by 600.

4. If you want to try changing the resolution, move the slider. To use fewer pixels, which essentially makes everything on your display larger, move the slider to the left. To use more pixels, which makes everything on your display smaller, move the slider to the right. Click OK, and this dialog box pops up:

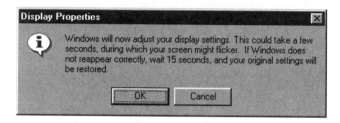

This piece of advice applies to everything about your computer: if you're satisfied, and if it's working, leave it alone. There's been many a slip 'tween the hand and the chip— sometimes to the great dismay of the person wielding the offending hand.

5. To continue, click OK. In a few seconds, your display will change to match the setting you specified. If you prefer not to mess with something that ain't broke, click Cancel.

Although you might never need to change the resolution or colors on your screen, keep this ability in mind, especially if you upgrade your equipment or switch to a different monitor. Do note, however, that very high settings require very high-end hardware to match. Don't try to push your equipment beyond its capacity. On the definite plus side, though, if ever you end up writing books about computers, this Settings tab will be one of the features of Windows you put high on your "I like it" list.

Before you go any further, here's your reminder to reapply your Web-style wallpaper:

1. Right-click the desktop, highlight Active Desktop, and click the View As Web Page option.

2. If, as is likely, your Active Desktop wallpaper does not reappear, right-click the desktop again and choose Properties. Scroll down through the Wallpaper list, click Wallpapr, and click OK. That should do it.

About Those Bits and Pixels

Depending on the capabilities of your equipment, your color list will include some or all of these options: 16 Color, 256 Color, High Color (16 bit), True Color (24 bit), and True Color (32 bit). Essentially, the farther down the list you go, the greater the number of colors displayed. The 16, 24, and 32 bits refer to the amount of storage used to describe each color to your computer.

As for resolution, you should note that, even though you can move the slider from side to side, you can't come up with a "custom" number of pixels to display. Computers display only certain resolutions, such as 640 pixels across by 480 pixels down, or 1024 across by 768 down. You can't, therefore, decide you want 852 pixels across by 700 pixels down, nor can you combine two, as in 800 across by 480 down. It won't work. Besides, the images on your screen would be grossly distorted—the effect would be like looking into a funhouse mirror.

Also, bear in mind that although Windows supports a number of different settings for both the color and resolution options, the actual choices available to you depend on your monitor and the display adapter card in your computer. Sorry, but even though this sounds like a rewording of "your mileage may vary," it's still true. It's one of the ways in which you can see how closely intertwined an operating system and the hardware are.

A Place of Your Own

Now it's time to turn from the display to your hard disk for a few minutes. Even though it's hidden inside your PC and you never actually look at it, your hard disk is the one part of your computer that will eventually become not only a reflection of your organizational abilities (or lack thereof), but the storehouse of your own personal documents, games, sounds, and pictures.

On current PCs, a hard disk is physically a closed box about 5 to 6 inches square and about 2 inches high. Small as it is, this device is still capable of storing billions of characters' worth of information. That's billions, as in a typical 3 billion to 6 billion or more—quite a lot of ABCs and 123s. Through the magic of technology and engineering, all this information is coded magnetically onto a few thin, CD-like platters that you will never touch or physically rummage through, looking for something you need.

Because this storage space is so vast, a filing system of some type is essential. True, Windows and other software can help you by finding files you tell them to find, but over time people tend to create, name, and save a lot of documents. And unless you have perfect recall, it's all too easy to eventually end up saying (1) "What on earth is *that* about?" or (2) "Cripes (or worse), where *did* I save that thing?" Neither question is likely to contribute to either your sanity or your good nature.

To start off on the road to organization, here are two different, useful ways to keep your work close at hand. Both will always be sitting right in front of you, so the items you place in them will never be more than a mouse click away from view.

An In/Out Folder on the Desktop

Windows gives you an easy way to create the equivalent of an In/Out box on your desktop. Even though you won't want to stuff everything you do into this one container, you'll probably find it handy for holding current projects:

1. Right-click the desktop.

2. Move the highlight down to New.

3. When the New submenu slides out, click Folder. Immediately, a folder icon appears on your desktop, with the text *New Folder* highlighted.

4. That highlight is your cue to give the folder a more interesting—and useful—name. Since you'll be using this folder for examples from the book, replace the highlighted name with *Book Samples*. Press Enter, and you're done.

Now, what's so great about cluttering up your desktop with an empty folder? The benefits are easy to see:

1. Create another new folder as you just did, but name it My Test Folder.

2. Drag My Test Folder to your Book Samples folder, and release the mouse button. My Test Folder disappears. Where?

3. Click your Book Samples folder. There it is. As you can see, it's neatly stored and yet only a mouse click away from view. Close the window.

4. To keep your desktop organized, drag the Book Samples folder off to the side. The upper right or lower right corner is a good spot that will leave the folder easily visible but still separate from your normal desktop icons.

My Documents, and a Shortcut to It

Windows creates—for you—a folder called My Documents, which applications are likely to offer as the default storage location whenever you save a new document. My Documents is a logical place to use as your main "filing cabinet" because you can create other folders inside it to hold various categories of related documents. If you decide to use My Documents as your starting point in building a file system, you might appreciate having rapid access to it on your desktop. My Documents doesn't appear on the desktop automatically, but you can keep it close at hand by creating a *shortcut* to it on the desktop. Here's how.

1. Click My Computer, and then click the icon for your hard disk.

2. In the hard disk window, there's a folder icon labeled My Documents.

3. *Right-click* the My Documents folder, and then drag it to your desktop. When you release the mouse button, this menu pops up:

4. Click Create Shortcut(s) Here. A copy of the folder labeled *Shortcut to My Documents* appears on the desktop, while the original stays right where it was.

5. Notice that the shortcut to My Documents is identified by a small arrow in the lower left corner of the icon and by the words *shortcut to* in the label below the icon. Every shortcut you create is identified in the same way. That's how you can always tell a shortcut from the "real thing"—the actual folder or document it's pointing to.

6. To see what's in your My Documents folder (possibly nothing right now), just click the shortcut on your desktop. Close your open windows.

As you'll see again later, shortcuts are really useful items that can "warp" you to all kinds of places from your desktop. Interests and needs change with time, however, and in many cases you'll find that a shortcut has outlived its usefulness. Are you stuck with it forever? Nope. Just as you can add a shortcut to your desktop, you can remove it anytime you want. To give this a try, delete the shortcut to My Documents. (If you'd prefer to keep the shortcut, just read the following steps instead of actually carrying them out.) The steps are few and simple:

1. Right-click the shortcut to My Documents.

2. Choose Delete from the pop-up menu that appears. Windows displays this dialog box, asking you to confirm the command:

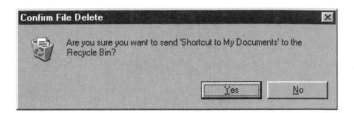

By default, Windows asks for confirmation whenever you delete information. It's not trying to either irritate or second-guess you, however. Because it's programmed to treat everything you create as if it were priceless, asking you to confirm your intent is just its way of adding insurance to a Delete command.

3. In this case, you do want the shortcut out of there, so click Yes.

All gone.

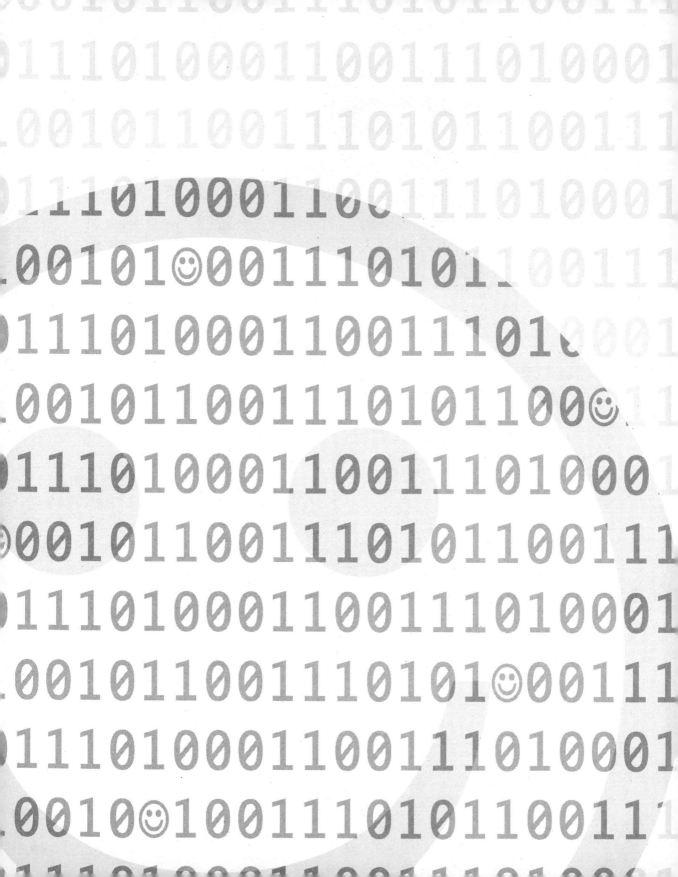

PC Work Is About Files

Ah, files. They're important—"everyone" says so. And "everyone" is right, for one simple reason: because every bit of information you commit to your computer's safekeeping is stored in some type of file. For example, when you start an application and create your own from-scratch document, that document becomes a file as soon as you use the Save As command to name it and tell the application your work is a keeper.

The fish pattern you made and the text in the screen savers you experimented with in the last chapter are also stored in files. Your changes were stored when you clicked the OK button. It's amazing how much helpful "housekeeping" of this type goes on without your having to supervise or do anything but click the mouse.

Think back to when you looked at your hard disk and your Windows folder. You saw files there, too—files representing some really important programs, as well as files representing other information, including graphics and (although you probably didn't recognize them) files containing important collections of data about your computer. And, of course, files are also where your PC keeps every other piece of information on your computer: every program you install, every game you play and save, and every set of instructions that help your PC work with your display, modem, CD-ROM drive, printer, and other hardware. PCs and files—they go together like chickens and eggs. You can have one without the other, but neither would be very useful, at least not for long.

Since files are so important to your computer, it's important to develop an understanding of what they are, along with the more practical knowledge of how to create, copy, move, delete, print, and otherwise work with them.

Try It

Before you dig into the art of naming and working with files and folders, you might enjoy a short introduction to the topic on your lesson CD. Among other things, the lesson shows you a way to create a folder within another folder. To run the lesson:

1. Start the CD by inserting it in the drive or by clicking the PCs For Beginners shortcut on your desktop.

2. Click 2 to reach the Windows Overview section, and click the left button to skip the Overview introduction (unless you want to see it again).

3. On the list of Overview lessons, click *Working with Files and Folders*.

4. When you complete step 13, click the lesson window's Minimize button *before* you click Next. (Clicking Next returns you to the Overview contents, and you can't minimize the window from there.)

5. Click Yes when asked if you want to minimize the window.

Now you've reduced the window to a button on the Taskbar—close at hand but temporarily out of the way. (If you want to quit at this point or after any other lesson, by all means go ahead and do so by pressing the Esc key. Just remember that whenever a Try It box tells you to *restore* the lesson window, you'll want to *restart* the CD instead.)

A File Is...

The best way to start investigating the idea of a computer file is by asking the most basic question of all: what is a file? The most graphic way to answer this is to take a look at a few for yourself:

1. Click the Start button, work through Programs and Accessories, and start the little program called Notepad. This window opens:

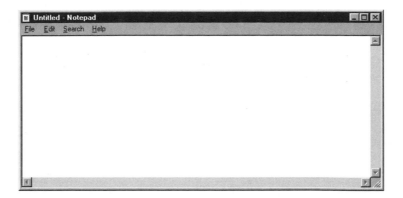

Notepad is a *text editor,* a program similar to a word processor like WordPad, but not as sophisticated or as capable of handling large documents. Despite its (intentional) limitations, Notepad is a great program for writing and viewing short text documents, as you can see now.

2. Click the File menu and choose the Open command. In the Open dialog box, double-click your Windows folder:

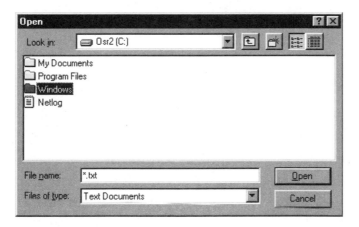

3. When the display changes to show the contents of your Windows folder, scroll to the right, if necessary. Double-click the file named Readme, and the following screen appears in the Notepad window.

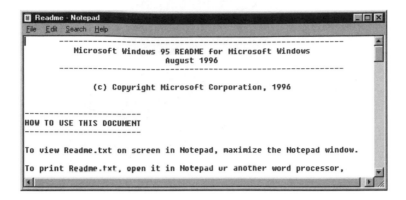

As you can see from looking at it, Readme is not a fancy document. It is a *text* file designed to be read with a minimum of fuss and elaborate software footwork. In keeping with that goal, its contents are made up of the computer equivalent of a child's block letters rather than the much more sophisticated fonts and formatting associated with word processed documents.

4. Now that you've seen a file composed of nothing but text, you can put Readme and Notepad away. The fastest way to get out of here is simply to click the Close button.

5. Next, click the Start button, work through Programs and Accessories, and open Paint. Although you used Paint to create wallpaper, you probably didn't realize that it works with graphics saved in a form known as *bitmaps*. Let's take a look at one provided with Windows.

6. Open the File menu and choose the Open command. As you did with Notepad, double-click your Windows folder. If necessary, scroll to the right, and this time double-click any of the colorful icons that look like pages "painted" with red and green shapes:

 IP Although the book hasn't yet covered how to install programs and you won't look for specific files until later in this chapter, keep the name Readme in mind. Many applications come with a Readme file that contains information of interest to you, the user. It's good practice to search program disks for a Readme before installing the software—you could save yourself some time and energy.

A graphic image appears in the Paint window. Although this image looks nothing like Readme, it too is stored as a file on disk. (Obvious, yes, but wait.)

7. Close Paint and put the bitmap away. Again, the fastest way is to click the Close button.

8. Now try something completely different. Click the Start button and open the Programs submenu. Click MS-DOS Prompt, and this rather uncolorful window opens:

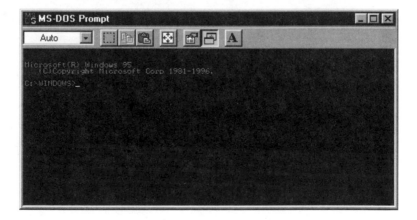

This considerably different window shows you what computer screens used to look like. It's displaying, for your benefit, the *prompt* (the blinking underline) at which people typed commands to the MS-DOS operating system.

> **OTE** MS-DOS, although no longer much in use, was for years *the* operating system on Intel-based computers. It was, in fact, the non-graphical ancestor of your Windows. Today, the parent has become the child in a sense, because MS-DOS is now part of Windows. If you find or decide to use an application created for MS-DOS, you can use the MS-DOS Prompt command to tell Windows to get lost and let MS-DOS run the show for a while.

9. Ready for some fun? Type this command, exactly as you see it here, including the word *type* (which is actually a command to MS-DOS):

    type c:\windows\notepad.exe

    The little MS-DOS window fills with an amazing assortment of symbols and blank spaces, and you probably hear a beep or two:

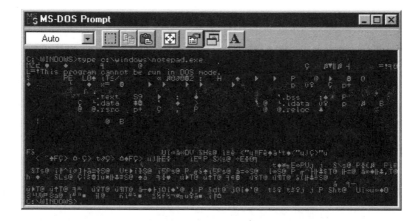

    What was the point of that, and what are you looking at? The point was to show you what an actual program—Notepad—looks like when your computer tries to display the file in which it is stored. Those symbols and spaces are the visible representation of the *executable* program that makes Notepad the functional text editor you saw earlier. Again, you are looking at the contents of—what else—a file.

10. You've finished with the MS-DOS window now, too, so click the Close button to put it away and return to Windows proper.

Well, there you have it. Three files, all vastly different, but each one of them a legitimate computer file nonetheless. So…back to the original question: what is a file?

The answer is: It is a collection of information, information that doesn't even have to be in words. It can be pictures or program instructions or even sound or video. Computer files are no different from the letters, notes, tape cassettes, drawings, recipes, or maps to buried treasure that can all be considered files stored in a filing cabinet. These files just happen to be stored electronically on a disk, rather than in a box or a piece of office furniture.

A Name for Every File

As you've seen for yourself, *content* doesn't define a file. And neither does size. A file composed of words can be as short as a single character, or it can be as long as a book (or even longer). So is there anything that all files from programs to graphics have in common? Yes, and it's a simple thing: a name.

And that, from a practical point of view, is how you can and should define a file—not only as a collection of information, but one that is stored as a unit and is given a *file name*. No matter what the file contains, its file name defines it not only to you, but to your computer.

File Names Then and Now

Once upon a time, a file name was a well-defined piece of work that had to be made up of no more than eight characters followed by a period (.) and an optional three letters known as the *file name extension*. A typical file name back then looked like this: MYFILE.DOC.

These days, since Windows 95 burst onto the computing scene, you have a lot more flexibility in naming files. The extension is still only three characters long, but you can be as wordy as you want with the name itself. So, for example, you can name a file:

> This Is the File I Decided To Give a Very Long Name To Just Because I Felt Like It and Besides It Was So Much Fun.doc

and both your computer and your applications will happily find it, store it, and retrieve it for you.

Rules for Naming Files

Short and sweet file names are generally a lot better than long and windy ones. If nothing else, very long file names are tedious to type and difficult to remember.

Although file names are very important, there are really only three simple rules to follow in assigning names to the files you create and save:

- Name a file anything you want, up to a maximum of about 200 characters. Capital and lowercase letters are both perfectly acceptable.

- Use any characters you want in the file name, including blank spaces to make the name more readable. You can also use any of the following symbols:

  +   ,   ;   =   [   ]

- Don't try to give the exact same name to two files stored in the same location—that is, on the same disk (such as a floppy) or in the same folder. It won't work. Windows will ask you if you want the new file to replace the older one with the same name.

A Look at Some File Names

Although you looked at file names each time you opened a file in the preceding set of instructions, take another look at some, both because you now know more about them and because you want to see the difference between some long file names and the older, shorter, 8-character ones:

1. Click My Computer to open it, and then click the icon for your hard disk. When the window opens, notice the labels beneath all the icons. Those are all file names, even the ones that identify folder icons. To your PC, folders are files, too. They just happen to be special-purpose ones that contain the names of other files.

2. Notice that some of the folders—Program Files is a good example— have relatively long names that include spaces to make the names more readable. That's what new-style, long file names look like.

3. Now scroll through the window if necessary and look at some of the nonfolder icons, all of which represent actual files. If you count the characters in the file names, you'll find that they are in the older eight-character form. That's the style most programs still use for their own files, and a lot of people do too, either out of habit or for convenience because they need to move files to and from computers running older operating systems that can't recognize long file names.

Psst...What's Your Alias?

If you never plan to use any computer but your own and you're sure your files won't end up on a computer running an older operating system such as MS-DOS or an earlier version of Windows itself, feel free to skip this box. If, however, there's a chance you'll be moving files to an older computer, read on to save yourself some time later on.

Although you can get as creative as you want with file names, there are two main ways in which long file names might trip you up with older software. Both are related to the need for Windows 95 and later versions to support *backward compatibility*, and both are related to the old eight-character-plus-dot-plus-extension file names (sort of affectionately known as the "eight-dot-three" format).

To maintain compatibility—the ability to work with and share files—with older operating systems, Windows 95 and later versions "see" file names in two different ways: as their long forms and as a shorter, eight-dot-three form known as an *alias*. Windows assigns the alias, so you don't ever have to bother doing so, but to create the alias Windows generally shortens the long file name by tossing out spaces and using only the first six characters, followed by a tilde (~) and a number. So, for instance, the file name

This Is the File I Decided To blah blah blah

becomes:

THISIS~1.DOC

Now here's the rub: aliases such as this one are the only form in which older software can open, save, or work on files with long file names. And what that means is that you'll have to work with those aliases too. This isn't necessarily a problem, unless you've been a little...careless...about naming your files. For instance, suppose you write a lot of letters. When you save your letters, you've gotten in the habit of naming them *Letter to* followed by the person's name.

(continued)

Psst...What's Your Alias? *continued*

> What would these file names look like when converted to aliases? This:
>
> LETTER~1.DOC, LETTER~2.DOC, LETTER~3.DOC
>
> and so on. How useful in figuring out which letter is which...
>
> If there's a possibility that you'll be working with the alias rather than the long file name at some time, keep the potential alias in mind when you name your files. For example, your file names would still be nicely identifiable (and somewhat more economical) if you named them Grandma letter, Aunt Mary letter, Bill Gates letter, and so on. The aliases, although still not as clear as the longer names, would at least be turned into:
>
> GRANDM~1.DOC, AUNTMA~1.DOC, BILLGA~1.DOC
>
> And so on.

A Brief Look at Extensions

Although every file has to have a unique file name—at least on the disk or in the folder where it's stored—extensions are a different breed of cat for two reasons:

- The same extension can be applied to many files on the same disk or in the same folder.

- The extension can be, and usually is, a generic label that identifies the file by type.

    For example, the file name and extension:

    MYFILE.DOC

    identifies one particular file named MYFILE, which is of the type DOC (short for document).

If you don't get carried away trying to find holes in the comparison, you can easily cement the concept of file name and extension in your mind by thinking of a file name as being like your first name and thinking of the extension as being like your last name. Thus, for instance:

Jane Doe

distinguishes Jane from Joe, Fred, and Janelle just as easily as the name MYFILE distinguishes it from HERFILE, HISFILE, and ITSFILE. And Jane's last name identifies her as a member of the Doe family, just as DOC identifies MYFILE as a member of the "document" family.

Putting Extensions to Work for You

You already know that an extension literally "extends" a file name by an additional three characters and that those three characters generally identify the type of file they're attached to: *doc* for documents or, as you saw in Chapter 4, *avi* for video files and *wav* for audio files. But aside from telling you what type of file you're looking at, do extensions serve any useful purpose? Absolutely.

By default, every application you use assigns its own preferred extension to the files you create with it, and every application searches for its own preferred extension whenever you tell it to find and open a file for you. So even though you don't have to worry about assigning file name extensions and, in fact, you don't even have to know which extension an application prefers, you do need to know that those three little letters are important. They are the "badges" that identify files to programs. And as you create hundreds or thousands of different files, those extensions are the tools your application programs are going to use in sorting the files they can use from the files they can't.

Where this all *does* begin to affect you is in knowing how to use extensions to:

- Start programs automatically

- Find files when you can't quite remember their names or where you put them.

Here are two good examples that show you what this means and that give you a little more practice with your PC at the same time. The first shows how to use a document (a file) to start the program designed to work with it; the second shows how to find documents (files again) whenever you need them.

Using a Document to Start a Program

Up to this point, you've always started programs by finding and clicking their names on a menu. There's another way to start them, though: by finding and clicking a document, and using the extension as a "key" to unlock the program you need. Here, give it a try:

1. Open My Computer, click the icon for your hard disk, and then click your Windows folder.

2. Scroll, if necessary, and click any file with the icon representing a bitmap (the icon with the red and green shapes, remember). As soon as you click the file, Windows automatically starts Paint and displays (opens) the file for you. That's because the bitmap extension, bmp, tells Windows which program to use in displaying the file.

3. Close Paint.

You can do the same thing with other file types, too. For example, clicking an avi file, as you did in Chapter 4, starts the Active Movie Control because Windows knows it is the program designed to display videos. Similarly, clicking a doc file is all you need to start any word processor that looks for the extension doc.

Using Find to Locate a File

Now, what about finding files? There's a lesson on your CD that neatly walks you through the process. To give it a try, head for the "Try It" box on page 153, and then come on back here.

Now, as long as you're becoming familiar with the Find command, imagine a "what if" situation that happens all too often, especially as you accumulate many files: What if you can't quite remember the name of the file you want? Oops.

> **Try It**
>
> This lesson shows you how to create a small file with WordPad, save it, and then quickly find and open it once again:
>
> 1. Click the PCs For Beginners button on the Taskbar to restore the window.
>
> 2. Click the Lessons button in the upper left corner of the window to go to the list of Overview lessons.
>
> 3. Click the lesson titled *Finding Information.*
>
> 4. When you finish step 14, minimize the lesson window again without clicking Next.

Actually, there's a solution, and it's really simple. All you need is one little character, the asterisk (*). This asterisk, which you type by holding down the Shift key and pressing the 8 key in the top row of the keyboard, is called a *wildcard character*. The reason it's so useful is that it can act as a stand-in for any other character or group of characters. Here are two examples that show how to use the asterisk in two related, but slightly different ways.

First, suppose you can't remember whether you named the book report in your CD lesson Thomas Hardy or Thomas Wolfe. If you can't remember the name, you can't find the file, right? Nope:

1. Click the Start button, highlight Find, and click Files or Folders again.

2. Both names start with *Thomas*, but the last names don't have anything in common. How, then, to tell Find you want the Thomas somethingorother file? In the Named box, type *Thomas** (don't type a space between Thomas and the asterisk) as shown in the following illustration.

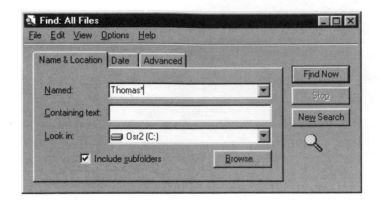

You left out the space, by the way, even though there's a space between the first and last names, because you're telling Find to look for any file in which *Thomas* is followed by any other characters, *including* a space. (A space is a valid character to your computer).

3. Check that the Look In box is showing your hard disk. If it is not, click the downward-pointing triangle to the right and choose the hard disk from the list.

4. Click the Find Now button, and in a second or two, *Thomas Hardy* should pop into view. Leave the window open for now.

And here's a second, often very useful way to use the Find command. This time, you don't give a hoot about having forgotten part of the file name, because that's not what matters. This time, you want Find to list all the bitmaps on your hard disk. That is, you want it to show you the names of all the files that belong to a particular group, no matter what their file names are. Again, you use the asterisk:

1. Click the New Search button in the Find window, and click OK when Find tells you you're about to "clear your current search."

2. This time, type *.bmp* in the Named box, as shown in the following illustration:

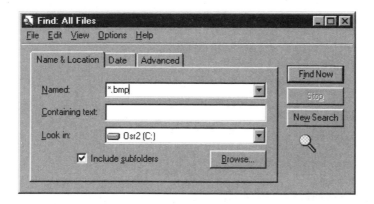

3. Check that the Look In box is showing your hard disk. If it is not, open the list and choose the hard disk again.

4. Click the Find Now button, and in a short time, the bottom of the Find dialog box fills with the names of all the bmp files on your hard disk. Click the Close button to put Find away.

You can use this same technique for finding any group of files, not just those with the same extension. Just substitute the asterisk for whatever characters the files in the group do *not* have in common. For instance, if you typed *dog*.doc*, Find would give you dog*star*.doc, dog*wood*.doc, and dog*gone*.doc. You can also use asterisks to represent both part of the file name and the extension. For example, typing *dog*.** would find dog*food*.*doc* as well as dog*fish.bmp*.

All About Folders

Earlier on, this chapter mentioned that a folder is a special kind of file— one designed to hold the names of other files. In addition to being the most useful tools you have for keeping your documents in some kind of order, folders are very easy to visualize and to use. All you really need to know about them is this:

■ They are used as containers for documents and other files.

■ They can contain other folders.

Often, people describe folders by comparing them to—surprise—the manila folders you would put in a filing cabinet. That's accurate enough as far as it goes. But take the idea just a little bit further. Aren't there two different ways you could approach your filing?

■ You could just stuff folder after folder into the cabinet and slam the drawer shut. That's quick, but it can make things a little difficult to find—say, at tax time or when the school insists on knowing when the kids were vaccinated and for what.

■ Or you can organize the files you put away. Maybe, for example, by putting dividers between your tax receipts and your papers related to family members. And if you're really on top of things, maybe you even have different folders in the family section for each child. (Gee, go ahead. Make a person feel...inadequate.)

At any rate, the same thing holds for the electronic folders you use to file your, uh, files. Formally, two terms are used to describe the organization of computer folders: *hierarchical* and *tree-structured*. Oh, yuk, right? Actually, both terms just refer to the form of an organization that has some structure to it. *Hierarchy*, after all, is just a fancy word for a pecking order, and all it means is that someone or something higher in the order is related in a certain way to someone or something lower in the order. Likewise, *tree-structured* is just a fancy way of saying that the structure branches from one level to the next just as your family branches from parent to child. Figure 6-1 shows a simple hierarchy in the form of a suit of cards; Figure 6-2 shows a tree structure along the lines of those you saw in Biology class.

Figure 6-1.   *This is a typical hierarchy.*

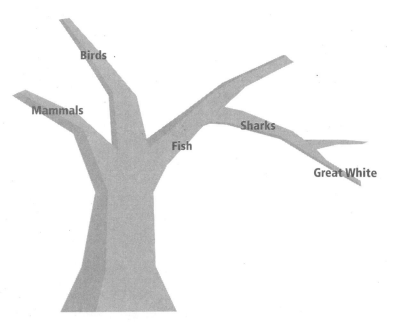

Figure 6-2.   *This is a typical tree structure.*

Here's an example that shows you the difference, as you would see it affecting your computer. You already know how to create folders, but to get a sense of why some structure is needed, create a few more:

1. Point to a blank part of the desktop, right-click, highlight New, and click Folder.

2. Name the new folder Fish.

3. Go through the same two steps to create another folder named Sharks.

4. And for good measure, do it again to create a third folder named Great White.

Now you have four folders scattered on your desktop. It's beginning to get a little messy, no? Just imagine what life would be like after you'd created a dozen or so of these beauties. And imagine how much fun you'd have searching through them to find one document in particular. Even though you'd assign more personal names to your folders, bear in mind that over time a well-used computer accumulates files the way a hound accumulates fleas in summer. Before you know it, they're *everywhere*.

Step one, then, in managing your files and folders, is to organize.

Getting Organized

These days, organizing folders is such a breeze you can change the way they're organized as often as you want. It's all thanks to the Windows feature called *drag and drop,* which you used earlier when you dragged a file to a folder in the lesson "Working with Files and Folders." As you saw, drag and drop literally lets you drag something from one place to another. It works with folders, too:

1. Drag the folder named Great White and drop it on the folder named Sharks.

2. Drag the folder named Sharks, which now contains the folder named Great White, and drop it on the folder named Fish.

3. Drag the folder named Fish, which now contains the folder named Sharks, and drop it on the folder you named Book Samples.

As simply as that, you've turned a collection of four folders into one. And, of course, they're all still available to you:

1. Click the Book Samples folder to open it. There's the Fish folder.

2. Click the Fish folder, and you see it contains the Sharks folder.

3. Click the Sharks folder, and you see it contains the Great White folder.

Drag and drop works in the other direction, too. Here's something that might prove useful to you in starting your own filing system. It will also show you how to change the name of a folder:

1. Drag the Great White folder from the folder window, and drop it back on the desktop.

2. Click the Up button at the top of the folder window:

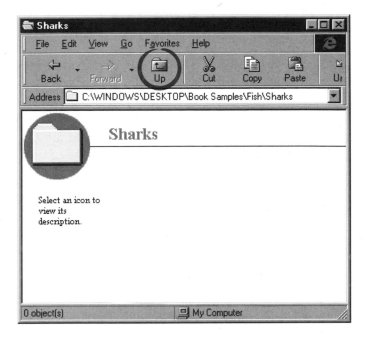

Using the Up button to move through a folder hierarchy is one of the many ways your computer turns concepts (here, hierarchical organization) into useful reality for your benefit.

The Up button moves you *up* through different folder levels. In this case, you're telling it to take you from viewing the current (empty) level that showed the Great White folder to the level (Fish) that contains the Sharks folder.

3. You should now be looking at the Sharks folder. Drag it onto the desktop, too.

4. Click the Up button again, and this time drag the Fish folder back to the desktop.

Now think about some way you, personally, could make use of two or three of these folders. If you share the computer with your family, you might want to give one folder to each family member. Or if you have your computer all to yourself, you might like to have different folders for different types of documents you plan to write. Whatever you decide, here's how to make these practice folders a little more meaningful:

1. Point to the Fish folder and *right-click*. When the pop-up menu appears, slide the highlight down the list and click Rename. When Windows carries out the command, it draws a small box around the folder name and highlights the name itself, as shown by the following.

It's waiting for you to give the folder a new name, so...

2. Type a name, anything that's appropriate to the use you plan to make of the folder—a person's name, for instance, or a word or two describing what the folder will eventually hold.

3. Follow the same procedure to rename the Sharks folder and, if you need it, the Great White folder.

4. When you're done, drag the folders to whatever part of the desktop you'd like to keep them on.

5. If you want to organize the folders again, create a new folder (or rename one of your samples) and place your other folders inside it. You know your own needs best, and you know the procedure now, so let your own preferences be your guide.

6. Click the Close button in the Book Samples window to close it.

Managing Files and Folders

In addition to creating, naming, and *nesting* folders one inside the other, you of course want to *populate* them with files. And, of course, you want the flexibility that you have with manila folders and filing cabinets: the ability to move, copy, and otherwise rearrange files whenever you want. Windows provides all that and more.

As usual, Windows gives you more than one way to accomplish these tasks. First, take what will probably seem the easier route because it relies only on what you already know about the desktop and about windows and their contents.

To start off, you need a file to work with:

1. Start WordPad. To create a small document, type the following (just so you'll know what this file contains):

> This is a sample document I'm using to try copying, moving, and printing files.

2. To save the file in a nice, easy-to-find location, open WordPad's File menu and click the Save As command. The Save As dialog box appears:

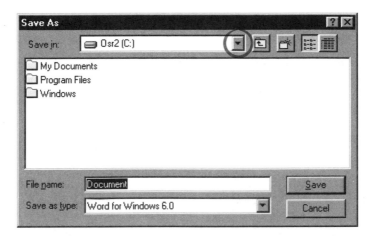

Click the downward-pointing triangle circled in the preceding illustration. When the list of possible places to *save in* appears, scroll down if necessary and click your Book Samples folder.

3. Click to the right of the word *Document* in the File Name box and drag to the left to highlight *Document*. Now you can type a name for your file, so type *My Sample Document*.

4. Click the Save button. Since you're through with WordPad, click its Close button to put the program away and clear off your desktop.

5. To see your sample file, click the Book Samples folder on your desktop. When the window opens, there's your file, just where you told WordPad to put it.

Copying Files

You might wonder why, if you've already created a file, you would want to copy it. Just as with paper files, there are lots of reasons. Perhaps you want to make a copy of an original document for safekeeping or later reference before you start editing it. Or maybe you want to put a copy on a floppy disk so that you can take it to another computer, give it to a friend, or have it professionally printed on high-quality printers and paper at a nearby copy center. For whatever reason, copies of files come in handy more often than you might think.

Suppose, first, you want to simply duplicate a file so that you have before and after versions available to look at. This is easy:

1. If necessary, make your Book Samples window larger so that you have some blank space in which to work.

2. Now right-click your sample document and drag it to a blank part of the window.

3. Release the mouse button. Notice that the popup menu gives you several options:

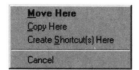

4. For this example, you want to copy the document, so highlight *Copy Here* and click the left mouse button. Immediately, Windows makes an exact duplicate of the file. Notice, too, that it's smart enough to name the duplicate Copy of My Sample Document.

5. To verify that this is, indeed, a duplicate, click the copy to open WordPad and display the file. Look at the title bar in the WordPad window, and you can see that, yes, the file is named Copy of My Sample Document. (In case you hadn't noticed earlier, the title bar always shows the name of the file you're currently working on.)

6. Close the WordPad window again.

 OTE Why name a duplicate "Copy of"? There are two good reasons: One, so that you always know which version of a document you're looking at or working on, and two, because (as mentioned earlier in this chapter) two files stored in the same location can't have exactly the same file name and extension, as would be the case if Windows duplicated this file, name and all. By naming the duplicate Copy of, Windows manages to take care of both concerns in one clever maneuver.

---

7. And what if you want more than one copy? Windows says, be my guest. Right-click the copy of your document, drag to another blank spot, and click *Copy Here* again on the popup menu. Now you have *Copy of Copy of My Sample Document* sitting there, too.

8. And if you don't care to have your copies named *Copy of, Copy of Copy of, Copy of Copy of Copy of*, and so on and on, it's easy to take care of that, too.

9. Right-click the second duplicate (Copy of Copy of) that you created, and choose Rename from the popup menu. When Windows highlights the existing name, type *Second Copy of My Sample Document* and press Enter. There you go. Notice that renaming files is the same as, and thus as easy as, renaming folders.

 IP You can also rename a file from within an application by using the Save As command and giving the file a different name. Bear in mind, however, that this does not change the name of the original file. It saves a copy of the file under the new name, so you essentially end up with file A (saved under the original name), and file B (saved under the new name). If this is what you want, great. But if all you want is a single copy of the file with a new name, use the Rename command from Windows instead.

Moving Files

Part of keeping your hard disk and your files organized involves moving them from place to place. Like copying, this is no more difficult than a little drag and drop. The process is a lot less tedious than it was before Windows 95, when moving a file essentially involved redefining the *path* to it, the path being the string of folders (then called *directories*) that led to the file. It was fun for people who enjoyed such things :-), but even they have to admit that moving is a lot easier now. To try it for yourself:

1. Point to the second copy of your sample document, press the *left* mouse button, and drag the document to your desktop. It's moved.

2. To put it back in the Book Samples folder, drag it back. Moved again.

And what if you want to move a file to an entirely different folder? No problem:

1. Leave your Book Samples folder open for a moment, but drag it out of the way if necessary so that you can see My Computer on your desktop.

2. Click My Computer, click your hard disk, open the File menu, and use the New command to create a new folder named Test Run.

3. Now arrange the Book Samples and hard disk windows on the desktop so that you can see both the new folder and the contents of Book Samples. (Resize one or both windows if necessary.)

4. Point to the second copy of your sample document, press the left mouse button, and drag the file to your Test Run folder.

5. Click Test Run, and you'll see that the file is, indeed, in there.

When Does It Move and When Does It Copy?

The examples in this chapter show you how to *right*-click and drag to *copy* a file but *left*-click and drag to *move* a file. That's generally the easiest way to guarantee that you copy rather than move, or move rather than copy. What you haven't seen, however, because the remembering can get a little convoluted, is that you can actually left-click and drag to *either* copy or move a file. What's so convoluted about that? Nothing, except that whether you copy or move depends on *where* you're copying or moving *to*. By default, Windows *copies* a file if you're dragging and dropping from one disk to another, but it *moves* the file if you're dragging and dropping from one location on a disk to another location on the same disk.

If you feel like experimenting with left-clicking and dragging and dropping, there's no reason not to. Any file you move when you meant to copy it can always be moved back, and any file you copy when you meant to move it can always (as you'll see later) easily be disposed of. Just bear in mind that the result of dragging and dropping a file can be either a copy or a move, depending on where the file ends up.

Sending a File Somewhere Else

In addition to copying and moving files, you can choose to send them somewhere else—to a floppy disk, for example, or to your printer. Sending is similar to copying in that you're sending a copy of the file to another location while the original remains right where it was. Sending just doesn't involve any Copy command or any drag and drop. It's just an incredibly useful way to "move" a file from here to there. To see how it works, send a copy of your sample file to a disk in your floppy drive:

1. Put a floppy disk in your floppy drive.

2. Right-click the second copy of your sample document—the one in your Test Run folder. When this popup menu appears:

   Move the highlight to Send To. As you can see from the Send To submenu, you can choose from several options specifying where (or to whom) you want to send the file. If you choose, you can even put a shortcut to the document on the desktop, where all you have to do is point and click to open both the file and the program that created it.

3. For this example, click *3½ Floppy (A)*. Your floppy drive whirs into action, indicating that a copy of the file is being sent there as you listen to it hum.

4. By now, your desktop is a little cluttered with windows. You won't need these anymore, so close them by clicking the Close button in each.

5. If you want to verify that a copy did, indeed, land on the floppy in drive A, click My Computer and click the icon for your floppy drive.

Windows Explorer "Sees" All, Does a Lot

Now that you've seen how to copy, move, and send files with "regular" Windows, you can take a look at a feature called the Windows Explorer. The Explorer (not to be confused with Internet Explorer) is a tool that some people come to rely on heavily, while others consider it nice but not all that necessary in the day-to-day use of a computer. Which you decide on is entirely up to you.

Try It

For an overview of Windows Explorer, what it does, and some of the many ways you can use it to organize your work, try the following lesson on your CD:

1. Restore the lesson window.

2. Click the Lessons button to see the list of Overview lessons.

3. Click the lesson "Exploring Files and Folders."

4. When you finish step 16, minimize the lesson window again (by clicking the Minimize button rather than clicking Next in the final step).

You've created a fair number of folders and files in this chapter. Use them to see how Windows Explorer can help you manage the information that, inevitably, collects on your hard disk over time. The lesson on the CD showed you much of what you need to know, but here are a few extras:

1. Start Windows Explorer by clicking the Start button and choosing Windows Explorer from the Programs submenu.

2. If you see a scroll bar along the right edge of the left pane, great. If you do not see a scroll bar, make the Windows Explorer window shorter from top to bottom until a scroll bar does appear.

3. Now drag the scroll box in the scroll bar up and down. Notice that no matter what is displayed in the *right* pane, the contents of the *left* pane scroll as you move the scroll box. This independent scrolling

can be enormously useful in managing files and folders, as you're about to see.

4. Scroll down, if necessary, and click your Book Samples folder in the left pane. Immediately, Windows shows the contents of the folder in the right pane. Yes, you've been there, done that. But now try this.

5. Scroll up in the left pane until you see your floppy disk drive. Notice that even though you scrolled the left pane, the contents of the right pane remain as they were. Why is that so great?

6. Drag My Sample Document from the right pane to floppy drive A in the left pane. Copied, just like that from one disk to another, and all because the two panes (a) scroll independently and (b) respond to drag and drop.

Try It

For a related overview of ways to move and copy single or multiple files in Windows Explorer, try the following lesson on your CD:

1. Restore the lesson window, and click the Lessons button for the list of Overview lessons.

2. Click the lesson "Moving and Copying Files."

3. When you finish step 15, minimize the lesson window again.

NOTE The "main" part of your hard disk—the part you see when you click the hard disk icon in My Computer—is something of a special place known as the *root directory*. This part of your hard disk really should be left to software, so when you save documents, make it a habit to put them in folders on the desktop or in folders you create in the My Documents folder that Windows creates for you when it is installed. Not only will your documents be easier to find, you won't run into problems with organization or overpopulation in the root directory.

And what if you want to move whole folders? That's easy, too, and also just a matter of drag and drop. You can, of course, display the name of the folder you want to move in the right pane, and then drag it to the destination folder in the left pane, but there's also a way to do it using the left pane only.

To see how this works, move your Test Run folder from the main part of your hard disk to your Book Samples folder. This will make for easier cleanup later on. Here's how you do it:

1. Scroll up if necessary until you see the name of your Test Run folder in the left pane. As you can see, Test Run is in among a lot of other folders, most of them devoted to programs. To move Test Run to a better spot for documents and document folders...

2. Drag Test Run down the tree in the left pane until you see your Book Samples folder. (Book Samples is toward the bottom of the items in the left pane, because that's where Windows displays the names of items on the desktop. When the mouse pointer reaches the bottom of the left pane, the pane will automatically scroll to reveal more files and folders.)

3. When you reach Book Samples, drop Test Run on top of it. As easily as that, you can move an entire folder from one location to another.

4. Click the plus sign to the left of the Book Samples folder icon, and sure enough the "tree" blossoms to show Test Run under (inside) Book Samples.

5. You've finished with Windows Explorer, at least for the time being, so close it by clicking the Close button.

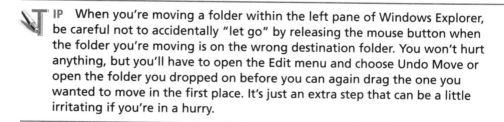 **TIP** When you're moving a folder within the left pane of Windows Explorer, be careful not to accidentally "let go" by releasing the mouse button when the folder you're moving is on the wrong destination folder. You won't hurt anything, but you'll have to open the Edit menu and choose Undo Move or open the folder you dropped on before you can again drag the one you wanted to move in the first place. It's just an extra step that can be a little irritating if you're in a hurry.

Printing

So far, this discussion of managing and working with files has studiously ignored one of the things people do most, even in this "paperless" computerized age: they *print* files to get good, old-fashioned, ink-on-paper copies of documents.

Printing is something so fundamental that any application that allows you to create a printable document will also provide you with a Print command that sends the document to your printer. So, then, is there anything more you need to know? Actually, there are two things:

■   How to tell your computer about your printer.

■   How to use Windows to print for you, if you choose.

Installing a Printer

Printers differ in the way computers "talk" to them. That's why you must choose the make and model you use. The choice you make ensures that Windows uses the right "language" in communicating with your printer.

First things first—you can't print anything if your computer is clueless about the printer to use. Luckily, this part is easy because printer setup is handled by a *wizard,* a Windows program especially designed to ask you for the information it needs and then use the information you provide (such as "my printer is a [fill in the blank]") to perform all the housekeeping required to make your PC work with your printer.

If your computer does not yet know about your printer, the following steps tell you what to do. If your printer is already installed, you can actually step through these instructions, too. Just click the Cancel button instead of Finish to back out at the end. Here's what you do:

1. Start off by (a) clicking the Start button, highlighting Settings, choosing Control Panel from the submenu, and then clicking the Printers icon in the Control Panel window, or (b) clicking My Computer, and then clicking the Printers folder.

2. Whichever way you start, the next step is to click the Add Printer icon in the Printers window shown by the following.

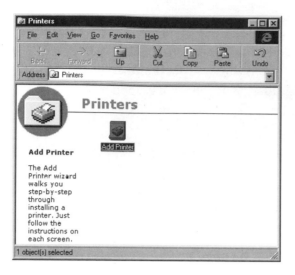

3. As soon as you click the Add Printer icon, Windows activates the Add Printer Wizard, which starts off looking like this:

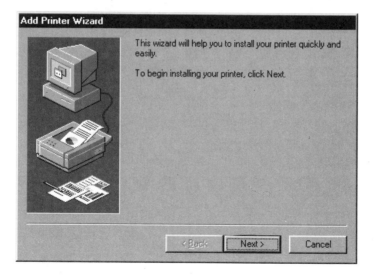

4. There's nothing to do here but read the instructions, so do that and click the Next button.

5. Now you see a screen asking how your printer is attached to your computer. Unless you're on a computer network and you plan to use a printer attached to another computer, choose Local Printer.

(Click the radio button to the left of Local Printer if the button is not already selected.)

6. Click the Next button, and you now see a screen asking you to choose the make and model of printer you're going to use:

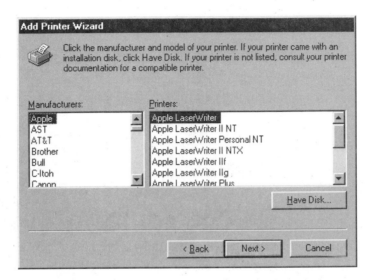

In the Manufacturers list, choose the make of printer you have; in the Printers list, choose the model you have. If the printer came with an installation disk, click the Have Disk button and place the disk in the drive you need to use. (If necessary, click the downward-pointing triangle at the right of the drive list and select the drive.) Click OK.

7. Click the Next button, and the wizard then asks which port you want to use. Don't get excited. Chances are, you want the one the wizard highlights for you (probably the one named LPT1). Leave the Configure Port button alone and click Next.

8. Now you get to the easy stuff. On the next screen, type a name you want to give your printer. It can be any name—even something silly like *I Am an Expensive Printer*. On the same screen, click Yes or No to specify that your Windows programs should automatically use this printer. (Click Yes if this is your only printer; click No if you have another printer and want to use this one as an alternate.)

9. Click Next, and the next screen asks if you want to print a test page to be sure Windows and your printer are working together properly. This is a good idea, so click Yes (if necessary; it's probably selected by default).

10. Now turn on your printer and click Finish. (If you've already installed a printer, remember to click Cancel here instead.)

11. The wizard now takes the information you provided and sets up Windows to work with your printer. At the end, a printed test page assures you that all is well.

Once your printer is installed, Windows adds to the Printers folder an icon with the name you gave the printer. You can see the icon in the Printers window.

Printing Documents

Now that you're all set to print, what're you gonna print first? Well, printing is printing, whether the document is a letter, a poem, a book, or a graphic image, so instead of wasting paper on the inconsequential files you created in this chapter, try printing one of the sample documents on your lesson CD instead.

Try It

To reach the CD lesson on printing:

1. Restore the lesson window and click the Lessons button.

2. Choose "Printing a Document" from the list of Overview lessons.

3. When you finish step 16, minimize the lesson window again.

Cleaning House

The last section of this chapter, "Know When To Say 'No'," shows you why you should never mess around with the files in your Windows folder. The same reasoning, of course, also holds for the files in any folder created by any software installed on your computer. Before you go on to that, however, think about what you've been doing so far in this chapter: You've been making a mess on your hard disk with a bunch of sample files you'll never need again. It's time to clean house, and the way you do so is with the Recycle Bin, conveniently placed right on your desktop.

Try It

Your lesson CD includes an introduction to the Recycle Bin and how to use it:

1. Restore the lesson window and click the Lessons button.

2. Choose "Using the Recycle Bin" from the list of Overview lessons.

3. When you finish step 16, minimize the lesson window again, or quit the CD.

Now what about using the Recycle Bin with all your sample files, not to mention the many others that your imagination and your applications will combine to create in the future? Try a few different ways to delete files:

1. Click your Book Samples folder to open it.

2. If necessary, drag the folder window to the side so that you can see the Recycle Bin icon.

3. Just so that you have lots of files to delete, right-click one of the documents in Book Samples, drag, and choose Copy Here from the pop-up menu. Do this again so that you end up with four document files in the folder.

4. Let's first use delete method number one: Right-click one of the files and choose Delete from the popup menu. Click Yes when Windows asks you to confirm the deletion. One down.

5. Now let's use delete method number two: Hold the mouse pointer still on one of the files until Windows selects it, and then open the File menu, and choose Delete. Again, confirm that you want to delete the file. Two down.

This time, delete a bunch at one go:

1. If necessary, choose Large Icon view and—again, if necessary—drag the remaining files (but not your Test Run folder) in the window so that they are nicely lined up.

2. Now place the mouse pointer at the corner of an imaginary rectangle that would include both files. Hold down the left mouse button, and drag to draw a dotted line around both files. Dragging like this is a quick way to select multiple files. It works in other views, too; Large Icon view just happens to be easiest here.

3. Place the mouse pointer on either one of the file icons and drag to the Recycle Bin. Both files you selected obediently tag along. Drop them in the bin. And, again, confirm the deletion.

 IP   If you prefer, you can also select a group of files by selecting the first one and then holding down the Ctrl key while you select the others. This is a nice way (the only way) to select files when the ones you want are not bunched together next to each other.

All your sample files are gone, but two folders remain, My Test Folder (which you created in Chapter 5) and Test Run:

1. Select one or both.

2. Delete them any way you choose.

3. Click the Recycle Bin to open it and confirm that everything's there.

Since it's very important to be comfortable recovering accidentally deleted files, try restoring some just for some additional practice beyond what you did in the CD lesson:

1. Drag one of the deleted files back to the Book Samples folder.

2. Right-click another file and choose Restore to recover that one, too.

3. To "undelete" a folder, select either of the folders you just deleted and either drag it back to Book Samples or use the Restore command.

The last step in this set is especially important, because it shows that you can restore an entire folder—*if* you have to. In real life, *don't* delete entire folders, especially ones that contain a lot of documents, unless you've reviewed the contents and are absolutely certain that the entire folder is expendable. Losing one file is bad enough; losing an entire folder can be cause for weeping. Truly.

All right, this time you're finished with the samples for good, so:

1. Delete 'em all except for Book Samples.

2. Close the Book Samples window.

3. Open the File menu in the Recycle Bin window, and choose Empty Recycle Bin.

4. Confirm that you do, indeed, want to delete the items.

5. All done except for one last chore: close the Recycle Bin window.

Know When to Say "No"

As you've seen it's very easy to delete files and folders. Some might say it's too easy. After all, documents are not the only files represented on your computer. Your hard disk, which is the main storage place for files and the first place Windows looks for them, is also home to some critically important program files—files that are not necessarily difficult to find. The main portion (the root directory) of your hard disk and your Windows folder both are home to many files that are absolutely essential if you want to enjoy a working computer (as opposed to one that sits around looking pretty but can't do anything, including start up and run).

Early in this book, you learned that an operating system performs some critical jobs. In terms of a functional computer, the two most important of these jobs are defined by Windows' ability to:

- Interact with the processor, memory, and other hardware.

- Enable other programs to perform input and output—to read from the keyboard and "write" to the display, as well as to read from and write to your disk drives.

Now that you've seen your computer in action and you know a lot more about files than when you started, you can understand how important these jobs are. If Windows could not interact with your hardware, who else would get that hardware to do anything? You couldn't, not on your own. You don't have either the language or the means of communication. And if Windows could not help your applications use the keyboard, display, and disk drives...well. Here, again, you couldn't do a thing, no matter how motivated you were. Knowing how your computer works certainly does put things in perspective.

To take this understanding of the operating system's importance one step further, you're now about to look at—just look at—a few Windows files. As you saw when you displayed the Notepad program early in this chapter, program files are incomprehensible to you even though they're highly meaningful to your computer, so you won't touch those. But in addition to all its *code,* Windows also relies on information stored in several text files that it keeps in the root directory of your hard disk, and a look at one of these files will serve nicely to show you why you should never monkey with Windows or anything belonging to it.

To start off, you're going to temporarily change a setting so that you can see the names of files that Windows normally marks as *hidden* to casual viewing and accidental tampering:

1. Click My Computer to open a window to it.

2. Open the View menu and click the Folder Options command.
   The Folder Options properties sheet appears:

Click the View tab.

3. Scroll down if necessary until you see a folder icon next to the words *Hidden files.* Underneath are three options.

4. If the option Show All Files does not have a dark dot in the radio button to its left, click the radio button to turn this option on.

5. Click OK to close the properties sheet.

Now to see what you can see...

1. In the My Computer window, click the icon for your hard disk. The folders and files that appear are those located in the disk's root directory. Those icons that are "grayed out" represent files whose names would not be visible if you hadn't turned the Show All Files option on.

2. Scroll through the files, and you'll see the names of several *log* files, including one named Bootlog. Notice that it is accompanied by a spiral-bound, memo-pad icon indicating that it is a text file. Ready to look at it?

3. Right-click Bootlog and choose Open from the popup menu. Because Bootlog is a text file, Windows opens Notepad and displays the contents of the file for you:

```
Bootlog - Notepad                                          _ □ ×
File  Edit  Search  Help
[000AF77B] Loading Device = C:\WINDOWS\HIMEM.SYS
[000AF77B] LoadSuccess    = C:\WINDOWS\HIMEM.SYS
[000AF77B] Loading Device = C:\WINDOWS\DBLBUFF.SYS
[000AF77D] LoadSuccess    = C:\WINDOWS\DBLBUFF.SYS
[000AF77D] Loading Device = C:\WINDOWS\IFSHLP.SYS
[000AF77D] LoadSuccess    = C:\WINDOWS\IFSHLP.SYS
[000AF77D] Loading Device = C:\WINDOWS\SETVER.EXE
[000AF77E] LoadSuccess    = C:\WINDOWS\SETVER.EXE
[000AF78F] Loading Vxd = VMM
[000AF790] LoadSuccess = VMM
[000AF790] Loading Vxd = C:\WINDOWS\SMARTDRV.EXE
[000AF790] LoadSuccess = C:\WINDOWS\SMARTDRV.EXE
[000AF790] Loading Vxd = C:\WINDOWS\system\VMM32\IOS.VXD
[000AF792] LoadSuccess = C:\WINDOWS\system\VMM32\IOS.VXD
[000AF792] Loading Vxd = vnetsup.vxd
```

A little technical? A little daunting? It should be.

4. Scroll down through the file. As you go, notice that lines such as *Loading Vxd* = are followed by lines that read *LoadSuccess*. Farther down, the text changes to lines such as *SYSCRITINIT* = followed by *SYSCRITINITSUCCESS*.

What you're looking at is the record Windows keeps of all the things that go on during startup. Obviously, you don't have to try to decipher any of this, but it *is* important to realize that this file contains references to an awful lot of Windows programs—programs whose purpose you might never know (or care to know), but that are essential to the working computer in front of you and for that reason *must not be tampered with or deleted*.

As you can see, there's a lot more to startup than blinking lights, a Windows 95 display, and a few beeps. Point taken? Good. It's time to put Notepad and Bootlog away and return to Folder Options so that you can return hidden files to their normal—and safer—obscurity:

1. Click the Close button on the Notepad window.

2. In the My Computer window, open the View menu and click Folder Options.

3. Click the View tab, scroll down if necessary, and click to put a dark dot in the radio button to the left of the first hidden files option, Do not show hidden or system files. (System files are operating-system programs—essential ones.)

4. Click OK to make the change.

Now you know. Don't mess around with files whose purpose you know nothing about. And don't mess around with files in your Windows or other program folders either. It's much better to be safe than sorry. Besides, if you ever want or need to remove an application program designed to run under Windows, the Control Panel offers a way to do it. You'll find out about that along with other ways to manage disks and hardware in the next chapter.

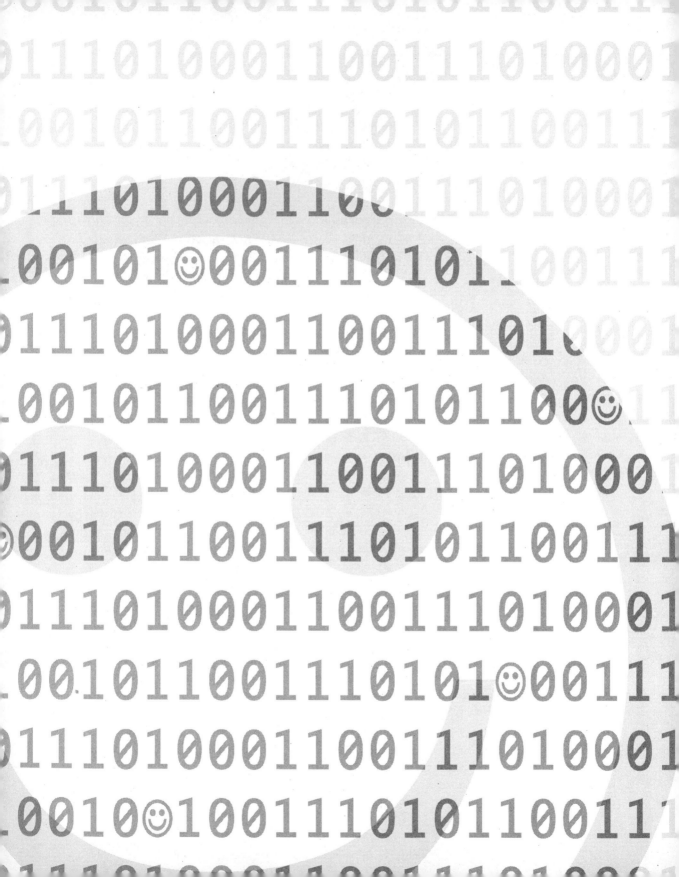

Maintenance and Easy Living

As you've seen throughout this book, a working PC is a combination of hardware and software. You've learned a lot about handling software, especially Windows. Does your hardware warrant the same attention? Yes and no. Yes, in the sense that your computer appreciates a little bit of common-sense care. No, in the sense that you'll never have to either know or care about how your hardware actually works. It just does.

Since your software can't function without your hardware, though, take a quick look at some basic ways to keep your hardware happy. It doesn't take much, and most of it you'd do anyway, and without thinking. But just for the record...

A Little TLC Is All It Needs

Complex as it is inside, a computer requires less care than the average car. It doesn't need oil changes or new tires, and not only does it not want a weekly wash and wax, it never needs one. Although a computer, like any machine, *can* break down, breakdowns don't happen very often. In fact, considering the sophistication of its parts and pieces, and the speed at which it all works, the fact that a computer functions at all is incredible. And it not only functions, it's as reliable as your TV and generally as undemanding as a pet rock. (Well, almost.) So what do you need to do to keep it running? The following is a top-10 list to keep in mind.

1. Keep it reasonably clean and free of dust—about a clean as your stereo, unless your stereo is really dusty.

2. Plug it and the monitor into a surge protector to prevent damage in case the power to your house or office flickers or goes out unexpectedly. Power changes can be hazardous to a PC's internal health. (If the power does go out and you don't have a surge protector, turn the computer off and wait until the power comes back on before you restart your computer.)

3. Don't shove the system around when the disk drives are running.

4. Don't open up the system without turning off your PC, and don't touch anything in it without first touching a piece of grounded metal to remove any static charge on your body. "Electrifying" might be a great description of your personality, but the circuitry in your PC won't appreciate it. In fact, if you don't know exactly how to proceed, don't open up the system at all. (See item 9 below.)

5. Keep food away from the keyboard. Spilled drinks, bubble gum, and cake frosting can turn the keyboard into a nasty—and unreliable—mess.

6. Try not to smoke in front of your PC. You won't be hurting its morals, but you will gunk up the screen over time. Speaking of the screen, clean it with a nonabrasive cleaner, the kind you use on your TV.

7. Store your floppy disks and CDs in some type of container. You don't have to get elaborate about it. The boxes your floppies come in work fine, and there's nothing wrong with sticking your CDs back in the "jewel boxes" they're shipped in. Loose disks have a way of getting dropped, buried, and—especially frustrating when you need them—lost.

8. If it ain't broke, don't fix it. Don't mess with success. If your computer is running well and your software is behaving as it should, leave it alone. Unless you know exactly what to do, don't be tempted to "tweak" the system for better performance. People have tried, and they have not necessarily been happy with the results.

9. Similarly, if you want to add a piece of hardware or more memory, either get good instructions or have a professional do the installation for you. There's no shame in asking for help, and there's a lot of pleasure to be had from having the job done right the first time.

10. If your PC starts making strange noises or has trouble running, shut it down and take it in for a checkup. The inside of a computer includes more than chips and circuitry. There's also a fan, a power supply, and your disk drives. If any of these runs into mechanical trouble, do what you would with any other appliance: get it fixed.

Of Disks and Discs

Although the word sounds exactly the same in both cases, you always spell the word for "traditional" computer storage like your hard drive and your floppies as disk. *However, when you're referring to a CD, you spell the word* disc.

Now to go from the ridiculous(ly simple) to the sublime(ly engineered).

In the last chapter, you found out quite a bit about computer files—maybe more than you ever thought you wanted to know. But those files, both program files and data files, are the be-all and end-all of a working computer, the kind you're glad you went out and bought. And because files are so important, it naturally follows that the hardware you store them on is pretty special, too.

Disks for Permanent Storage

Disk storage is where you file whatever information—programs, documents, sounds, pictures of the kids—that you want to keep and use again. This type of storage is available not only on your computer's hard drive but on floppy disks as well. Each has its own place in your computing toolbox.

- Floppy disks, which once upon a time were 8 inches across and truly floppy, typically offer about 1.5 megabytes (1.5 MB) of storage, which translates roughly to about 1.5 million characters. Although they don't hold as much information as hard disks, floppies do have the advantage of being portable.

- The hard disk, or hard drive, is your PC's primary storage location. These days, a typical hard disk offers anywhere from 1 to 6 or more gigabytes (GB) of storage, which—again roughly—means about 1 to 6 *billion* characters. The place where your PC automatically looks for a program you want to use, the hard disk is also the medium on which your PC's manufacturer probably installed a considerable amount of software. Hard disks hold far more than floppies do but are obviously not anywhere near as portable.

And What About the CD-ROM?

Your CD-ROM drive is something of a special case. True, it's used for storage, but that storage, at least with the currently available state of the technology, is typically *read-only*. Read-only, as you'd assume, means that your computer can read information *from* the disc but it cannot *write* information *to* the disc the way your floppy and hard drives can. Just like the music CDs you buy, CD-ROMs can be played, but most cannot be recorded on. Thus, you use your CD-ROM drive to feed programs and other information *to* the computer, but you do not save any new data on a CD-ROM.

By the way, CD-ROM stands for *compact disk-read only memory*. (Don't be misled by the "memory" part; computer storage of most types is often referred to as memory.) Compact though they are, these discs can also hold vast amounts of information—about 600 MB per disc, which is about equivalent to a stack of floppies more than 4 feet high. Sturdy, light, and spacious, CD-ROMs are rapidly replacing floppy disks as the medium on which software providers deliver their programs.

Since CDs are generally read-only, but floppy and hard disks are the places on which you store your own data, the remainder of the disk coverage in this chapter concentrates on disks, rather than discs.

 OTE   Although both disk drives and CD-ROM drives store information for use by a computer, they differ dramatically in the way they work. Floppy and hard drives read and write information to disks magnetically. CD-ROM drives, in contrast, use light—laser optics. All types of disk/disc drives are engineering marvels. Yet, although they are internally both complex and delicate, they are highly reliable and typically run trouble-free for years.

How Files Are Stored on Disk

Disk storage is a wild and wonderful thing that involves some seriously interesting terminology, including words like *platter, track, sector,* and the methods of storing information about files known as *FAT* and *FAT32* (pronounced "fat" and "fat thirty-two"—more about these later). All of these terms and more are woven together in disk storage like threads in a tapestry to explain two things: how a disk is structured and how a file is stored within that structure. Although the terms can be daunting when you encounter them in a bunch, if you just concentrate on the essentials you will find that disk storage is easy to understand. It also serves as a great example of the type of housekeeping that an operating system handles in the process of keeping you "up and running."

The basic component of a disk, whether hard or floppy, is a flat circle something like a CD. In a hard disk, two or more such circles, known as *platters,* are stacked one above the other and held in place by a rod called the *spindle* through the center. The arrangement is a lot like records stacked on a phonograph spindle (back when people actually used such things). In fact, a hard disk works something like a phonograph. The platters spin and, as they spin, the *read/write heads* that actually write your files to the platters and read them back off at your request move back and forth like phonograph arms from the outer edge to the center of each platter.

Hard disk platters are—no surprise—hard. They are also very finely machined and operate at unbelievably close tolerances. The platters, for instance, spin at more than 5000 RPM. As they spin, they create a cushion of air on which the read/write heads "fly" back and forth. This cushion of air is tiny, so the heads themselves are flying above the platters at a distance far, far less than the diameter of a human hair. And as they fly, these heads busily pour information onto the platters or read information from them— programs, data, Windows itself. This is how all of it gets from disk storage (where it's saved) into memory (where it's worked on).

As for floppy disk drives, they work in much the same way, although they deal with single disks rather than multiple platters, and the disks they read from and write to are actually thin, flexible rounds of plastic encased in the rigid *jackets* that you normally slide into and out of the drive itself.

So that's how the drive mechanism works. What about the way all your millions and billions of characters worth of programs and data are actually stored on those disks? That, too, is amazing, especially when you consider the speed at which everything happens. Basically...

Every disk—floppy disk or hard disk platter—is divided into numbered rings called *tracks,* and each of these tracks is divided into equal-sized pieces called *sectors*. To form a mental picture of all this, picture an onion cut in half crosswise. Each onion "ring" would be equivalent to a disk track. Now, cut the onion like a pie into equal-sized pieces. Each of those pieces would be a sector. The actual number of tracks and sectors varies, depending on the type and capacity of the disk, but the basic structure is the same in every case. This basic structure looks something like the illustration in Figure 7-1.

When the read/write heads fly across the disk, they are looking for tracks and sectors that either contain the information you want or that are empty and can be filled with a file you're saving. How do they find the right ones? Windows, using the file-storage method called FAT or FAT32, refers to exact tracks and sectors by number—for example, track 9, sector 12. The FAT or FAT32 (which is an improved version of the older FAT) is like a logbook. (Indeed, *FAT* stands for *file allocation table*.) Windows maintains a FAT for each disk you use, in a special part of the disk's storage area, and in the FAT it records the track and sector locations of every file on that disk.

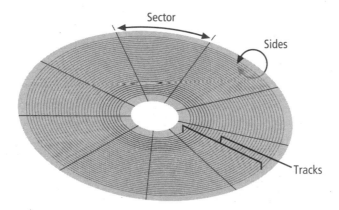

Figure 7-1.   *The basic structure of a disk.*

So, for instance, when it is finding a file for you, Windows consults the entries in the disk's FAT and then sends the read/write heads to the tracks and sectors in which that file has been stored. When it is saving a file for you, Windows consults the FAT to figure out where there are empty sectors on the disk and tells the read/write heads to put your file into them. This goes on flawlessly, time after time after time.

Now, how and when do you put all this theory into practice? Certainly not in actually storing or retrieving files. That's up to Windows, and Windows alone. You, however, are the ultimate keeper of your disks, and so there are two times in particular when you take charge: when you *format* a disk to prepare it for use, and when you check a disk to see how much storage remains available on it. Take a look at formatting first.

Reformatting and Recycling Disks

When you format a disk, you tell Windows to set up its FAT logbook on the disk and to divide the disk into the tracks and sectors it will use for actual storage. Formatting is simple, and you can do it to either a new or a used disk (one that already has information on it), and you can do it to either a hard disk or a floppy. However, because formatting wipes out all existing information on a disk, Windows protects you in one vital way:

It does not allow you to format your primary hard disk.

Know why? Because that's where Windows lives, and it will not allow you to wipe out program files that it is using and that it needs in order to keep running. Clever operating system—at one time, it was not only possible but easy to format your hard drive. When that happened, "oops" was far too calm a response to the situation.

However, even though you can't (and shouldn't) format your hard disk, there's absolutely no reason why you can't reformat floppies. Reformatting wipes the disk clean and prepares it for the next use, so it's a great way to recycle floppies containing information you know you don't want anymore. Just remember to check the disk for any files you might want to keep *before* you format it. Afterward is too late.

If you happen to have a floppy disk on hand—new or used is fine—here's the procedure to follow:

1. Put the floppy in your floppy disk drive.

2. Open My Computer, and click the floppy drive icon so that you can see what's on the disk.

3. If the floppy contains files you want to keep, either replace the floppy with another or move the files temporarily to your Windows desktop for safekeeping. (To move them, open the window's Edit menu, click the Select All command, right-click one of the file icons, and drag them all to the desktop. Choose Move Here from the pop-up menu that appears.)

4. If the floppy is blank, copy something to it so that you can see what happens during formatting. The Book Samples folder on your desktop will do fine.

5. Now to format the disk. Click the Up button on the toolbar to return to the My Computer window.

6. Right-click the icon for your floppy drive, and choose Format from the menu. This dialog box appears:

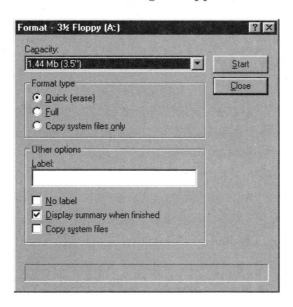

By default, Windows chooses the best capacity and type of format for the disk in the drive, so you can generally accept both the capacity and the type of format it displays.

Under Other Options, however, you can choose to *label* the disk with an identifying name or title. The label is much like a file name, but it is limited to 11 characters. You can see this label when you check the disk *properties* (as you'll do in the next section), so assign a label just for the practice.

7. Click in the Label box, and type *Test Disk*.

8. Now format the disk by clicking the Start button, and watch the bottom of the dialog box. You'll see messages telling you what Windows is doing. When formatting is complete, this summary appears:

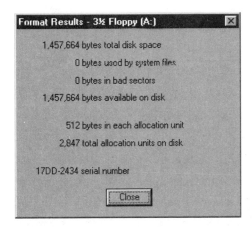

This is telling you how many *bytes* (roughly characters) are available for storage; whether any parts of the storage are set aside for system files, which Windows can use for starting up from the floppy (there are no system files on this disk); whether any of the storage has been "deactivated" because of bad spots (bad sectors) on the disk; and how the disk is divided up into *allocation units,* which indicate how the tracks and sectors will be parceled out to files. At the bottom, Windows displays the serial number—unique to every disk—it has assigned this floppy. (And yes, if you see the letters A, B, C, D, E, or F, those are, indeed, "numbers"—they're just in a form known as *hexadecimal* that computers use.)

9. Your formatting is done, so click the Close button on the summary and the Close button on the Format dialog box.

10. Leave My Computer open, and leave the floppy in the drive—you'll be checking on it soon.

Other Format Options

As you've seen, Windows displays the correct disk capacity and the most convenient format type for a disk when you choose the Format command. You might be wondering, however, about the other options in the Format dialog box. Here's what they mean and when you might want to use them:

■ Capacity: You can click the downward-pointing triangle at the right of the Capacity box and choose a different capacity if you want to format the disk to hold a different amount of information than it normally would. When would you do this? Only if you were preparing a disk for use in a drive *without* the ability to handle the disk's normal capacity—essentially, if you were preparing a 1.44 MB floppy to work with a lower-capacity 720 kilobyte (KB) drive. That's unlikely to happen with current computers, on which 1.44 MB floppy drives are standard.

■ Format Type: Sometimes a quick format, which erases a previously formatted disk but uses the old file structure and track/sector layout, does not work on a disk. This is always the case with a disk that has never before been formatted. If you have such a disk, you can choose Full for the "soup to nuts" version of a format, which tells Windows to do it all. If the disk is already formatted but you want it to have the *system files* Windows uses at startup, choose the Copy System Files option. This doesn't format the disk, but it does copy the necessary files to the disk.

■ Other Options: If you don't want a label on the disk, choose No Label. If you aren't interested in seeing the summary you saw in the hands-on practice format, click the Display Summary When Finished check box to clear the check mark Windows puts there by default. If you want to both format the disk and copy the system files to it, choose the format type you want in the Format Type section, and then click the check box to the left of Copy System Files in the Other Options section. (Yes, it seems as though choosing Copy System Files in the Format Type section should be the way to go, but this is actually the way it works.)

How Much Empty Space?

As you've just seen, formatting a disk is a piece of cake, especially because Windows is smart enough to keep your system safe by refusing to format your primary hard disk. There's more to disks than formatting, though. There's using them, too, and that means not only storing information on them but being able to see how much more you can cram onto a particular disk.

Although disk storage that is measured in millions and billions of characters seems practically endless, rest assured that a floppy can fill up pretty fast if you're saving graphics or other large files on it. And even a hard disk soon accumulates files that seem to sprout out of nowhere (which they don't, of course). Windows doesn't tell you when a disk is *nearing* capacity, but it does tell you when a disk is too full to hold anymore. To avoid being told that, especially when you're trying to save an important file:

■ Check your hard disk periodically, especially if you think it's beginning to get full.

■ Check a floppy before trying to save a large file on it. For that matter, check the file's size too, which you can do in Details view, either from Windows Explorer or by opening a window that displays the file. Some files are simply too big to fit on a floppy. (If you habitually save large files, you might want to consider either getting a utility program that compresses files or investing in an add-on, such as a ZIP drive, that uses high-capacity, removable disks for storage.)

Everybody tells you to keep your disk storage neat and to delete unwanted files so that they don't clog your disks. Of course, everybody also tends to be better at telling you to do it than they are at doing it themselves. Still, the advice is valid.

■ Delete unwanted files so that your disks don't end up like pack rat heaven.

That said, here's how to check a disk for storage. In this set of steps, you'll check both the floppy you just formatted and your hard disk:

1. Start with the quick way to check the storage available on a floppy. Enlarge the My Computer window if necessary, and look at the left side of the window. You should see a report on the capacity of the floppy you just formatted, along with notes on the space used (none) and free (all the rest). If you don't see this report, select the icon for the floppy drive. The report will appear and look like this:

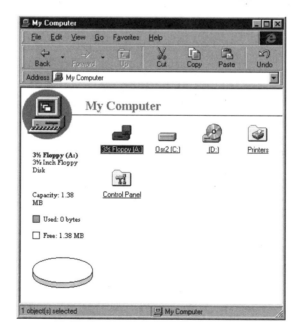

2. To see what your hard disk looks like, try looking at a more detailed report. Right-click the icon for your hard disk, and choose Properties from the pop-up menu that appears. This time, you see a report like the following:

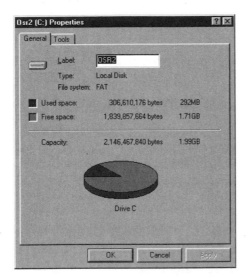

3. While you're here, notice that the label for your hard disk is highlighted. If you'd like to change the label—to your name, for example, just type a new label, using no more than 11 characters, including spaces.

4. Click OK to close the report and, if you typed a new label, to change the name of your hard disk.

5. Close My Computer.

A Little Peace of Mind

In addition to being able to format and report on disks, Windows also includes some valuable tools you can use to check on their health and keep them performing as well as possible. In this section, you'll take a look at two "peace of mind" tools.

If you open your Start menu and then open the Accessories submenu, you'll notice an entry called System Tools. Although the name might bring wrenches and screwdrivers to mind, these tools are actually—of course—utility programs designed to help you help yourself by keeping your system and your data in good shape.

The number of items in a System Tools "kit" varies from one computer to another because different manufacturers include different tools in this category. Some, for example, include antivirus software, such as McAfee

VirusScan, that checks disks for those renegade and potentially destructive sneak programs called viruses. (If you have an antivirus program, it most likely starts automatically whenever you start your computer.) On the same menu, you might also see the Windows Backup program, which automates the process of selecting and copying files from your hard disk to floppies for safekeeping. And, too, you might see items with names like Resource Meter or System Monitor. These are also valuable tools, but ones that you're unlikely to use except out of curiosity. They're designed for programmers and other technically oriented folk to check on software and how it is performing.

Even though this chapter covers only ScanDisk and Disk Defragmenter in any detail, don't feel you're being shortchanged by not learning how to use any other system tools you have. Remember: programs come with their own help.

Despite all the programs you might or might not find in System Tools, however, are two named ScanDisk and Disk Defragmenter that are almost certain to be there. These are the tools you're going to check out and use.

Checking on a Disk

ScanDisk, as its name tells you, scans a disk. Why? Primarily to check on Windows' "log" of file-storage data to be sure it's accurate. So what? Well, problems with entries in this log can make files—especially program files—unreliable and possibly not even usable. So what does ScanDisk do about any problems it finds? It corrects them.

And what, exactly, does ScanDisk check? If you want, it can check the entire surface of a disk for bad spots and mark any it finds as "off limits"— unusable for storage—to prevent possible problems in the future. By default, however, ScanDisk checks file names and folders, and it also checks for little waifs known as *lost clusters,* which, like lambs that stray from the flock, are small bits of programs or data that become separated from the files to which they belong. Lost clusters aren't common, and they aren't dangerous, but they can be created when a program "glitch" or an abnormal shutdown prevents Windows from putting files away correctly, and they do take up storage space. Because lost clusters are essentially useless to you, ScanDisk—again by default—finds them and releases the storage space they occupy for use by other files.

Where Did This Come From?

It's possible that, sometime in your computing career, you'll see a bright blue screen appear instead of Windows when you boot the computer. The blue screen tells you that the non-Windows version of ScanDisk is checking your hard disk for errors. If you see this, it just means that you started the computer without having shut Windows down properly the last time you quit—for example, if you forgot about the Shut Down command and just turned off the power switch. Remember that part of shutting down involves Windows putting files away correctly and updating its internal records. If Windows isn't given the chance to do this, its file-system "log" becomes unreliable. And if that happens, ScanDisk runs the next time you start up so that it can check for—and fix—any problems in file storage caused by the abnormal shutdown. If this version of ScanDisk finds any problems, it will prompt you with options that tell you what to do next. Follow the instructions on the screen. When ScanDisk finishes its job, it will hand you over to Windows for startup as usual.

You don't have to use ScanDisk often, or even at all, but it is a useful and reliable tool for periodically checking on the health of your hard disk. It's also handy if Windows or another program has trouble reading from or writing to a floppy disk and you can't figure out why. ScanDisk might be able to tell you and, possibly, do something about it.

A disk scan can take a fair amount of time, especially if you choose to inspect both the storage and the surface of a hard disk, but you can see what happens by checking out the floppy you recently formatted:

1. Check to be sure the floppy is still in the drive.

2. Click the Start button, and work through Programs and Accessories. Highlight System Tools, and then choose ScanDisk from the submenu. The following window appears, showing the possible drives to scan.

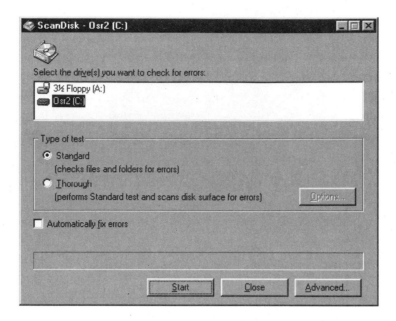

3. A standard scan of the floppy would take about 2 seconds and wouldn't show you that much, so opt for a thorough scan instead by clicking the floppy drive in the box headed *Select the drive(s) you want to check for errors* and the radio button to the left of Thorough.

4. Click the Start button, and watch the gauge and messages at the bottom of the window. ScanDisk runs through the standard scan on your floppy very quickly, because there is little to check in the way of file storage. When it launches into the surface scan, however, you can see it begin to work its way over the disk, *cluster* (storage unit) by cluster. This part of the scan will take a few minutes.

When it's over, ScanDisk most likely won't have found any problems because your floppy is freshly formatted. Now try a standard scan of your hard disk:

1. In the ScanDisk window, click your hard disk in the box headed *Select the drive(s) you want to check for errors.*

2. Under Type Of Test, click the radio button to the left of Standard.

3. Click the Start button, and ScanDisk again swings into action. On a large hard disk, this scan will take awhile. It is, however, a good thing that you're doing, so be patient.

And remember to do this every now and then.

By the way, although ScanDisk does fix problems in file storage, don't assume it can fix everything. Sometimes, two unrelated files get "joined at the hip," so to speak, when the same storage location is logged for both. If this happens, the problem—known technically as *cross-linking*—is knotty enough that neither ScanDisk nor any person can untangle it. ScanDisk tells you which files are involved, so the best—only—solution is to delete the files and copy them back to the disk. If one of the files is a program, reinstall the entire program, to be sure everything works properly.

If/when ScanDisk finds a problem, it notifies you with a message like the following:

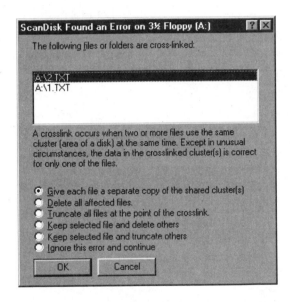

This message had to be specially created in order to show you how Scan-Disk responds to a problem. You'll probably never see such a message, but if you do, accept the default option (create copies of the shared information in both files), and then check the files themselves by opening them (if they are documents) or by running them (if they are programs). The file that originally owned the shared information should be fine. The file that accidentally inherited the shared information will either have to be re-constructed (if it's a document file) or replaced (if it's a program file) as described above.

"Defragging" a Disk

In addition to making sure that file storage and, indeed, the physical surface of a disk are both in good condition, you'll probably want to periodically (every six months or so) *defrag* your hard disk. *Defragging* (short for *defragmenting*), as a word, sounds a little on the mean and nasty side, but it actually refers to something that can speed up the performance of your hard drive. It doesn't have much, if any, effect when a disk is new, but defragging can improve file storage and speed on a disk that's been worked hard for awhile. This is why.

When a disk is newly formatted, its storage space is like a vast, empty field—easy to "plow" and easy to "plant" with row after row of files. And, at first, that's exactly the way things work. Files are laid down neatly, one after the other. But not all files are the same size, are they? A program file can be huge. A letter can be considerably smaller. Each needs a certain amount of storage space, but giving the letter the same amount as the program would be wasteful. Conversely, the program couldn't possibly fit into the same space as the letter. So, Windows assigns each the amount of room it needs. That's all well and good, and no problem at all.

Disk storage, however, is not like an open field in one important way: it is divided into equal-sized pieces, none of which is actually large enough to hold an entire file. (This sounds inefficient, but it's really not, as you'll see.) So, now you have disk storage divided into…oh, think of it now as row after row of pigeonholes. How does Windows stick a big file into these little pigeonholes? It divides the file into pigeonhole-sized pieces and pops those pieces neatly into as many pigeonholes as the file needs. It's all very neat, very tidy, and very reliable because, remember, Windows keeps track of where all files—and all pieces of all files—are stored in the log it maintains on every disk.

Now, what has all this got to do with defragging? Think about how you use a disk. Over time, you don't just create and save files. You change some. You delete others. And each time you delete a file, you make its storage available for another file, which almost certainly won't be the exact same size as the one you deleted. To make the best, most efficient use of disk space, Windows ends up switching from storing files in *contiguous* (side-by-side) groups of pigeonholes and instead begins reusing vacated space by tucking pieces of files in this available hole and that one. Eventually, on a well-used disk the pieces of any one file can become—physically—widely separated.

This separation of file segments is called *file fragmentation,* and it's absolutely no cause for alarm, because Windows tracks the location of every piece of every file in its log, and it can find the pieces without problem. But what fragmentation does mean is that the read/write heads of the disk must do a lot more traveling to find and retrieve entire files. Even though the *access speed* of a disk drive is so fast it's measured in *milliseconds* (thousandths of a second), a lot of head movement necessarily means slower access times. To improve the situation by storing widely separated file segments close together—and thereby help your disk work faster—you use Disk Defragmenter, like this:

1. From the Start button, work through Programs and Accessories to System Tools. On the System Tools menu, click Disk Defragmenter. Two small windows appear, one probably on top of the other:

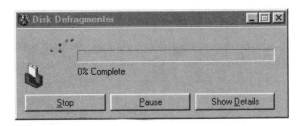

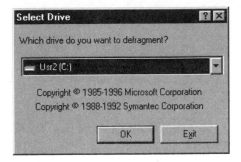

2. As the Select Drive window requests, you choose a drive to defragment. By default, your primary hard disk is selected.

That's a good choice, both in real life and for the purposes of this example, so accept the proposed drive by clicking OK.

3. Now the defragmenter goes to work and begins checking file storage on your hard disk. After the check, it displays a window like this one, telling you what it found and what it recommends:

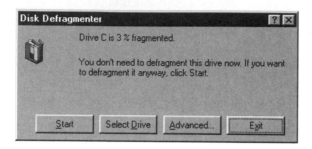

On a new or nearly new hard disk (which this book assumes yours is), chances are that "Defrag" will find little or no fragmentation and will therefore tell you there's no reason to proceed, unless you really want to. (It's very polite.)

If Defrag reported that your disk needs defragging, you might want to wait until you won't need the computer for an hour or so. When you're ready, run Defrag again, and when you see the message telling you the hard drive needs defragging, click the Start button.

4. On the assumption that Defrag has reported "you don't need to defragment," you're going to skip the actual defragmentation. Instead, click the Advanced button to see a little more about what Defrag can do.

5. The Advanced button causes Defrag to display this list of options:

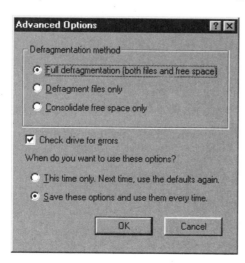

What is all this stuff? Ask Defrag.

6. Click the question mark (?) button in the upper right corner, point to the first option (for full defragmentation), and click the left mouse button for an explanation.

7. Click the question mark button again, point to another option, and click the left mouse button for an explanation of that option.

8. Click away with the question mark until you feel you've found out enough, and then click the OK button to close the Advanced Options dialog box. (Yes, this has been a way to show you that you can rely on yourself, rather than on a book to find out what you need to know.)

9. Click the Exit button in the Disk Defragmenter window to close Defrag.

Finally, just to reassure you that you figured it out right:

■ A full defragmentation collects all the pieces of fragmented files and puts them together, and it collects all available storage space and puts *it* together so that everything is neatly stored away. This is the most time-consuming, but also the most effective, method of defragging.

■ The Defragment Files Only option pieces fragmented files together but leaves available free space wherever it happens to be. This leaves you with all the pieces of existing files stored together in contiguous locations, but it also leaves available free space scattered around the disk. Defragmenting only is faster than a full defragmentation, but it can mean that files you save in the future will be fragmented (as Windows puts them into the scattered bits of free space for storage).

■ The Consolidate Free Space Only option is essentially the reverse of the Defragment Files Only option. Consolidating free space means that files you store in the future can be put into contiguous storage locations (and therefore won't be fragmented), but it also means that existing files on the disk can end up being even more fragmented (if Windows has to wander farther afield to find free space to store those that change in size).

Aced it, did you? Good. Now for some stuff that's a little more fun.

Shortcuts and Some Nifty Ways to Use Them

Shortcuts are one of the friendliest features in Windows. Appearing in Windows 95 for the first time, they are small files that include nothing more than the information, called the *path*, that tells Windows how to find whatever document, program, or icon you create a shortcut to. The beauty of a shortcut is that you can put one wherever it's most convenient for you, and then you can use that shortcut as a quick means of opening or using whatever item the shortcut leads to. So, for instance, instead of having to open My Computer whenever you want to see what's on a disk in your floppy drive, you can put a shortcut to the drive directly on your desktop, where a single click is all you need to open a window to it.

In Chapter 5, you experimented with shortcuts by creating one on the desktop to keep your built-in My Documents folder within easy reach. In this chapter, you'll create a few more that can make life easier when you're working with your computer.

First, suppose you've been working on a long document, one that's going to take several sessions to complete. One easy way to find and open recent documents is built right into Windows: open the Start menu, highlight Documents, and choose the one you want from the list of recently used documents Windows automatically keeps for you. Here, however, is a way to zero in immediately on the one document you want to work on.

First create a sample document:

1. Click the Start button, work through Programs and Accessories, and click Notepad.

2. Type some text into the Notepad window. Anything will do, even *hi there*.

3. Open the File menu, and choose Save As.

4. In the File name box, type *Test Document*.

5. Now click the downward-pointing triangle to the right of the Save In box. Scroll down, if necessary, and click Book Samples.

6. Click the Save button, and then close Notepad.

Now for the shortcut:

1. Open the Book Samples folder on your desktop.

2. Right-click Test Document, drag it to the desktop, and choose Create Shortcut(s) Here from the pop-up menu. That's all it takes to create a shortcut. Notice that Windows automatically identifies it as a shortcut with a small arrow in the lower left corner and the label *Shortcut to Test Document.*

To see how it works:

1. Close the Book Samples window (just to clean up the desktop).

2. Click the Shortcut To Test Document icon on the desktop.

Within seconds, Windows starts Notepad and opens your test document, eliminating the need to find and start Notepad and then to find and open the document. This type of shortcut is so easy and so useful that all the chapters of this book were kept close at hand in just this way.

To clean up:

1. Close Notepad.

2. Drag the document shortcut to the Recycle Bin, and click Yes when you're asked to confirm the deletion.

3. For good measure, open the Book Samples folder and drag the document itself to the Recycle Bin, too. Again, click Yes to confirm.

Now for some more shortcuts you might find handy:

1. Place a floppy disk in your floppy drive.

2. Open My Computer.

3. Right-click the icon for your floppy drive, drag it to the desktop, and click Create Shortcut(s) Here from the pop-up menu.

4. Click the shortcut, and within seconds a window appears showing you the contents (if any) of the disk in the drive.

5. If you want, use the same right-click, drag, and create shortcut method to create desktop shortcuts to your hard disk and your CD-ROM drive.

6. Now, here's another good one. Click the Printers folder in the My Computer window.

7. Find the icon for the printer you normally use and...exactly. Right-click, drag it to the desktop, and create a shortcut to the printer. How do you use this shortcut? If you want, you can print a document by dragging it and dropping it on the shortcut. Or, check the status of a document you're printing by clicking the shortcut to open a window that displays the information you need.

8. If you don't want to keep any of these shortcuts, drag them to the Recycle Bin to dispose of them, and confirm the deletion.

In addition to shortcuts, there are a couple of other ways you can make life easier for yourself. You can add to the Send To list that opens when you right-click an item, and you can put favorite or often-used applications at the top of the Start menu, where you can reach them without having to work through one or more submenus.

Try adding your printer to the Send To list. That's another easy way to print a document without finding and starting the program and document first. Here's how to do it:

1. Click the Start button, open the Programs menu, and click Windows Explorer.

2. In the left pane of the Windows Explorer window, scroll down if necessary and click the Printers folder. It's near the bottom of the window, below Windows and other program folders. Your printer should now be listed in the right pane of the window, like this:

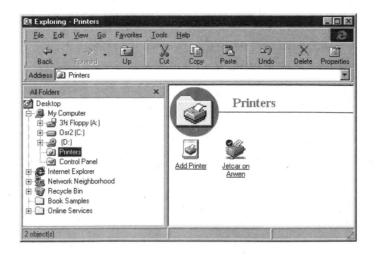

3. Scroll up in the left pane—again, if necessary—and click the plus sign to the left of your Windows folder.

4. Now scroll if necessary until you can see the subfolder called SendTo in the left pane. (Yes, you're going to "tamper" with part of your Windows folder, but only with the SendTo subfolder, and Windows doesn't mind if you add to it.)

5. Right-click your printer in the right pane of the window. Drag the printer to the SendTo folder, drop it, and choose Create Shortcut(s) Here from the pop-up menu. You've just added the printer to the Send To list.

To see the list:

1. Drag the Windows Explorer window out of the way if necessary, but leave it open—you'll be using it again shortly.

2. Right-click your Book Samples folder, and click Send To on the pop-up menu. A shortcut to your printer should be sitting there, along with all the items that originally came on your Send To list.

From now on, you can print a document simply by right-clicking it on the desktop or in an open window and choosing the printer from the Send To list.

To finish up, try adding and then removing a program from the top of the Start menu. This is really easy and a great way to customize the Start menu, especially for someone who isn't very comfortable with computers yet. Just for practice, you can add Notepad to the Start menu and then remove it to keep your Start menu clean:

1. Windows Explorer should still be open on your desktop. Scroll if necessary, and click your Windows folder.

2. Just so you can see exactly what you're doing, change the view to details by clicking the View menu and choosing Details.

3. In the right pane, scroll until you see Notepad. It's identified by the familiar spiral-bound notebook. Look to the right, and you see Notepad listed as an Application in the column headed Type. That's the item you want.

4. Drag Notepad to the Start button, and drop it there. That's it.

5. Click the Start button, and Notepad appears, right at the top of the Start menu.

6. Click Notepad, and the program starts—without your having to work through the Programs and Accessories menus to find it first.

7. To finish up, close both Notepad and the Windows Explorer window.

Adding a program to the Start menu doesn't mean you're stuck with it forever. To see how to remove a program from the menu, take Notepad off. You don't need it there anyway:

1. Right-click a blank part of the taskbar, and choose Properties from the pop-up menu.

2. Click the Start Menu Programs tab, and click Remove. The Remove Shortcuts/Folders dialog box appears:

Here you see a list of all the programs on your Start menu and its various submenus.

3. To remove Notepad, scroll down if necessary until you find the Notepad icon with the shortcut arrow in the lower left corner—the icon that looks like the circled item in the preceding illustration.

4. Click the Notepad icon, and then click the Remove button.

5. Click Close, and then click OK on the Taskbar Properties sheet.

6. Click the Start button. Notepad is gone.

Well, that's it for this section on shortcuts and other labor-saving devices. As you become more experienced, you'll no doubt think of other ways to customize your PC and the way it works for you. These small "tricks," however, should have given you a start. Now, it's on to looking at a little wizardry.

Running with the Wizards

Very proficient, high-level programmers are often called "wizards." So are a group of small, useful programs included with Windows that help you through the details of procedures that some people find a little daunting because of the technology involved. This section deals with both, in the sense that it gives you a look at two special wizards of the software kind that help you install the programs and hardware created by wizards of the human kind. In the process, you'll also be able to see and appreciate some of the thought and care that went into making Windows the "user-friendly" operating system it happens to be.

 OTE The term *user-friendly,* used so often in relation to computers, might strike you as a rather *un*friendly term in its own right, because it can seem to imply that humans are so incapable of understanding computers that the computers must make a special effort to be nice to those poor, two-legged user critters. Balderdash. Humans made them; humans understand them. Heck, humans *control* them.

Adding and Removing Software

As you work with Windows, especially when you try to do something new, a Windows wizard just might pop up to lend a helping hand. For instance, if you installed a printer in the last chapter, the wizard known as Install Printer appeared to guide you through the process. In Chapter 9, you'll see another wizard, one that helps with Internet connections. And, in the future, if you decide to use your computer to call up another computer, you'll encounter still another wizard that handles dial-up networking. Whenever you meet such a wizard, use it. It's been programmed to know exactly what you have to do and to guide you through the steps in the order they should be performed.

On the other hand, if you want to go looking for a wizard, one of the best places to find one is in the Control Panel. Why? Because some of the utilities in Control Panel deal with procedures that, at least historically, have not been all that easy to handle. In fact, you can have a friendly get-together with one right now.

Try It

Your CD includes a lesson on adding and removing software that makes use of one of Windows' wizards. To try the lesson and actually use the wizard:

1. Start the CD either by inserting it in the CD-ROM drive or by clicking the PCs For Beginners icon (a shortcut, actually) on your desktop.

2. On the opening screen, click item 2, the Windows Overview section.

3. Click the left mouse button to skip the Overview introduction, and, in the list of Overview lessons, click *Adding and Removing Software*.

4. When you finish the lesson, quit the CD. You won't be using it again in this chapter.

There's not much more this book can do that the lesson didn't, so you won't be seeing any more of this wizard. In fact, you might not see it all that often, because new software—especially the kind shipped on CD-ROMs—often includes an autoplay "switch" that automatically starts the program's setup procedure for you. However, if you need to help a new program get installed or, especially, if you want to *remove* a program you no longer want to keep on your hard disk, remember Add/Remove Programs. It's the way to go with programs designed for Windows.

Adding New Hardware

Once upon a time, installing and getting new hardware to run with a PC was not always the easiest job in the world. Aside from the screwdrivers and, often, patience and manual dexterity required to physically install the device, you could very well find yourself tinkering with exotic settings—things with names such as interrupt request (IRQ) or input/output range—that the operating system and other software needed to know about in order to use the device.

These days, adding new hardware to a computer is much simpler—at least the software end of it is—thanks to a feature called Plug and Play, which is often abbreviated PNP. Plug and Play is neither software nor hardware. It is a specification, a blueprint that hardware designers and manufacturers can follow in building add-on devices for computers. Why is it so great? Because Windows can automatically detect and set itself up to use Plug and Play hardware. This is a good thing, a very good thing, especially because a certain rather formidable ally of yours called the Add New Hardware wizard makes installation of Plug and Play devices especially easy.

Although this book can't, for obvious reasons, take you all the way through installation of any new hardware, it can give you a look at the wizard and, in the process, show you what kinds of hardware the wizard is designed to help you with. Here's what to do:

1. Click the Start button, highlight Settings, and click Control Panel.

2. In the Control Panel window, click Add New Hardware to start the wizard, which looks like this when it first appears:

3. Even though you can't work through the entire wizard, you can see how it starts its work. To do so, click the Next button. The wizard's display changes to this:

As you can see from reading this screen, the wizard and Windows are fully prepared to set up your hardware for you.

4. In real life, you should keep the default option and let Windows search for your new hardware. Now, however, just so you can see a list of hardware types, click the radio button to the left of No, and then click the Next button:

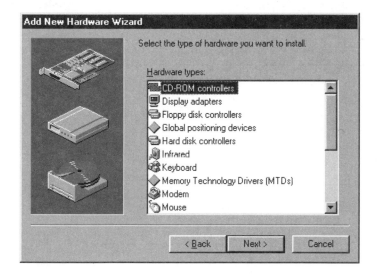

Scroll down the list if you like. There's a healthy assortment displayed here.

5. When you've seen enough, click Cancel. This is the end of the line for you, at least for now.

You interrupted your look at the wizard here because from this point on the wizard gets serious about details, such as the make and model of hardware you're installing. You really wouldn't want to go any farther without some actual hardware to install. You did, however, manage to see what the wizard looks like, and maybe someday you'll be returning to it, to walk through the entire installation process with some brand-new hardware of your own. If and when you do, just remember:

- Install the hardware—physically—before calling on the Add New Hardware wizard. (It can't install what it can't detect, and it can't detect what isn't there.)

- Let Windows check for your new hardware.

After that, you should be home free.

 IP If you have trouble using hardware you've installed, turn to Help before you start pulling out your hair. Look up *Plug and Play hardware, trouble-shooting* in the index. You might be able to resolve the problem there. If not, call the manufacturer or contact a professional who can help you out.

All About Applications

Up to now, you've been finding out about your computer: how to use it and what to do with it. But computers are not *just* about operating systems, or even files or folders or disks. They're about applications—the programs that actually make computers do the things you want them to do. Applications are where you turn when you want to use your computer to write, draw, play chess, learn a different language, design a garden, remodel your kitchen, or brush up on anything from calculus to chemistry.

Despite all the work that applications can help you do, a chapter about applications can't do a lot in the hands-on area for the simple reason that, in order to help you learn how to write or draw or design a landscape or solve an equation, the book would have to assume that an appropriate application was either on your computer or ready for you to install. And unfortunately, a book can't make that assumption or provide you with the necessary applications.

What this chapter *can* do is take you on a tour of some popular types of application software. It can show you what they look like, roughly how you use them, and, more importantly, explain why or when you might want to put them to work—why, for example, you would turn to a database program instead of a word processor to create an inventory of your books or tapes, even though all you plan to do is type words in the form of names, titles, and so on.

Because reading isn't nearly as much fun as doing, this chapter will help you keep from twiddling your thumbs in boredom by providing some hands-on sessions that help you get a feel for working with application software. For instance, you'll use WordPad to experiment with a word processor, you'll be able to watch some "movies" that show a word processor and a spreadsheet in action, and you'll learn how to install and use two free pieces of software in the Goodies folder on your CD. One of these is a trial version of the home finance program called Microsoft Money; the other is a trial version of the venerable arcade game called Pac-Man. (And yes, games are application software; they're just more fun than some other kinds.) So, if you're ready to go...

How Come It's Microsoft This and Microsoft That?

This chapter deals with Microsoft software. But that's not only because this is a Microsoft Press book; it's because the software really is good. And Microsoft's Home Essentials 98, which forms the basis of this chapter, includes a useful program called Microsoft Works. Why turn to Works to show you applications in action? Because Works is *integrated* software, meaning that it includes several applications in the same easy-to-learn, easy-to-use package. Furthermore, Works is not only designed for everyday, nonbusiness use; it is also preinstalled by many manufacturers on new PCs. As a result, there's a good chance it's already on your computer, ready and willing to work when you want it to. Finally, because all applications described here come from the same source, they present a consistent "look and feel" that will help you spot the similarities and differences between applications as you look at the illustrations of each.

You should not, however, end up feeling that this focus on Microsoft products is an attempt to force you in the same direction. Although you wouldn't go wrong with the software described here, the shelves at your favorite computer store are loaded with hundreds or thousands of products to choose from. When it comes to buying software for yourself, read some reviews, listen to recommendations from friends, and then let your own preferences and needs guide your choices. That's the way to be *really* happy with the software you invest in.

The Big Three

To start off, take a look at the "big three" applications: word processors, spreadsheets, and databases. All three applications are widely used both at home and in business. All three also come in different "strengths," from what you might consider Lite (perfectly adequate for everyday use) to really heavy-duty (highly sophisticated, programmable, and—consequently—larger and generally harder to learn).

Works, the integrated Home Essentials 98 package that will take you on a walk-through of these three applications, falls in the Lite category, but don't think that means it's either limited or fit only for babies. Works is more than equal to the job when it comes to writing letters, setting budgets, or doing inventories and homework, and it can even help you "mail" documents via modem. To give you an idea of what it can do, Figure 8-1 shows some of the jobs Works can take on. The list in the illustration is also a good introduction to the kinds of work that computers do in general.

Similar to Microsoft's Word (word processor), Excel (spreadsheet), and Access (database), but smaller and easier to use, the applications included in Works function well on their own. But because common tasks often involve different types of data, these applications can also share information among themselves, to save you time and to make it really easy to move,

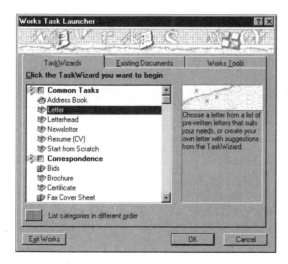

Figure 8-1.   *Works "wizards" and what they can help you do.*

say, a "numbers" document such as a budget into a "words" document such as a report. In short, if you have Works on your computer, you might want to give it a try. You'll probably like it.

The best place to start looking at applications is with what's probably the number one use for computers: word processing.

The Write Stuff

Word processors need little introduction. You use them to write things. This book, for example. Or a newsletter. Or a book report. Or anything else made up mostly of words.

Are there serious advantages to using a word processor? You bet. With a word processor:

- You can shape and reshape both what you say and the way it looks, until you're 100 percent satisfied, and then print it out.

- You never have to worry about running lines off the bottom of the page or staying in the margins—the program takes care of it for you, breaking lines and pages as you type. All you have to figure out is where to end one paragraph and begin a new one.

- You can make titles and headings bigger or darker than the rest of the text, and you can even print them in a different typeface if you want.

- You can print as many copies as you want, and each one looks like—indeed is—an "original."

- And best of all, you *never* have to use an eraser.

And the list goes on. As you work with your chosen word processor, you'll discover many other ways it makes writing faster, neater, and more efficient.

But if word processors are so great, aren't there *any* disadvantages to them? Actually, there's one: you have to learn to use them.

But it's not hard.

What Does It Mean to "Process" Words?

To use a word processor successfully, there's only one idea you need to get used to. It's something that comes to you automatically whenever you write with a pen, but you probably never took the time to think anything of it: As you write, you are shaping both the content of your writing and its format. You are controlling not only *what* you say, but how it *looks*.

To a word processor, however:

- *Content* is what you write.

- *Formatting* is what it looks like.

Content comes from you alone. Formatting is something that your word processor applies according to your commands. Furthermore, your word processor doesn't assume that just because you typed a word in all capital letters that it has to stay that way. All the little formatting extras can be applied whenever you want—as you write, or later on.

What this all means to you is that, when you're in the heat of some creative frenzy, all you have to think about is just plain typing. There's no need to worry about what your document will eventually look like, even if it's currently an ugly block of text on the screen. Once you've had your say and are satisfied with the way you said it, you can spend whatever time is necessary to change the formatting so that the printed document looks exactly the way you want it to. And you can format or reformat over and over again, as many times as you want. That's the big difference between writing with a pen or a typewriter and writing with a word processor: Nothing is done until you say it is.

When you need to indent paragraphs or line up columns of words, use the Tab key, not the Spacebar. It's not only easier, it produces accurate results.

Although this distinction between writing and formatting is easy to understand and might not seem like such a big deal, many people—including some who ought to know better—spend more time than they need to when it comes to spacing their words and paragraphs. Or they bang the Spacebar over and over to line things up. *It's not necessary*, as you can see from a simple hands-on practice of your own, with the little WordPad word processor.

1. Click the Start button, work through Programs and Accessories, and start WordPad.

2. Widen the WordPad window, if necessary, so that you can see the entire *Formatting* toolbar:

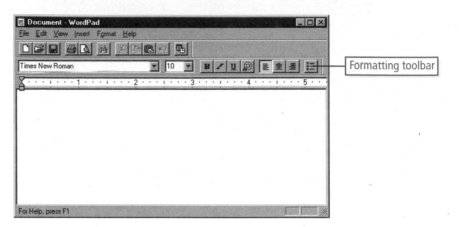

3. In the WordPad window, type the following sentence:

   What do you want?

   There's your content. Now to "paint" some formatting onto it.

4. Press the Home key to move the *insertion point* to the beginning of the sentence. Now hold down both the Ctrl and Shift keys, and press the Right arrow key to highlight the first word in the sentence:

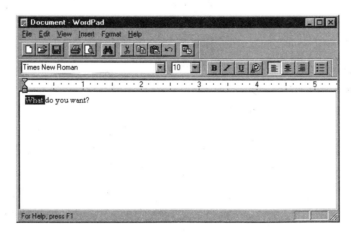

5. Now, click the Italic button (marked with a slanted capital I) on the formatting toolbar. As easily as that, you've italicized the word *What* and added a little oomph to the sentence.

6. Click the Italic button again to undo the formatting. Now see how formatting can make a big difference not only in the way your writing looks, but in how it strikes the reader.

7. Press the End key, press the Left arrow key once, hold down Ctrl and Shift, and press the Left arrow key again. This time, you highlight the last word of the sentence. Click the Italic button again. Changes the emphasis a little, doesn't it?

8. Of course, formatting is not just a matter of making words italic. You can also change their size. You can even change the way the paragraph is placed on the page with nothing more than a mouse click.

9. Try this. Find the Center button (the one with centered lines of "text" on it). It's the middle one in the group of three near the right end of the toolbar. If you're not sure you've got the right one, hold the mouse pointer still on it for a second and a tooltip saying *Center* will appear.

10. Click the button, and you tell WordPad you want the sentence centered between the left and right edges of the page.

11. Click the Preview button (the one with a white page and a magnifying glass) in the main toolbar underneath the menu names. This button tells WordPad to show you what your document will look like when it's printed.

12. You probably can't see much, so place the mouse pointer near the top of the preview "page." Click when the pointer becomes a magnifying glass, and WordPad will *zoom in* to give you a close-up. Your sentence looks a little teeny, doesn't it? Time to fix that, so click the Close button in the Preview window.

13. In the main WordPad window, click at either end of your sentence and drag to highlight the entire thing.

14. Now, click the downward-pointing triangle to the right of the Font Size box (the one with the number—probably 10—in it). This is where you can make highlighted text larger or smaller. Smaller won't do much for you, so make the sentence BIG. Move the highlight down the list of numbers, and click 36.

15. Much better, as you can see by clicking the Preview button again. Close the Preview window so that you can do a final little bit of formatting.

16. Click to place the insertion point between *want* and the question mark, and then drag to the left to highlight *want*. Now, click the Color button (the one with the artist's palette on it). Click a nice, bright color like red in the list that opens.

17. Click a blank part of the window to see the result. The italics, the centered paragraph, the font size, and the color are all different types of formatting you applied to your sample sentence. Imagine what you can do with a whole document.

18. If you want, try playing with the other buttons on the Formatting toolbar. Just remember to highlight the text you want to format

---

It's Whizzy

You might have noticed, when you tried the Preview button to look at a sample document, that the preview "page" looked exactly like a sheet of paper with your document printed on it. You might also have wondered at the way WordPad (and other applications) displays your text and your formatting on the screen in a way that's so close to the printed version that you don't have to guess where a line will "break" at the right margin or what your formatting will look like when you finally send the document to the printer.

These examples and more are all aspects of a feature known as WYSIWYG, which is pronounced "whizzywig" and stands for What You See Is What You Get. It means exactly what it says: the document you see on the screen is the document you'll fetch from the printer.

before applying the formatting. When you've had enough practice, click the window's Close button and click No when WordPad asks if you want to save the document.

Hopefully, you had a little fun here, and you've seen the difference between content and formatting for yourself. Now you can take what you've learned about the essence of word processing and see how more sophisticated word processors than WordPad not only distinguish between content and format but use that distinction to make life much easier for you.

Tools for Creating Documents

Works, the application software on which much of this chapter is based, includes a word processor that comes with a considerable number of predesigned *templates* that act as formatting and layout "blueprints" for creating your own documents. Using one of these beauties, you could turn an idea into a professionally designed and formatted document in a few short steps, which are summarized in the following list and illustrated on the next few pages:

- Tell Works which template you want to use as the basis for a new document.

- If it asks, provide "boilerplate" information (name and address, for instance) that it can insert for you.

- Tell Works to run a program called the *TaskWizard,* which actually creates the new document.

- Fill in the text that only you can supply (the body of a letter, for example).

- Change any formatting you want to change.

- Print the document.

Now here are the high points of the process, from beginning to end, as you can see in these illustrations and short descriptions showing how Works helps you create a letter.

Deciding on the template is easy, because all you do is pick the one you want from this list (the same one shown earlier in this chapter).

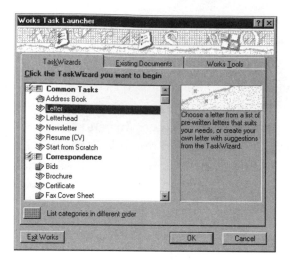

Works then asks if you want to have the TaskWizard take care of the grunt work for you. You say "yes."

Works displays a colorful window showing a few options and a sample document:

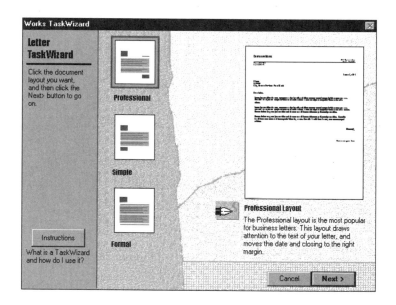

So far, so easy. Here, all you do is click the layout you want, and then click the Next button. Now, the screen changes to display a set of options covering various boilerplate items:

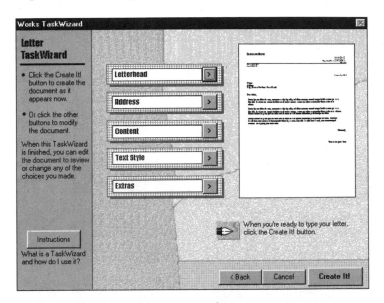

All you do now is click each item you want Works to handle for you, and then answer a few questions (such as "Do you want to create your own letterhead?") and provide requested information (such as "What is your name?"). Difficult it's not.

When Works has gotten your responses to all the choices it provides, and it has gathered all the information it needs for the document you're creating, you click a can't-miss button named Create It! that turns the information you provided into something like the following screen.

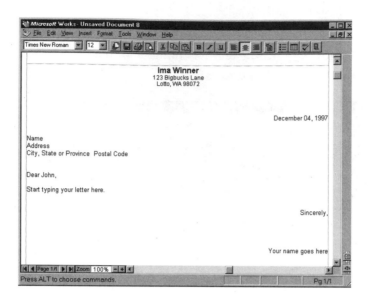

And, of course, once it's done, you have all the freedom you want or need to change the formatting or add a *clipart* picture to liven up the scene:

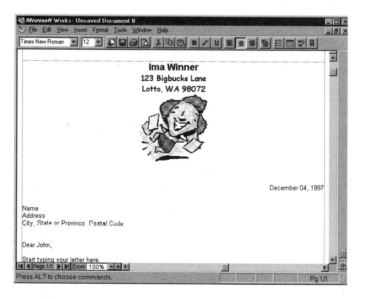

Oh, yes. And you can even write the letter. To replace the "placeholder" text for things like the name and address of the person you're writing to, you just highlight whatever you want to replace and then type away.

Try It

The emphasis in this description of word processors has been on distinguishing content from format, because that distinction is important in learning how to use a word processor as something more than a typewriter. In addition to formatting, however, today's word processors help with everything from spelling to grammar, and even adding pictures to your documents. Take a look:

1. If necessary, place the lesson CD in your CD-ROM drive. Click Exit when the CD begins to play.

2. Click My Computer, right-click the icon for your CD-ROM drive, and click Explore on the pop-up menu.

3. Click the Goodies icon (not the folder, the white "page" with the big blue *e* on it).

4. Click the item that reads *Click here for video* in the left pane.

5. In the right pane of this window are five word processing videos. To see them in sequence, click and run them in this order: Correct01, Correct02, ClipArt, List, and Bullets.

If you remember (from early in the book), the function keys labeled F1 through F12 are those special-duty keys that programmers can dedicate to making certain tasks faster and easier to perform.

In fact, if you find yourself typing the same thing over and over in different documents, you can even use a feature called Easy Text, which allows you to type the item once, store it under an abbreviation you choose, and then insert the text whenever and wherever you want by typing the abbreviation and pressing the F3 key. With Easy Text, you'd only have to type "Dynamite Dancing Dervish Deli" once. By storing this mess under, say, the abbreviation dddd (which is unlikely to show up in anything else), you can from that day forward just type *dddd* and press the F3 key to insert the text wherever you want.

The Numbers Game

A spreadsheet program is the electronic equivalent of as many ledger books as you can imagine, each one full of ledger sheets. You don't however, have to wear a green eyeshade and stick pencils behind your ear to use a spreadsheet—not even if you and numbers aren't the best of friends. In fact, as you'll see in this section, some of the tasks you can assign to a spreadsheet seem to have very little to do with calculating balances or profits and losses. Yet, they are ideal jobs for a spreadsheet because of the way such a program organizes and works with information. Whenever you have numbers to work with, or information—say, a football pool or a student grade sheet—that's best presented in a grid you read both across and down, that's the time to think about using a spreadsheet. But to begin at the beginning…. On your computer screen, a spreadsheet "page" looks like the one shown in Figure 8-2.

Some spreadsheet programs, such as Excel, allow you to bundle related sheets together in electronic "workbooks" and quickly share information across those workbooks whenever you want. What a feature for things like monthly budgets…or political fund-raising tallies.

Unlike a word processor, which is designed to deal with lines and paragraphs of information, you can see here that a spreadsheet is designed to deal with "nuggets" of information that are entered into the spaces, known as *cells,* that march across the sheet in *rows* and down the sheet in *columns.* This basic organization is the hallmark of every electronic spreadsheet.

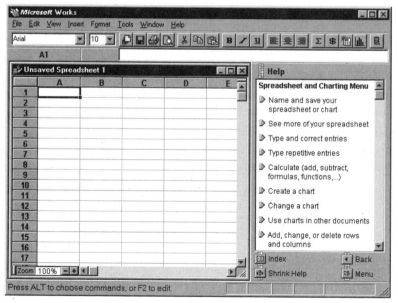

Figure 8-2.   *A blank spreadsheet, ready to be filled with information.*

So what goes into those cells? Not counting graphs and pictures, which are special items you insert, you can enter three basic types of information:

■ Text. This is any information that is not used in calculations. If you were creating a spreadsheet and you typed words to identify the contents of rows and columns, those words would be considered text.

■ Values. This includes all numbers (and sometimes dates) that are used in calculations. Values can be added, subtracted, multiplied, and so on. Essentially, they're the numbers that make a spreadsheet meaningful.

■ Formulas. This is the part that does math for you. You create formulas, and they take over the job of adding, subtracting, and otherwise calculating results based on the values you type into a spreadsheet. Formulas are the crowning glory of a spreadsheet program. Truth to tell, they can also be its most demanding feature when people begin creating formulas for complex calculations—especially formulas that rely on other formulas to do their work.

At any rate, that's what a spreadsheet is: it's text that identifies numbers; numbers that represent values; and formulas that use those values to calculate results for you. Figure 8-3 on the following page shows you a very simple spreadsheet, created with Works, that shows you all three of these elements. (The rather odd-looking notation =*AVG(C5:C7)* at the top of the window is the formula that calculates the person's bowling average for the week of June 1; a similar formula calculates the average for each of the other weeks, too.)

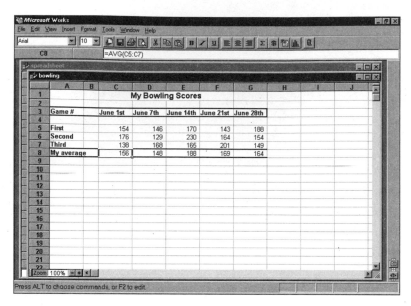

Figure 8-3.   *A simple spreadsheet that lists—and averages—bowling scores.*

Calling All Cells

Seeing that formula, by the way, brings you to something else about spreadsheets: how they know which cells you're working with.

Spreadsheets can be made up of many, many cells. A Works spreadsheet, for example, can contain as many as 16,384 rows and 256 columns, which means a single spreadsheet can contain 256 individual pieces of information about 16,384 different items. If you multiply the number of cells down by the number of cells across, you get a grand total of 4,194,304 cells per spreadsheet. That's a lot of cells, and a Works spreadsheet is actually smaller than a heavy-duty version such as an Excel spreadsheet, which contains 65,536 rows and 256 columns, for a total of 16,777,216 cells per sheet. Yow. Picturing all those cells is mind-boggling enough. Figuring out how to fill them all with information becomes, well, almost unthinkable, at least for the average person. Happily, however, a complete spreadsheet doesn't have to be anywhere near that big. It can, if you want, contain information in as few as one or two cells, although such a small sheet would have a hard time presenting anything meaningful.

But now think of this: If a single spreadsheet—the equivalent of one sheet of ledger paper—can contain millions of cells, how do you tell the program which cells you want to fill with text, values, or formulas? And how does the program refer to those cells itself, when it's storing, displaying, or calculating for you? Both you and the program use the same *cell notation,* which gives the position of each and every cell on the spreadsheet as an *address* made up of the cell's row number and column letter. (Rows are always numbered; columns are always referred to by letter. That way, you never have a cell address such as 111, which could refer either to the cell in row 1 and column 11, or to the cell in row 11, column 1. What a headache that would be.)

If you look at the bowling spreadsheet illustrated earlier, you can see that the information on the sheet is entered into rows 1 through 8, and columns A through G. Thus, by reading across and down, you can see that the scores for the first week of June are entered in the cells in column C, rows 5 through 7—or, in spreadsheet notation, cells C5 through C7. And if you look at the top of the window, you can see that the formula that calculates the average score is entered into cell C8. (That cell, by the way, is *selected* in the illustration—that's why the lines above and below don't show.) At any rate, knowing how to read these addresses, you can now easily figure out what the formula itself means:

=AVG(C5:C7)

	=	AVG	(C5:C7)
The value calculated	equals	the average	of the values in cells C5 through (:) C7

Piece of cake.

In the Eyes and Mind of the Beholder

Is there a lot more to learn about spreadsheets? Oh, yes. Tons. Spreadsheet programs offer as much variety as word processors in the types of help they give and the ways in which you can format them. And, as already mentioned, they can become really elaborate documents filled with complex formulas. But the complexity of a spreadsheet, though based on the capabilities of the program, is strictly the result of the skill and objectives of the person creating the sheet. Just as anything from hot dogs to a French chef's masterpiece can be called dinner, anything from a bowling tally to a company's financial report can be called a spreadsheet. The program provides the tools. The creator of the spreadsheet provides the information and the talent. Overall, however, here are a few things that a typical spreadsheet like the one in Works can do to help you out:

- It can create a colorful chart from the text and values you specify.

- It can add borders, underline, boldface, and otherwise format your text and values.

- It can add and remove rows and columns whenever you want. (You have to be a little careful about this, though, because if a formula requires a value in a deleted row or column, the formula will need correcting.)

- It can add clipart to a spreadsheet to liven up your presentation.

- It can create simple formulas for you. (That's how the AVG formula was created in the bowling spreadsheet.)

- It can check your spelling.

- It can display and calculate as many, or as few, decimal places as you require.

- It can refer to groups of cells by name, rather than address, once you tell it what name to use.

- It can protect whatever cells you indicate so that their contents cannot be changed.

And, as with word processors, the list goes on.

Try It

The Goodies folder on your lesson CD contains some video clips that show you what a sophisticated spreadsheet program—in this case, Microsoft Excel—can do. Take a look, and then come back to see some interesting ways that Works can use the capabilities of its spreadsheet program to create some useful but distinctly un-spreadsheetlike documents for you. Here's what to do:

1. If necessary, insert the lesson CD in your CD-ROM drive and click the Exit button when the opening lesson screen appears.

2. Click My Computer, right-click the icon for your CD-ROM drive, and click Explore on the pop-up menu.

3. As you did for the word processing videos, click the Goodies icon (with the big blue *e* on it).

4. Click the item that reads *Click here for video* in the left pane.

5. Click the spreadsheet videos in this order: Apples, Add, and Sums.

Now, to finish up this quick look at spreadsheets, a look that barely scratched the surface of what they can do, here are two different "spreadsheets" created with (and by) Works that don't look anything like an accountant's ledger. Yet, because of the way information is organized—across and down—both are natural candidates for this type of program. In both, you'll also see how the tools built into a spreadsheet program can produce some graphically different results.

First, here's how a Works TaskWizard can quickly create a monthly calendar for you to print and use. It starts from the same TaskWizard window illustrated in the section on word processing for creating personalized letterhead. This time, however, the choice begins in a section titled *Household Management*, which opens the list in Figure 8-4 on the following page. (The calendar entry is highlighted to show you which wizard will be put to work.)

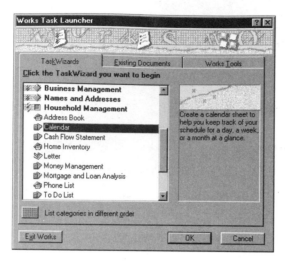

Figure 8-4.   *The TaskWizard list, with the calendar "wiz" highlighted.*

Now:

Clicking OK and requesting the TaskWizard brings up this window, which, as you can see, offers three different calendar layouts:

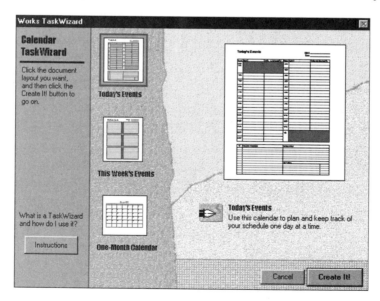

From here, clicking the One-Month Calendar and then clicking the Create It! button is all it takes to produce this:

To change the month and year, all you do is click cell B2 and type what you want. You don't even have to figure it out, because the instructions appear right at the top of the calendar—when you're working with the spreadsheet, that is. When you preview (as in the illustration) or print the calendar, the instructions "magically" disappear.

And here's another example: a To Do list also created by a Works Task-Wizard. Here, the picture has been zoomed in so that you can see some detail:

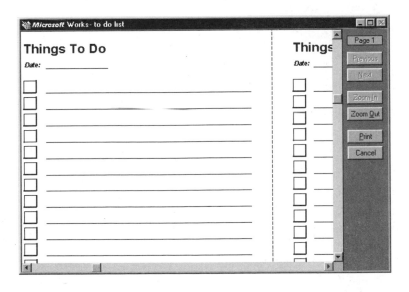

Aside from the name of the TaskWizard, the procedure needed to create this was identical to the one used to create the calendar. The result, though, is vastly different. Again, however, note that items are arranged both across and down the page—the type of organization a spreadsheet is designed to handle.

Records, Records, and More Records

Now you come to the last of the big three: databases. These programs come in multiple "strengths" from Lite to Colossal. You've probably read, for instance, that the government relies on databases for keeping track of information—taxes, social security, veterans' benefits, and so on. Databases like those fall into the Colossal category, and they require armies of trained professionals to update them and to keep them accurate. (No jokes, please.) On a lesser scale, although still in at least the Jumbo category, are databases like inventories, employee information, and sales that are maintained—again by professionals—in large corporations around the world. These, too, require trained professionals.

But, hey. People can and do use databases for much smaller, everyday projects. They are great for organizing and keeping track of:

- Phone numbers and addresses
- Recipes, books, music, stamps, coins, jewelry, butterflies, yoyos…anything collectable
- Household items, warranties, and serial numbers
- Auto maintenance and repair records
- Contributions to a garage sale or bazaar
- Teenage slang words and their definitions

Database programs are for any collection of related information that you want to organize, sort through, and be able to update whenever you want.

To nail the idea of a database, think of a telephone book. Imagine all those names, addresses, and phone numbers written on separate slips of paper. And imagine all those slips of paper stuffed into a box. And then imagine sorting through that box to find the phone number of your favorite pizza palace. Ick.

Now, imagine a program—on your computer—that could alphabetize those names, addresses, and phone numbers. And imagine that the program could sort all that information any way you chose: by name, by address, by ZIP code, by telephone exchange, or by telephone number. And, finally, imagine that the only work you'd have to do is type the information. Once. That's a database.

How Does It Work?

If a database program is for organizing information and making specific pieces of information easy to find, how does it make that happen? Well, just as a spreadsheet relies on a grid of cells, a database relies on a particular type of structure based on the idea of *records* and *fields*.

A database record is any collection of information about one particular item. It's comparable to a single entry in the phone book—say, your name, address, and phone number. A database field is any item of information *within* a record. A field is thus comparable to the phone number part of your "record" in the telephone book. Fields are pieced together to form a record, and records are pieced together to make a *table,* which is the combined information gathered together in all the fields and records related to a particular subject. A table would therefore be similar to the telephone book.

All this is pretty easy to understand, especially because the only hard-and-fast rule that applies to all tables is that each record within the table must contain exactly the same fields. The information in each field is different, of course, for every record, and each record is different from every other record. But the *way* the information is broken out into fields must always be the same. If that sounds a little too abstract, just picture the telephone book again. In the phone book, this would be a single record:

Last name	First name or initial(s)	Address	Phone number

Each of the boxes here would represent one field. These fields would be the same for every single person listed, even though the information in each field of each record would be different:

Adams	Alexander	111 Database Rd	555-1111
Bonilla	Joseph	222 Field Drive	555-2222
Lyon	Samantha	333 Record Avenue	555-3333

Regardless, each record would contain the same fields. And the accumulated records, for all the people listed, would make up the phone book "table."

That, essentially, is what a database is. Figure 8-5 shows one—a personalized name and address book—created in a few simple steps by the Works TaskWizard.

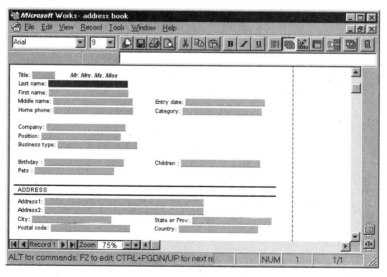

Figure 8-5. *A database address book.*

What you see in the illustration is an onscreen *form* designed by the TaskWizard to give you a page-like area in which to enter your information. To use the form, you would:

- Click a field to highlight it. (The Last Name field is highlighted in the illustration.)

- Type the information.

- Press the Tab key to move to the next field.

- Type.

- Continue typing and pressing the Tab key to fill out the rest of the form.

- Press the Ctrl and Page Down keys at the same time to move to a new record.

What If I Don't Like It?

In addition to creating a database and entering data into it, you can work with it—tinker with it, tamper with it, add a field you forgot (something that was once very difficult), remove a field you don't want, change the size of a field to make it longer or shorter, alter the formatting, and so on.

Depending on what you want to do, Works and its more sophisticated sibling, Microsoft Access, provide different views for working with a database and its contents. In Works:

- *Form* view, which is the view shown in Figure 8-5, displays one record at a time. You can use it for either entering or viewing information.

- *Form Design* view displays the form itself so that you can alter it—for example, by rearranging fields or by changing their formatting. You can also use this view to insert or delete fields. The following illustration shows what Form Design view looks like.

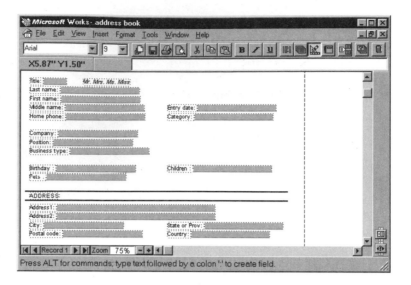

■ *List* view presents database fields and records in a spreadsheetlike format (logical, since database information is also arranged in an across-and-down pattern). You use List view for working with or viewing multiple records. You also use this view for formatting, adding, and deleting fields. This is what List view looks like:

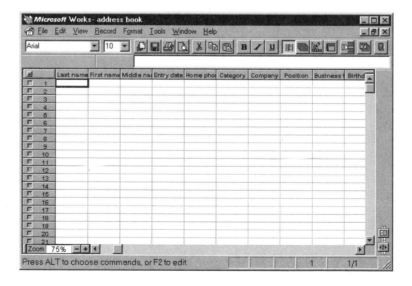

Suppose, for example, you didn't need the fields named Category, Company, Position, or Business Type. After all, this is supposed to be a personal address book. By switching to List view, you could quickly get rid of these fields this way:

- Select them, and then delete them all at the same time. The removal would be reflected in every view (and leave a gap in your form), however, so you could then...

- Switch to Form Design view and rearrange the fields to close the hole:

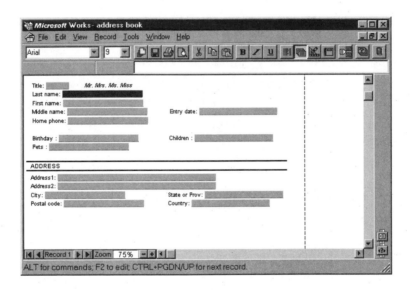

Now That I Have It, What Can I Do with It?

Of course, the whole point of creating a database is being able to use it. For that, Works offers a *Report* view, which produces a printed copy of your database. And it includes a sorting feature that allows you to sort the contents of the database by different fields, according to your needs of the moment. The ability to sort records is the greatest strength of a database, but because learning how to sort records might be confusing at first, Works offers a little help when you first try to solo, as demonstrated by the following illustration.

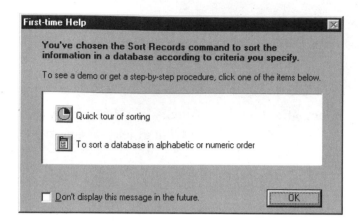

Basically, sorting rearranges the records in a database, to present them in whatever order you decide is most useful (and usable) in finding the record(s) you want to look at. The electronic equivalent of having, say, the recipes in your favorite cookbook rearrange themselves so that all the recipes that contain chicken, tomatoes, and peppers group themselves together at the front of the book. (If you're not into cooking, think of sorting as the equivalent of having all the names and addresses in your little black book rearrange themselves on any given night to list, oh, all the available people you know who enjoy beaches, movies, and hamburgers.) Because a database does just this kind of rearranging for you, it beats the heck out of a printed list. It also beats having to print and then "eyeball" a large group of records, scanning for those that meet your needs of the moment.

In your address book database, for example, you could choose to display records alphabetically—from A to Z *or* from Z to A), basing the sort on any field you chose, including:

- By birth date—to list people according to when they were born.
- By ZIP code—to group people by ZIP code.
- By city—to group people according to where they live.
- Even by pet—to group dog owners, cat owners, canary owners, and so on together.

The advantages of a database are obvious. For real-life ways to use one, think about being able to sort your music collection by artist. Or being able to sort items for a garage sale alphabetically and by price. Or being able to sort your valuables by date of purchase, by type (electronics, jewelry) or by cost. Using a database for organizing and sorting any kind of information is limited mostly by how much effort you want to put into it. And...really...how organized you, yourself, happen to be.

Some Other Helpful Applications

In addition to the big three applications, there are dozens of other, more specialized types of programs that can enhance your computer's ability to be a well-rounded household appliance. There are programs that help you produce brochures and newsletters, crop and touch up digitized photographs, and help your students prepare for college entrance exams. The rest of this chapter gives you a brief look at a few other applications included with Works in the Home Essentials 98 package and ends with instructions for taking a well-deserved break by installing and playing a game or three of Pac-Man.

However, work before play.

Cards and Newsletters

One of the applications included in Home Essentials 98 is called Greetings Workshop. It's a joint effort between Microsoft and the Hallmark card people, and it produces the kind of results you've probably come to expect from Hallmark. Although the program's name might make you think it's just for creating greeting cards, the software is actually quite a bit more flexible than that. It's also a bit different from the rather no-nonsense, down-to-business applications you've met so far, as you can see in Figure 8-6 on the following page.

Figure 8-6.   *Greetings Workshop. (The little guy in the corner is named Rocky; you can tell him to shoo if you want.)*

As you can see from Rocky's comic-book balloon "dialog," Greetings Workshop is really easy to use. All you do is click your way through choices and, if you want, personalize the card or banner or announcement or stationery you're creating with text or artwork of your own.

Pictures are said to be worth a thousand words, and such a graphical program is an obvious choice for saving on text and letting the software just show you the type of card it can create for you. The card shown in Figures 8-7 and 8-8 is one that Greetings Workshop makes automatically, without requiring you to type anything. It does, however, give you the option (not accepted in this case) to replace its built-in choice of text with whatever you would prefer the card to say.

To create the card, a single mouse click is all you need to start the ball rolling and display this screen:

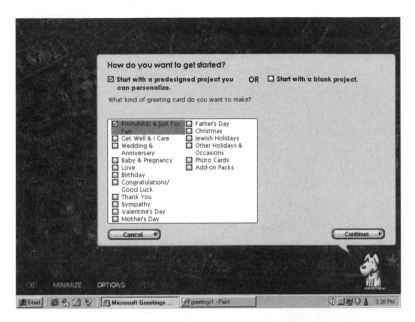

Figure 8-7.   *How you start a greeting card with Greetings Workshop.*

A few mouse clicks later, you're done. Figure 8-8 shows the result.

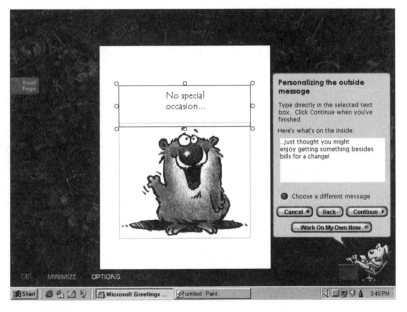

Figure 8-8.   *The finished product.*

Clever, isn't it?

Of course, Greetings Workshop can require just slightly more thought if you want to start from scratch by building a card or notice or other item on a blank page. The process is not difficult even then, however, because the program—or rather, Rocky the dog—steps you through the entire process, offering choices and prompting you all the way. 'Nuff said.

Balancing That Checkbook

In the home-finance arena, there are two major programs available. Both are popular, and both are often preinstalled on new computers. One is called Quicken. The other, which is included in Home Essentials 98 and is also bundled in a 90-day trial version on your lesson CD, is Microsoft Money 98. For the obvious reason that you can choose to install the trial version if you want, this section deals with Microsoft Money.

Installing the Trial Version of Money

If you want to take a look at Microsoft Money for yourself, here's what to do:

1. First, click the Start button and check the various programs listed on your Start menu and its submenus. Money might already be installed on your computer. If it is, there's no need to install it from the CD. If you don't find Money, you can install the trial version as described in the following steps.

2. If necessary, place the lesson CD in your CD-ROM drive. Click Exit when the opening lesson screen appears.

3. Click My Computer, right-click the icon for your CD-ROM drive, and choose Explore from the pop-up menu.

4. Click the icon (with the big blue *e*) labeled Goodies.

5. On the Goodies screen, click the item that reads *Click here for free software*.

6. On the free software screen, click Money Setup. Doing this launches the Money setup program, which begins by displaying the message *Do you want to install Microsoft Money 98 Trial Version?* You do, so click Yes.

7. Setup moves on to extracting (basically, puffing up) the files it needs from the compressed version on the CD, and then it swings into setup proper. You'll be asked to click Yes or OK in response to some dialog boxes, and you'll be asked to accept a license agreement to use the software. To accept, click I Agree.

8. After agreeing, click the large button next to Continue when this dialog box appears:

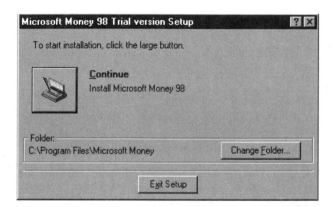

This is where Setup actually installs the software for you and prepares it to run on your system. At the end, it displays a dialog box asking if you want to install the Online Banking component of the program. You need a modem for this, but otherwise the choice is yours, so you can click either Yes or No.

9. When setup is complete, a dialog box appears to tell you so. At this point, click OK to finish up and then close your Windows Explorer and My Computer windows.

Using Money

Now, assuming that you either already had or have just installed Money 98, take a look at it. The following descriptions are based on the trial version provided on the lesson CD:

1. Click the Start button, open the Programs menu, and click Microsoft Money. The first thing you see is a welcoming message. Click OK to

continue. Money then swings into creating a new file for you—one that it will use to hold your financial information.

This section is based on the latest version of Money, which is known as Money 98. If you already have Money installed but it is an earlier version, it might not work exactly as described here. If you see differences, be sure to check out your program's Help menu.

2. When the file has been created, Money displays its opening screen. (The tour mentioned on the opening screen is available only in the full product. However, Money is easy to use, so don't worry about it.)

Where your finances are concerned, one of the first things you'll do is tell Money about your bank account(s). To show you how easy it is, here are the steps involved:

1. Click either the Accounts item at the top of the Money window or the item titled *Set up Your Accounts* in the window itself. Both take you to the Account Manager:

2. To create an account for your checkbook, click the New Account button at the bottom of the window. (If necessary, lengthen the window so you can see the button.) Doing this starts the New Account wizard, which opens like this:

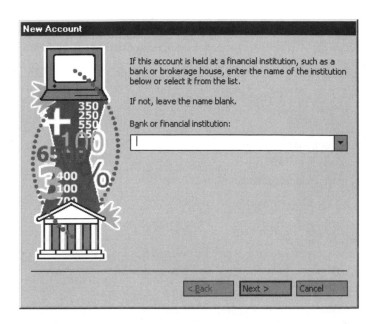

3. From here on, just provide the information the wizard requests. Click the Next button to move from one screen to the next. When you reach the end, click Finish, and within seconds, the Money window reappears, with your new account displayed in it:

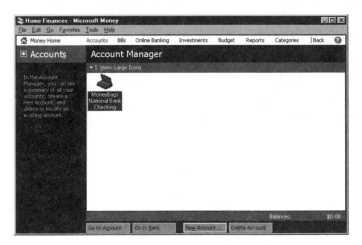

4. To begin entering transactions, click the Go To Account button at the bottom of the window.

From this point on, your finances are your own business, so this series of steps won't take you any farther. As you're investigating Money, however, there *are* three items you might want to pay special attention to. You reach them by clicking Planner at the top of the Money window. When the Planner screen opens, it gives you a set of options related to managing, as opposed to just tracking, your finances. Among these options are three you'll probably find particularly useful:

- Tell Money About Yourself
- Get Out Of Debt (for planning ways to pay off high-interest loans and credit cards)
- Make A Budget & Savings Plan (for managing monthly income and expenses)

Here, for instance, is the first of Money's fill-in-the-blanks screens for budgeting:

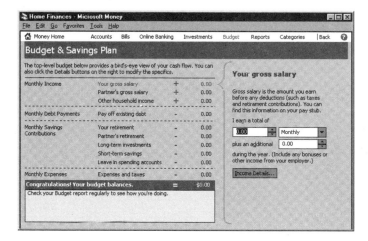

If you're like most people, these are all financial aids that will probably come in handy. One final note: if you click Money Insider at the top of the Money window, you'll gain access to a number of articles and worksheets on financial planning and management. And don't forget that if you need more information about Money, Help is there at the top of the window to give you a hand whenever you want one.

Winning That Bet (or Helping with That Homework)

Now, before you get to Pac-Man, here's a chance to wind down a little by switching from applications that *make* you think to a couple of nifty applications that *help* you think. Specifically, here's a look at two *online* reference works: an encyclopedia named Microsoft Encarta, and a set of basic references called Microsoft Bookshelf. Products like these can really come in handy in certain situations, for example, when:

- You find yourself gnawing at a question over and over. ("What does DDT stand for?")

- You've made a bet that glue is a form of gelatin.

- You can't remember who wrote "double, double, toil and trouble."

- Your kids suddenly inform you that they need everything they can find about the moon for a project that's due tomorrow.

(Ah, not to prolong the suspense: DDT is chemical shorthand for dichloro-diphenyltrichloroethane, pronounced "dye-kloro-dye-feenul-try-kloro-eth-ayn"; glue *is* a form of gelatin; and Shakespeare wrote that line in *Macbeth*. As for the moon...sorry. Been there, done that already—now it's *your* turn.)

But to get back to the subject, which happens to be reference information available via computer. Figure 8-9 on the following page shows what Encarta looks like and what it has to say about a particularly likable animal.

As you can see, the encyclopedia itself is impressive. Figure 8-10, however, shows that there's a little more to Encarta than meets the eye.

And what about Bookshelf? Well, it's not as endearing as Encarta—not as colorful and a little less intriguing to "browse" when you have a few minutes of spare time. But...it includes a dictionary, a thesaurus, an almanac, quotations, an atlas, and even a directory of interesting Internet sites.

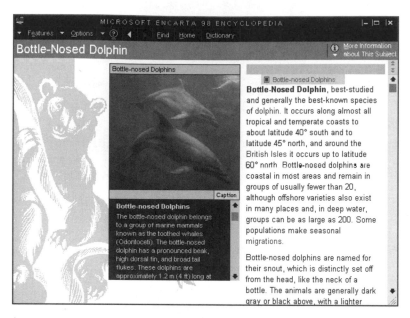

Figure 8-9.   *What Encarta has to say about everybody's favorite water "sport."*

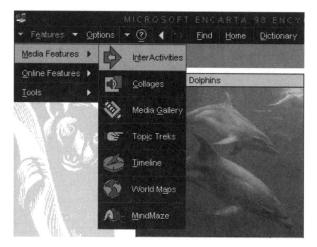

Figure 8-10.   *Encarta offers more than just text.*

Suppose, for instance, you've never bothered to look up the word *puce*. You know it sounds kind of yucky, but what exactly does it mean? Here's what the dictionary has to say about it:

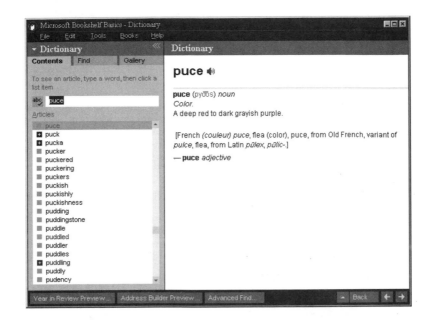

Hmm. So it's sort of flea brown. Maybe there's a more appealing way to describe that color? Try the thesaurus:

Well, purplish-brown isn't all that much better, but these illustrations at least give you an idea of what you'll find in a product like Bookshelf. Because both Bookshelf and Encarta run from CD-ROMs, they hold a considerable amount of information, and they put that information literally at your fingertips.

And now, it's time to finish up this chapter.

Take a Break!

If you were anywhere on the planet during the early 80s, you no doubt remember at least hearing about this big-mouthed, ghost-gobbling blast from the electronic past. The version of Pac-Man provided on your lesson CD is the real thing, PC-style. Although it's not the complete game, you've got more than enough to stay entertained and challenged for a while (and to get really fast at using the direction keys on your keyboard).

Installing Pac-Man

To give this 90s Pac-Man a try, you'll first have to install it from the CD. The process involves a number of steps, but it doesn't take long, so if you're game (no pun intended), here's what to do:

1. If necessary, insert the lesson CD in your CD-ROM drive and click Exit when the opening screen appears. (If the CD is already in your drive, skip this step.)

2. Click My Computer, right-click the icon for your CD-ROM drive, and click Explore on the pop-up menu.

3. When the contents of the CD appear in the window, click the Goodies icon with the big blue *e*.

4. On the Goodies page, point to *Click here for a game* and click.

5. The right-hand side of the screen starts off with some rather complex instructions for *downloading* the Pac-Man trial version (copying it to your computer). Don't get excited—you can skip over that part. You *do,* however, have to read through the license agreement that follows the instructions. If you agree to the terms and conditions,

click *I Accept These Terms* when you reach the end. Doing this causes a dialog box like this one to appear on your screen:

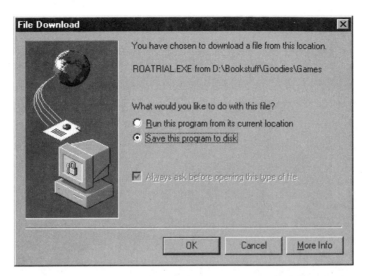

6. The default choice is to save the file to disk, but you already have the game on your lesson CD, so run the setup from there by clicking the radio button to the left of the text that reads *Run this program from its current location* and then clicking OK.

7. Next, you'll see a message asking if you want to proceed, even though an *Authenticode signature* was not found. Such a signature is valuable on the Internet, because it verifies the creator of software you download and protects you from potentially harmful programs. In this case, however, the creator is Microsoft, and you need not fear, so click Yes.

8. Click Yes again when a dialog box asks if you want to continue installing the trial version of Pac-Man.

9. As happened with Money, the setup program will then extract the files it needs and install the program on your hard disk. When setup is complete, a dialog box tells you so. Click OK.

10. Close the open Windows Explorer and My Computer windows. It's time for some fun.

Playing Pac-Man

The version of Pac-Man you have lets you play the first two levels of the game. Here's how to find and start it:

1. Click the Start button, open the Programs menu, and highlight Microsoft Games. Highlight the item labeled *Return of Arcade Trial*, and then click the item that reads *Pac-Man Trial*.

2. This is how Pac-Man looks when it starts up:

   Read this little Help screen to get an idea of how to play, and click OK. If you're still not sure what to do, just sit for a few minutes until a game demonstration begins to "play" out on your screen, like this:

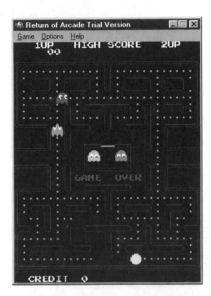

3. When you're ready to play, get your hand comfortable on the direction (arrow) keys on your keyboard and press the F2 key to start a game. It's fast, so don't be surprised if it takes some time to get used to.

The Pac-Man you have on the CD is just one of a number of trial versions of Microsoft games and other software available for free on the Internet. Chapter 9 will show you how to visit the Microsoft Internet site to look for (and download) some more.

From here on, you're on your own. And just as lots of people did with the original Pac-Man, you'll probably find yourself becoming totally absorbed in manipulating the hungry little mouth—to the extent of putting some body English into your efforts. (As if it would help.) Enjoy yourself. And don't forget to take a break now and then. Your hand and arm muscles will need it.

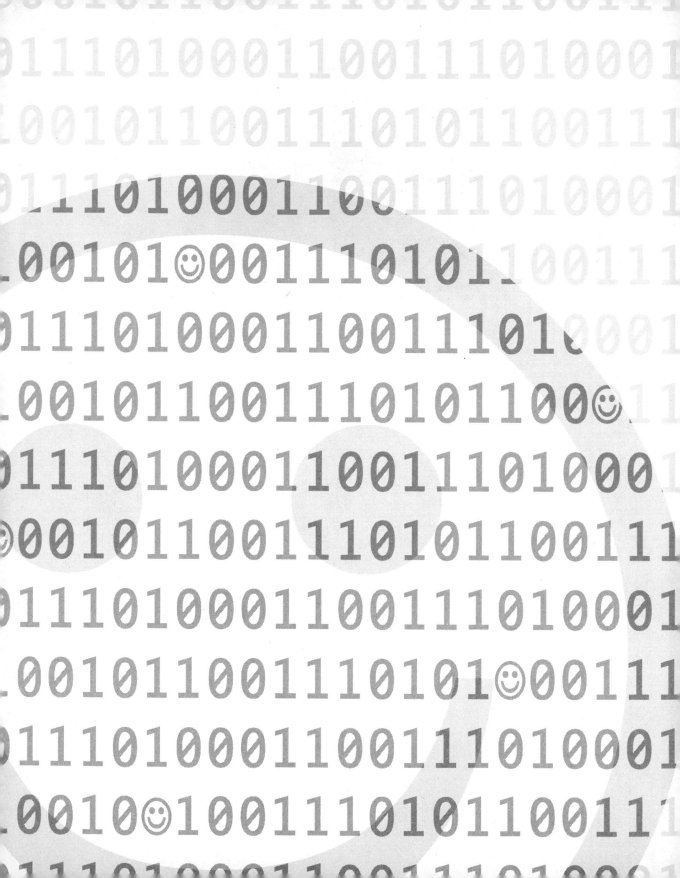

9

Hello, World

Throughout this book, you've been concentrating on ways to work with your PC in contented, if solitary, splendor. Now it's time to turn your attention outward—to communicating with your friend's PC, or with the main computer at work, or with the virtual outposts all over the world that you reach through the global network known as the Internet. It's time to step into the world of cyberspace.

Since you can't go anywhere (electronically, that is) without a modem, that little device will serve nicely as a starting point for your trip into the seemingly endless universe that becomes visible to you with the help of your PC.

Modems

A modem is the communications hardware that enables your PC to send and receive information over a telephone line. Depending on make and model, a modem can be connected to your computer either internally or externally. If the modem is internal, as yours probably is, it's a skinny little adapter card about the size of a small paperback book. If the modem is external, meaning that it sits on the desk and plugs into one of the openings on the back of the computer, it's a somewhat larger box more closely resembling a small transistor radio.

No matter whether it is internal or external, however, a modem always connects to both the computer and, via a phone cable, to a telephone jack in the wall.

Why You Need Them

The word *modem* is a made-up word that comes from two others, *modu-late* and *demo*dulate. Those two words both describe the way a modem works and explain why you need one to communicate. Although a deep understanding of modem technology involves a significant number of technical matters, the broad outlines are easy to understand and can—if you're interested—help you appreciate some of the complexity hidden behind the "ease of use" that marks a working PC.

Basically, a modem modulates (alters) the stream of information that comes from your computer by loading it onto a carrier signal—an ear-piercing sound—that can travel over a telephone line. When the information reaches its destination, which is always another modem, the receiving modem *demodulates* the information by unloading it from the carrier and converting it to a form the computer can use.

Why a Modem Works the Way It Does

Why does a modem have to bother modulating and demodulating? Why can't a computer just shoot information into a telephone for sending and slurp information from the phone when it's receiving? It's because telephones are *analog* devices—they work with signals (sound waves) that can vary both constantly and over a broad range, as shown in Figure 9-1.

Figure 9-1. *A sound wave.*

Computers like yours, on the other hand, are *digital* devices. They work with streams of data, the *bits* you've probably heard of, in which all information is represented by either of two *digits,* the numbers 1 and 0 (which you can think of as equal to on and off, or high and low). A computer's way of communicating, then, is more like what is shown in Figure 9-2. (Of course the computer's way of communicating is far more complex than this, but it's not necessary to know exactly how it works.)

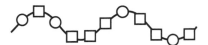

Figure 9-2.
The flow of information to, from, or within a computer.

In order to send these bits along the phone line, the modem takes them from the computer and pops them onto a carrier signal, something like what is shown in Figure 9-3.

Figure 9-3.
The conversion of computer information into a carrier signal.

Now the computer is happy because its stream of data is ready to travel; the bits are happy because they still represent the information being sent; and the phone line is happy because it has received the data in a form it can handle. This is the modulation part of the job.

When the data arrives at its destination, a receiving modem essentially reverses the modulation process by "unloading" the bits from the carrier signal and sending them to the receiving computer in the familiar stream of digital signals it expects. This is the demodulation part and, again, everybody's happy.

That's what the modem does for you, and it does it accurately, at speeds these days of 56,000 bits (1s and 0s) per *second* (or more).

How You Tell Your PC About Your Modem

Your PC's manufacturer has probably already set up your modem, so there's a very good chance that you don't even need to call on Windows' Install New Modem wizard. Someday, however, you might want or need to replace your modem with a newer or faster one, so here's a quick look at the wizard...just in case.

Unlike the step-by-step descriptions in the preceding chapters, this list of steps is not "hands-on." Rather, it is "this is what to do." You can, of course, start the wizard if you want to see it for yourself by following along through step 4 and clicking Cancel when you're told to.

1. To get to the wizard, click the Start button, open the Settings menu, and click Control Panel.

2. In the Control Panel window, click Modems. When you do (assuming you already have a modem installed), you see this:

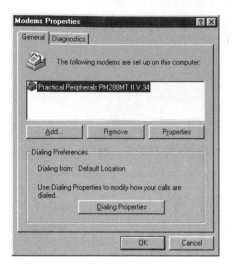

3. If you're replacing an older modem, you'll probably want to remove the entry for your old modem and then install the new one. To do this, you first highlight the name of the old modem (if necessary) and click the Remove button. To install the new modem, or to add a second modem to your computer, you click the Add button. Doing this calls up the Install New Modem wizard:

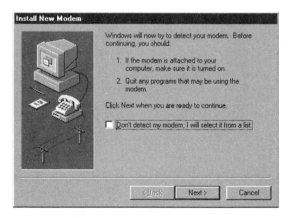

4. Follow instructions 1 and 2 displayed by the wizard, and then click the Next button. (Click Cancel here if you're following along but not really installing a new modem.)

5. The wizard then hands the ball to Windows, which checks your *communications ports* (connections) to find the new modem:

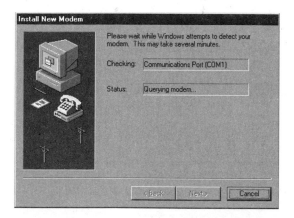

6. When Windows finds the new modem, the wizard displays the result:

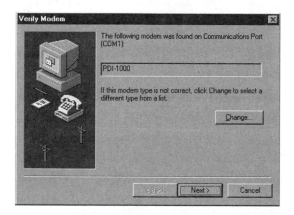

Unless the result of the search is wrong (unlikely), all you have to do now is click the Next button.

7. The wizard finishes up the installation and lets you know with the message *Your modem has been set up successfully*. It really couldn't be much easier.

And now, assuming your modem is installed and ready to go, you can take a look at the "intimate" side of communicating—a link between your computer and another one you specify.

A Network of Two

Your modem and your PC give you two different ways of reaching out to the world: person-to-person connections that you make through *dialup networking,* and the global networking that connects you to the millions of places in the virtual world of the Internet.

Dialup networking is what you turn to whenever you need to reach a specific computer via telephone—when, say, you want to send a computer file to a friend. Or you want to check your work email from home. Or your student needs to use some information posted on a school computer. It's also very easy to set up and use. All you need are:

- The telephone number you want to call.

- The Make New Connection wizard, which you use each time you want to set up a link to a different phone number.

Here are the actual steps you go through. As before, complete the instructions only if you're actually setting up dialup networking. If you're just practicing, click Cancel when you're told to.

1. To get to dialup networking, click the Start button, work through Programs and Accessories, and then click Dial-Up Networking. The following window opens:

2. To create a new connection (to a new phone number), click the Make New Connection icon. This starts the wizard you need:

3. The rest is just as straightforward. First, replace the highlighted text (*My Connection*) by typing a name that will identify the connection you're setting up—something like *Work Computer* or *Jack's PC* works just fine.

4. If you have installed more than one modem and the wizard is not displaying the name of the one you want, click the downward-pointing triangle at the right of the Select A Modem box and choose the modem you want. Click the Next button to move on to this:

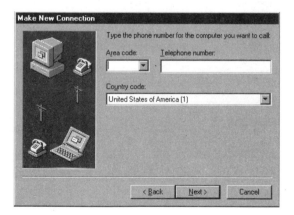

Type the area code and number you want to connect to in the form, and choose the country if necessary. Click Next.

5. On the final screen, just click Finish. (Click Cancel here if you're just pretending.) A few seconds later, a dialup icon with the name you assigned appears in the Dial-Up Networking window.

6. To use the connection you just created, click the icon to open a Connect To window:

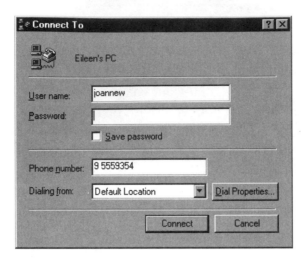

7. Type and save your password, if you use one, to identify yourself to the computer you're calling so that you can gain access to information its owner has *shared*. (If you're not sure what sharing is all about, refer to the box titled *What's Mine Is Yours*.)

8. Click Connect, and all you have to do now is wait for the other computer to answer. When it does, you'll be able to use any shared items on the computer you've connected to.

Now, on to the fun stuff.

What's Mine Is Yours

People who are used to working on computers that are connected to large networks not only use, but expect to use, shared information. That's what networks are all about—to make information available to many people. On a *stand-alone,* or non-networked, computer, sharing isn't normally required, so you might be wondering why, when, and whether you would ever want to share anything on it. In most circumstances, you won't. If someone ever needs to connect to your machine via telephone, however, you might want to make some, but not all, of the information on your computer available to that person.

In order to do that, you share out the folder, drive, or device the other person needs to use. This is how:

1. First, decide what it is you want to share. This is important, because the calling computer will be able to "see" only what you've decided to share. So, for example, if you share your entire hard disk, the person calling your computer will be able to see—and access—everything on your hard disk. This is probably not what you want, so instead share out only the folder or folders the person needs. That way, when the person connects to your computer, only those shared folders will be visible.

2. To actually share a folder or a device such as your printer, open a window to it, and right-click its icon. If sharing is turned on, choose Sharing from the pop-up menu.

3. If sharing is not turned on and you don't see a Sharing command on the menu, open Control Panel and click the Network icon. Now you can turn sharing on, as follows (the process sounds kind of technical, but it's really easy). Click the Access Control tab and check that the radio button to the left of share-level access control is dark. Then, click the Configuration tab and click the File And Print Sharing button and specify whether you want to share files, printers, or both. Go back to the item you want to share, and right-click its icon as described in step 2, above.

4. On the item's Sharing properties sheet, click the Shared As radio button, and then click the type of access you want to provide: Read-Only, which allows people to use, but not change, shared files; Full, which allows people to both use and change shared files; or Depends On Password, which lets you specify two different passwords (presumably for different people)—one to provide read-only access, the other to provide full access. Type and confirm the password(s), and close the properties sheet. A small hand will appear under the icon for the shared item, to show that it is shared out.

5. To stop sharing an item, right-click its icon, click Sharing, and click Not Shared on the item's properties sheet.

What *Is* This Thing Called Internet?

You've heard about it, read about it, and seen it on TV. You might have had friends, family, or coworkers encourage you to become part of it. And maybe you even bought your PC so that you, too, could see what this new frontier is all about and whether it's worth the fuss. But perhaps you're not quite sure what the Internet is or how this World Wide Web everyone talks about fits into the picture. For that matter, maybe you're a little fuzzy on exactly who—or what—even populates this place and how you find your way around in it with only a computer to guide you. Well, come along....

The Internet and the World Wide Web

A little hesitant? That's OK. Most other people were too—even those who now prefer shopping on the Internet to battling crowds at the mall.

To get a sense of this global resource, start with a quick—and painless—look at the Internet and the World Wide Web: what they are, how they came to be, and how they're related.

The Internet, or "Net"

The Internet is, essentially, a worldwide *network* of computers that can communicate with each other. It's vast, and it's structured in several layers, beginning with a sturdy *backbone* and working outward to smaller *midlevel* and *stub* networks. The overall organization looks something like the illustration in Figure 9-4.

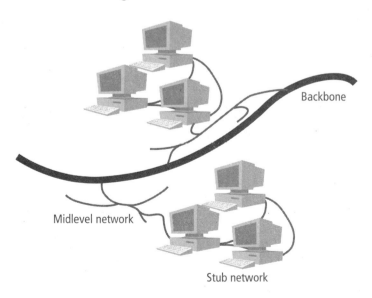

Figure 9-4.   *The overall organization of the Internet.*

Your little PC, by the way, doesn't actually fit into this picture. The computers that make up the Internet are known as *servers*. Their job is to store things and "serve" them up on request to computers known as *clients* that call up saying, "show me suchandso." You and your PC will be the clients.

But back to the Internet. Even though it's the hottest computer-related news of the mid-to-late 90s, the Internet has actually been around since 1969. What got it started in the first place? It was created as a means of linking universities and research labs so that they could share information via their (large) computers. Originally a single network of linked computers known as ARPANET (for Advanced Research Projects Agency NETwork), this early Internet eventually grew into the massive collection of interconnected networks—computers talking to computers—illustrated in Figure 9-4. Essentially, you can think of the computers making up today's Internet as being the "nervous system" that carries signals around the world.

The Web

And what of the World Wide Web you hear so much about? It's part of the Internet, but it's not the whole thing. The World Wide Web is a huge collection of *sites,* those places with names starting with *www* that you see and hear about everywhere these days. Each of these sites is a collection of colorful, often animated, and sometimes noisy Web *pages* that let you take a virtual (seemingly real) tour of whatever the site has to offer—from a look at the daily paper to a tour of a cyberspace shopping mall. Some sites are personal and small; others contain anywhere from dozens to thousands of individual pages. Each page, however, shows you something new about the site you happen to be visiting.

As for the kinds of sites you find on the Web. Whew. The list seems endless, and it ranges all over the map from businesses to schools, government agencies, publications, merchants, sports teams, horse farms, dog breeders...to practically anything else you can imagine. Who's represented there? Here's a short—a very short—list:

- Microsoft, IBM, Apple Computer, Intel, and other major high-tech companies.
- Nasdaq and Dow Jones.

- Hollywood High School, Harvard, Yale, the University of Hawaii, and many other schools.

- The White House, the Internal Revenue Service, and hundreds of local government agencies and organizations.

- The *New York Times,* the *Los Angeles Times,* the *National Enquirer,* and multitudes of other publications.

- Land's End, Wal-Mart, Tower Records, Barnes and Noble, and the Disney Store.

- The Seattle Mariners (yea!) and the other major league teams.

The Underpinnings and What You Need to Know About Them

What pulls all these different sites together into the universe known as the Web? It's the way in which they all present information to you—a way that is based on two imaginative and very easy-to-use features known as *hypermedia* (or *hypertext*) and *linking.* Uh-oh, is that starting to sound complicated? Actually, it isn't at all, because you don't have to dig into the nitty-gritty. A little understanding is all you need, enough to help you figure out the Web and how to use it.

Here goes. If the computers that form the Internet can be considered its nervous system, think of the sites and pages making up the World Wide Web as the "face" of the Internet. These sites and pages are, in fact, the part that provides all the colorful flash, dash, and sparkle that everyone expects (and makes so much of).

To go back a few years…the World Wide Web began in 1989 in Switzerland as a way for researchers to share not only text, as on the "regular" Internet, but pictures and other kinds of information. In order to make this type of sharing happen, the creators of the original World Wide Web turned to a way of combining different kinds of information in a single document type known as *hypertext* or *hypermedia.* Hypertext, which is illustrated in Figure 9-5, is what makes up a page on the World Wide Web. It is created with the help of a technology known as HTML (a word you might hear, and which is pronounced "aitch-tea-emm-ell"—short for HyperText Markup Language). Hypertext is one of the two things that actually define the Web.

Figure 9-5.   *Hypertext is the combination of text, pictures, and (in some cases) sound, animation, or video.*

So if hypertext (or hypermedia) is one of the defining features of the World Wide Web, what's the other? It's the concept of *linking* documents. A link, as its name suggests, is a connector between the Web page you're currently viewing and another, somewhere else, that you might also want to take a look at. Figure 9-6 on the next page shows you what some typical links look like.

And how are links added to a Web page? HTML again. HTML not only allows Web designers to bring life to your screen with pictures and sound, it also allows these designers to *embed* links to other documents within the body of the ones they create. The linked documents can be at the same site or at many sites around the world. It doesn't matter. If the designer feels you would like to see those documents too, in goes a link.

And here's the real magic of the Web: these links respond to a simple mouse click. As easy as they are to use, they are also the "vehicles" that take you from one document to another, one Web site to another so that you can literally jump your way around the world simply by clicking your way from one Web page to another. Linking lets you bop around the World Wide Web much faster than any jet-setter in a Concorde could even dream of.

Figure 9-6. *A link takes you somewhere else on the Web. So that it's easy to spot, it's usually underlined or displayed in a different color. If the link happens to be an image, the mouse pointer turns into a "hand" to show that the image is also a link.*

Getting to the Web

But enough chatter. Knowing about sites and pages, hypertext and links helps you figure out what goes on *when* you use the Web, but it doesn't yet explain *how* you use it—a rather important little detail, don't you think?

First of all, how to get to the Web. For that, you need:

- A modem, which you probably have.

- An Internet browser, which you have, thanks to the lesson CD.

- An Internet Service Provider, or ISP, which you *don't* have unless you've already signed up with one.

You already know about modems, so move on to check out browsers and ISPs to see how they relate to getting you online with the world.

A Browser

Just as you need a word processor to help you see and work with text documents, and you need a program like Paint to help you see and work with drawings, you need an Internet *browser* to help you see and explore the Web. It's the browser that finds the Web sites you want to visit, displays the pages you want to see, and follows the links you choose to follow.

Inside your computer, a browser "reads" and "translates" HTML instructions; outside (where you can see the results), it turns those instructions into the spiffy displays that everyone associates with the Web. Figure 9-7 shows Internet Explorer, one of the two leading browsers, as it looks when you connect to the Web.

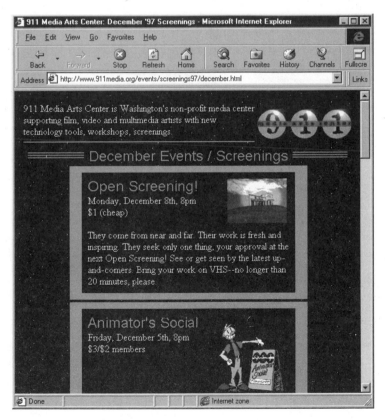

Figure 9-7.   *A Web page displayed in Internet Explorer. Illustration courtesy of 911 Media Arts Center (http://www.911media.org). Web authoring and written word by Peter Mitchell; graphic design (911 logo) by Adam Chapman; cartoon illustration by Braden Lamb.*

This is the browser that's been running on your system since you installed the lesson CD and turned on Active Desktop back at the beginning of the book. Here, though, instead of limiting itself to the lessons on your CD-ROM drive, IE ("eye-eee" as it's often called) is turning outward to the entire world.

Browser Battle?

If you've followed computer-related news at all, you probably know that the two leading browsers are Microsoft's Internet Explorer and Netscape's Navigator and that they are serious competitors for the hearts and minds of Web fans everywhere.

In point of fact, both are highly capable yet easy-to-use programs that bring the Web alive for you. Because the Web is a hugely big deal these days and both Internet Explorer and Navigator are so popular, you might well have icons for either or both on your PC right now.

At the moment, however, you definitely have Internet Explorer version 4.01 installed on your computer, because this version of IE is the only way you could have been using the lesson CD. Way back when you ran the CD's setup program, one of the things it did was check your system for IE 4.01. If it did not find the program or if it found an older version of the browser, it prompted you for permission to install IE 4.01. Without this particular version of IE, you could not have been working with the Active Desktop and, therefore, with any of the hands-on practices in the book. And without IE 4.01, you could not have used the lessons on the CD either.

This chapter, like all the others in the book, is based on IE, but the final section of the chapter tells you how you can choose IE, Navigator, or both when you "graduate" to working on your own. In the meantime, though, continue using IE for just a little longer. That way, the chapter and the CD lessons you're referred to will continue to work as advertised. Fair enough?

An ISP and How to Get One

You know that you have a working browser. Now what about an ISP? An ISP—Internet Service Provider—is an organization that has the communications and computer facilities needed to connect you to the Internet. (That's for a fee, of course.)

Even though much is made of the freedom and accessibility of the Internet, it's easier for ET to phone home than for you to call up the Internet directly. The only way for you to reach the server computers that dish up all the good stuff on the Web is by signing up with an ISP. So the only decision for you to make is which ISP to sign up with.

There are a lot of ISPs to choose from. Local, independent providers might limit their services to Internet access and email and require a little more work up front, but they can be excellent choices if you want to set up a Web site of your own.

Others, such as the Microsoft Network (MSN) and America Online (AOL), are well-known and widely used national or international providers that can be easier to set up and that offer not only Internet access and email but a significant amount of members-only content, such as games and shopping, as well as features such as live chat rooms, where you can communicate with other people in "real time," and bulletin boards, where you can see and respond to messages about subjects that interest you.

If you haven't yet signed up with an ISP, this book is not about to try to tell you which one is best. That's your decision, and it's one that only you can make. So that the process won't be terribly lonely, however, talk to your friends, especially those who have been using the Web for a while or who are technically knowledgeable. Their experiences should give you some basis for judgment.

Although this book won't attempt to influence your decision, it can show you the sign-up options sitting right there on your desktop. There are two:

- The MSN icon, for the Microsoft Network.
- The Online Services folder, which contains icons for the providers shown in Figure 9-8 on the next page.

Figure 9-8.   *Service providers included in the Online Services folder.*

If you want to sign up with one of these, the CD can help you get started, but before you go on to the Try It box, take a few minutes to prepare so that the process will go quickly and smoothly:

■ First, have a credit card handy. You'll be asked to indicate the method of payment, and the provider will want to know your card number. The usual cards are acceptable—MasterCard, VISA, American Express.

■ Also in the payment category, think about how you're going to use the Web. You'll probably be offered a choice of rates, depending on the amount of time you expect to spend in cyberspace. If you think you'll just be an occasional visitor, a low rate for X number of hours plus an additional charge for any extra time might be best for you. If you think you'll be a frequent visitor, a higher rate (typically, about $20 per month) for unlimited access might be more economical in the long run. In thinking about this, bear in mind that a *lot* of people who thought they'd use just a little bit of access time ended up rather expensively finding out that the Web drew them in quite a bit farther than they'd expected.

■ Finally, think up a *user name* and a *password*. You'll be asked to come up with these, so you might as well know what they are in advance. Both will identify you to the provider you choose, but there's a big difference between the two. Your user name will be *public*. It's the name that others on the Web will know you by, so think before you decide on something like *loverboy* or *GreatOne*. (Many people use some combination of initials and part or all of their last names.)

Try It

The lesson CD walks you to the door of the sign-up process and then picks up again once you have Internet access. To use it:

1. Either place the lesson CD in the CD-ROM drive or start the CD from the PCs For Beginners shortcut on your desktop.

2. Click Windows Overview on the opening screen.

3. Click to stop the Overview introduction, and then click the lesson titled "Connecting to the Internet."

4. Step 4 in this lesson has you open and read a document describing the services in your Online Services folder. At that point, you might want to minimize the lesson window temporarily to make the document easier to read.

5. When you finish using the document, close the window to clear your screen a little bit, and then click the PCs For Beginners button on the taskbar to restore the lesson window.

6. Beginning with step 6, the lesson switches from signing up with an ISP to taking your first cruise on the Web. At this point, you are of course free to continue. If you prefer, however, you can instead minimize the lesson window again and come back to the book for a little explanation before you go on.

7. Whether you work through the entire lesson in one go or take a break in the middle, when you reach the end of the lesson (step 14 of 14), click the lesson window's Minimize button instead of clicking Next.

Your password, in contrast, will be *private,* ideally known only to you and the provider. It will be the way the provider verifies that you are you and not an impostor using your account. A word of advice: *don't* be clever and come up with a password like *love, sex,* or *money.* They're way too easy to guess.

Getting Around

Once you have Internet access, the fun begins, especially because getting to a particular site is no harder than typing its Web address. This address always comes in the form:

www.sitename.xxx

- The *www* identifies the site as part of the World Wide Web.

- The *sitename* is a unique name that identifies the exact site you want to visit.

- The *xxx* part is a three-letter "extension" that identifies the site by type. There are several such identifiers, but the most common are *com* (for commercial sites), *edu* (for schools), *org* (for noncommercial organizations), and *gov* (for government agencies).

For example:

www.microsoft.com

When you pronounce a Web address, you pronounce the "w" three times, and you call the period "dot," as in "double-yew, double-yew, double-yew dot microsoft dot com." Some extensions are spoken like a word (com and gov) and some are spoken as letters (edu).

identifies Microsoft as a commercial member of the World Wide Web. (Yes, that's Microsoft's actual Web address.)

Every Web site is identified by an address in just that form, so whenever you see a www. something.com (or org, or gov, or whatever), you know the address represents a Web site you can visit whenever you want.

But how do you actually go about getting there? First, you connect to your service provider, and then you type the address you want in the browser's address bar, as shown in Figure 9-9.

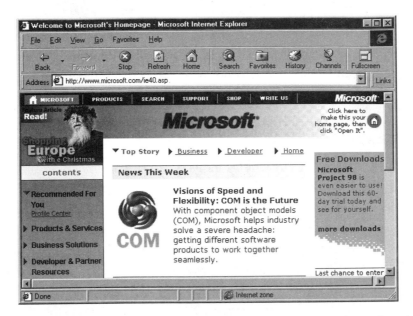

Figure 9-9.

The address bar, showing a Web address (www.microsoft.com) and the name of the page displayed (ie40.asp).

Press Enter when you finish typing, and off you go. If you have a service provider and Web access, try the following lesson on the CD for a real-life trip that includes a stop at Microsoft.

Try It

This lesson uses Internet Explorer to give you a hands-on experience with the Internet. To try it:

1. Restore the lesson window by clicking the PCs For Beginners button on the taskbar. (If the window is not currently minimized, start the CD either by inserting it in the CD-ROM drive or by clicking the shortcut to the CD on your desktop.)

2. If you restored the lesson window, click the Lessons button at the top of the window. If you started the CD, click Windows Overview to reach the list of Overview lessons.

3. Click *Exploring the World Wide Web.*

4. When you finish the lesson, minimize the lesson window.

"Earls" and How You Use Them

Once you've arrived at a site, you click links to skip from page to page—or even from site to site. If you look at the address bar as you move around in a site, you'll see that the display changes to show longer entries that look like this:

http://www.microsoft.com/games/puzzle/

This is what a link actually looks like. In cyberspace terminology, it's known as a *URL,* which is short for Uniform Resource Locator. Once always pronounced "you-are-ell," URL is increasingly being pronounced "earl" instead. The *http* part (pronounced "aitch-tea-tea-pea") that appears at the beginning essentially identifies the document as a Web page. Technically, http stands for *hypertext transfer protocol* and refers to the set of rules used by your browser to access and display the page. The remainder of the URL, reading from left to right between the slashes that act as dividers, identifies the site (*domain*) and any subdomains within the site, and it ends with the name—like a file name—of the page itself.

You don't have to either know or care how URLs are created or saved, or how your browser actually follows one to the page you want to see. If you become an active netizen, though, it helps a lot to know what a URL is, because people will often say things like, "check out this URL," or "what's the URL," or (since a lot of URLs are distributed via email) "send me the URL." Well, now you know.

Places to Go, Things to See

The people you know are among the very best sources of Web sites to visit. It's a rare "surfer" who doesn't want to spread the word about a particularly interesting site.

The World Wide Web is a gigantic place where you can find information on everything from ants to artichokes or zithers to zoos, so it's impossible for a whole book, much less a single chapter in a book, to even begin to show you around—especially because your interests are so individual. If you see or hear an advertisement or commercial that lists a Web site you think might be interesting, by all means check it out. That's a good way to start building up a "library" of Web sites you enjoy. And don't forget to add the ones you like to your list of favorites (click the Favorites menu, and then click Add To Favorites) so that you can go back with a simple click of the mouse.

As you saw in the lesson, another way to find information on the Web is to search for specific sites. When you do this, you use a rather amazing program called a *search engine*. To help you zero in on Web sites and pages that contain the information you're looking for, search engines rely on indexes—databases—of key words compiled by actual searches of what's out there on the Web. In some cases, these indexes are compiled by people. In other cases, the indexes are created by clever programs variously called *spiders* or *Web crawlers,* which roam the Web looking for juicy tidbits to bring home. Regardless of where or how they're found, those key words are what the search engines use to list pages that match your request for information.

Because search engines cover so much territory, they are a fantastic way to begin exploring the Web on your own. To have some fun and see just how much you can uncover, try another search, this time a *full-Web* search for something that interests *you*:

1. If necessary, start Internet Explorer and connect to your service provider, and then click the Search button:

So far, you haven't done anything that the lesson didn't show you. But notice that the top of the left pane shows a *link* (underlined so that you know what it is) that tells you *Choose a Search Engine*.

2. Click the link to display the following array of search tools. If the link opens to show you a menu, click the item that reads *List of all Search Engines.*

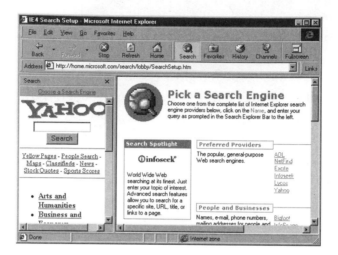

3. Scroll down in the right pane if necessary until you see the heading titled *Full-Web* above two items, AltaVista and HotBot.

4. Click AltaVista (a personal favorite), and the display in the left pane changes to this:

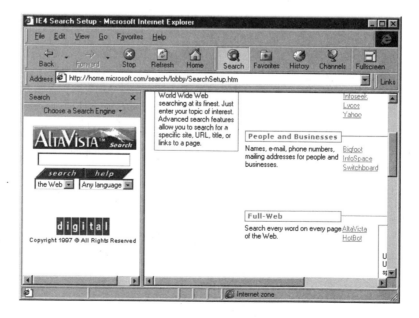

5. Now, tell AltaVista to search for something you want to see. Type a descriptive word or two. Try to be as specific as possible—for example, *ants* or *red ants* rather than *bugs*. Click the blue Search button in the left pane, and click Yes if a Security Alert dialog box appears to tell you you're about to send information to the "Internet zone" (the Internet at large). In a few seconds, the results of your search appear in the left pane.

6. Now go play. To see as much as possible, click the Maximize button in the upper right corner of the IE window, and then click away on whatever links in the left pane seem interesting to you. As you click, the Web page belonging to the link appears in the right pane.

7. As you poke around on the Web, add any two pages you want to your Favorites list so that you have something to work with when you take a look at another neat feature coming up. To add to your favorites, remember, you click the Favorites *menu* at the top of the window and then click Add To Favorites.

8. Ready to move on? OK, disconnect from the Web now if you want. What you're going to try next works both when you're connected and when you're not.

9. Click the Favorites button—the one with the folder icon. Now, the left pane lists your favorite sites, including the two you were asked to add in step 7.

10. As you roam the Web, adding to your favorites list, you'll find that the list can become both extensive and disorganized. Hah. Not for long. Point to the last item on your favorites list, whatever it happens to be. Now, drag the item up in the list a notch and drop it. As quickly as that, you can move favorites around to organize the list the way you want.

11. You can also reorganize favorites with the Favorites menu, and there's something even better you can do with them there. To try it, click the Favorites menu. When you do, the menu shown at the top of the next page opens.

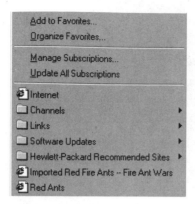

12. Click Organize Favorites, and this dialog box appears:

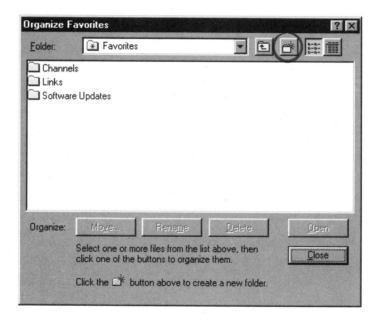

13. First, put the two links you added to your favorites in a folder of their own. The list stays a lot neater that way. Click the Create New Folder button (circled in the illustration) at the top of the dialog box. When the new folder appears in the large pane at the top, type a name for it and press Enter.

14. To move the two links to the folder, just drag them and drop them in. To confirm that they've been moved, double-click the new folder.

15. If you want to keep this folder and your links, go ahead and click the Close button in the dialog box now. You might, however, prefer to try removing them instead, just so you can see how to do it.

16. To remove both the folder and the links it contains, click the Up One Level button at the top of the dialog box. When the new folder appears in the pane, click it, and then click the Delete button. Confirm that you do want to delete the folder and its links, and in a second your entire experiment ends up in the Recycle Bin.

17. Close the Organize Favorites dialog box, and then close the Internet Explorer window.

Is It Safe?

Once you have Web access and the freedom to roam, there's one question that might sit in the back of your mind: Is it safe? You've probably heard or read a fair amount about safety and the Internet, especially with respect to kids and finance.

Basically, the Internet is just like anywhere else. Where kids are concerned, there are good places, some designed just for them, and there are not-so-good places, ones you wouldn't want any young people to see or go near. Figure 9-10 on the next page, for example, illustrates one of the good places. It's a popular chat room—a place where kids can go on line and "talk" to each other—run by Headbone Interactive, a maker of children's software.

Even though fairness might suggest that an adults-only site receive equal time here, that's left up to you and your imagination. Seek, and no doubt ye shall find....

If you have kids who might like to check out this site, they (and you) can find it at *www.headbone.com.* (By the way, the site is *monitored,* so you can rest easy about what's being said there—no meanies, no spoilers, and no real names allowed.)

In addition to self-monitored sites and those designed especially for children, various types of controls—similar to movie and television ratings—have been devised to help parents. IE, for instance, includes a Content Advisor that helps you control the types of content that can be viewed on your computer. Here's how to enable the Content Advisor.

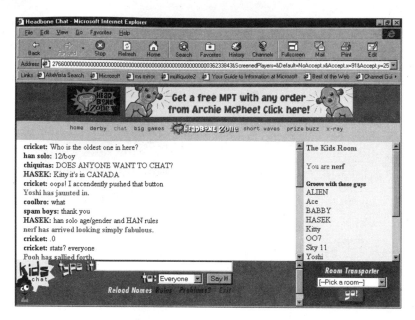

Figure 9-10.   *Illustration courtesy of Headbone Interactive.*

1. Click the Internet Explorer icon, open the View menu, and click Internet Options.

2. In the Internet Options dialog box, click the Content tab, and then click the Enable button in the Content Advisor section of the tab.

3. When you're asked for a Supervisor Password, type and confirm a password and then click OK. (And *don't* let the kids know what the password is.)

4. Creating a password brings up a Ratings tab. Click the category you want to control, and then move the Rating slider to the right, to whatever level of language, nudity, sex, and violence you consider acceptable. (The default, level 0, blocks the most content; the maximum, level 4, blocks the least and is therefore the most permissive.)

5. When you finish, click OK, and click OK again when a dialog box appears to tell you that Content Advisor is installed. (When you're not connected to the Internet, you might want to come back to Internet Options and disable Content Advisor—it can get a little intrusive sometimes.)

Ultimately, however, whether you rely on ratings or your kids' own common sense, remember that the best guides are parents themselves. If you have children, watch what they do and check the sites they want to visit. Stay involved, and never let them give out personal information.

As for finance, that depends on your judgment too. There are places, such as the online bookstore called Amazon.com, that are used comfortably by many people. To guarantee privacy, such sites take orders—and credit card numbers—over what is called a *secure server*. That's a computer on the merchant's end that receives all information in *encrypted* form, meaning that the information has been scrambled by software to make it unreadable by anyone but the receiving computer.

In addition, Web browsers including both Internet Explorer and Netscape Navigator include security features that let you know when your connection is secure and when it is not. And, too, security-conscious organizations and their servers rely on digital *certificates* that assure you of their good name, good intentions, and trustworthiness.

All told, however, if you have any misgivings about the Internet in combination with either your children or your finances, the best advice is simply: don't, at least until you're comfortable with the situation. Remember, you don't have to jump in the deep end. Tiptoe your way in, going only as far as you want, when you want. And just as you do in a strange city, watch where you go and what you do. A huge number of reputable, well-known organizations ranging from schools to government agencies to mall-type stores are all on the Web. They'll keep you plenty busy.

Communicating via the Internet

Figure 9-10 showed you a children's chat room. There are many such for adults, too—places where people communicate about all kinds of things from computers to games to more...personal...matters. The number one means of communicating on the Internet, however, is *email*. Some people live by and for it, and many find it the best way to keep in touch with family and friends scattered around the country or around the world. What's so great about email?

- It's fast—usually faster than "snail mail" sent via the post office.

- It's easy.

- It can be sent and read whenever you're in the mood.

- It does away with licking stamps and envelopes.

And when you connect to your service provider, it can lift your spirits to see a message saying *You have new mail.*

So how do you go about setting up email capability on your computer? The details will depend on the email program you use and on your service provider. Setting up can be very simple, or it can require a little help from you and your ISP. When you're setting up a mail *account,* for example, you might be asked to provide information such as the name of your *mail server* (the computer that collects and delivers your mail) or the name of your *newsgroup server* (the computer that provides you with access to mail postings from numerous interest groups on the Internet). Such information can be provided only by your ISP, so if you encounter such questions, don't frustrate yourself trying to find the answers. Write down what you need, and then don't be shy about calling your ISP for the answers.

You might have read about email services "going down" and causing misery to their users. Yes, it does happen. But not often, and the problem is usually resolved within a few hours to a few days. It's annoying and can result in lost messages, but given the amount of traffic and the hardware and software support involved, it's kind of understandable, too.

Sending Mail

Once you're set up for email, sending and reading your messages are equally simple and straightforward. First, on the assumption that you'll be eager to announce your "online-ness" to the world, take a look at sending mail. To get going, all you do is start your mail program and choose the service's "compose a new message" option. For example, starting Outlook Express, the email program that comes with Internet Explorer, opens a window like this:

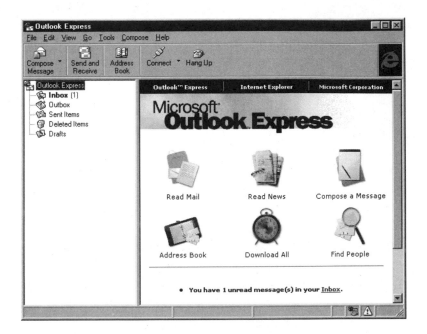

To create a message here, you would click the Compose Message button, to display this window:

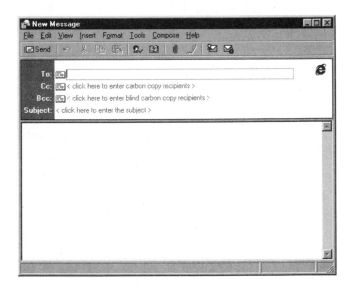

The top of this window is where you type the message *header,* which contains the information that will appear on your recipient's screen. The header is the electronic equivalent of writing a name and address on a letter envelope.

The only really essential part of the header is the *email address* of the person you're sending mail to. This is information you must either already know or be able to find out—for example, by consulting the program's equivalent of a phone book or address list. However you come by the address, it always takes the form:

emailname@destination

where *emailname* is the person's user name and *destination* is the place where the person receives email. The @ is also required; you type it by holding down the Shift key and pressing 2 in the top row of the keyboard. In addition to the main recipient (or recipients, because you can send mail to more than one person), you can also send a copy of the message to someone else by filling in the person's email address on the Cc: line. When you send a copy, the name of the person receiving the copy appears in the message header of both the recipient and the person you send the copy to. If, for whatever reason, you don't want the recipient to know that you sent a copy, type the email address of the person receiving the copy on the Bcc: (blind carbon copy) line instead.

Next—and this is always the polite thing to do—type a short description of your email on the Subject line. That way, the person you're mailing will know what the message is about. And finally, type the body of your message in the large open part of the window, and finish up by using the program's Send command.

So that you can see what email looks like, here's a sample message created in Outlook Express:

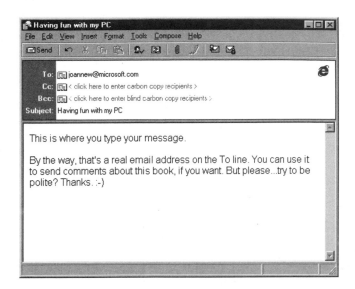

Reading Mail

In addition to giving you a way to compose and send messages, your email program (with the help of your electronic post office and mailbox, of course) also takes care of fetching your mail and displaying your messages for you. Just as your word processor and other applications go to great lengths to preserve every file you create—indeed, every character you type—your email program will be careful never to lose a piece of mail either by misplacing it or accidentally "forgetting" to save it. Although the features available to you depend entirely on the mail program you use, any self-respecting email software will ensure that you, and you alone, have the power to organize your messages and to delete them. The program, like a good dog, will fetch and then leave the thinking to you.

If an email program keeps both read and unread mail, however, you might be wondering how you can tell one from the other. It's easy. Typically, the program uses a visual cue to let you know which is which. In Outlook Express (and other email programs), for example, unread mail appears in boldfaced, dark type, whereas mail you've already read appears in normal type. Figure 9-11 on the next page shows what the *Inbox*—the collection point for your mail—looks like in Outlook Express.

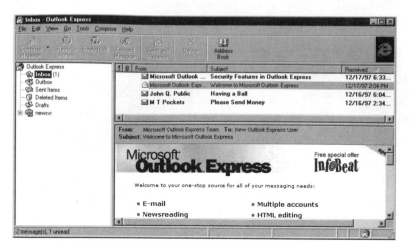

Figure 9-11.   *The electronic inbox in Outlook Express. (Just because you have email doesn't mean all your messages will be pleasant ones.)*

The easiest way to actually read your new mail is to simply start your mail program and use its Read Mail, Show New Mail, or Download New Mail option. (The actual name of the command, of course, will vary.) From there, either click or double-click the message you want to read. The mouse action depends on the program. In Outlook Express, for instance, clicking a message header in the top of the window causes the body of the message to appear in the lower portion of the window.

Once you've read a message, your email program should also give you ways to delete it (as with the Delete button in Outlook Express), reply to the sender (the Reply To Author button), reply to everyone listed in the header (the Reply To All button), or send it along to someone else (the Forward Message button). Experiment with your email program, and don't forget to consult its Help menu if you find yourself puzzled by some feature.

Other than that, have fun. Once you try email, you'll probably find you like it a lot.

Netiquette

The online world is often quite outspoken, sometimes even to the point of rudeness. Such behavior isn't any more acceptable in cyberspace than it is in the real world, although it's frankly easier to get away with because there's no face-to-face contact involved. Still, there are a few rules that people follow (or try to follow) when they go online—especially when they *post* email messages to large groups they've joined. If you plan on becoming an active *netizen,* here are some tips to help you get started:

- Don't type in ALL CAPITAL LETTERS. That's considered shouting.

- If you reply to a message, especially a long one, do everyone a favor by not resending the entire thing. Quote only the part you're responding to.

- If you respond to something in…fiery language, stop and take a breather before hitting the Send button.

- Don't send pointless messages, such as "This is a test. Anybody there?" You'll hear from a lot of people, but you won't like what they have to say.

- Don't create some huge, elaborate, graphic signature in some weird typeface, and don't include graphic images in your message unless you have to. Such things take time to download, and wasting people's time like this can cause a lot of irritation. In fact, many people check the size of a message before opening it; if it's too big, they delete it.

- Be nice. Just because it's the Information Superhighway doesn't mean that road rage is acceptable.

Finally, don't hesitate to let people know that you're a "newbie" on the Net. They'll be more inclined to explain and forgive mistakes…as long as you're willing to learn from them.

Active Channels: Push Me, Pull You

And now, before you move on to finding out what your choices are in the way of browsers and their functionality, take a look at something special offered by the version of Internet Explorer running on your computer. You already know that IE is closely tied to the Active Desktop, which has been allowing you to single-click your way through all the lessons and hands-on practices in the book. Where the Internet is involved, however, IE also supports a feature you'll probably find intriguing and might find highly desirable: *channels.*

What are channels? Comparable to the TV channels that deliver broadcasts to your home, these channels are a means of helping you find information on the Internet without having to go and search it out. Instead of waiting around for you to come to them, these channels represent special Web sites that are designed to deliver information to you and to update it periodically so that you're always able to see the latest and greatest they have to offer.

There's a good chance that you've been staring at the entry point to channels for quite some time now, if you've had Internet Explorer's *channel bar* sitting on the desktop:

(Your channel bar is probably vertical. The one illustrated has been prodded with the mouse into a side-to-side shape to save space on the page. It shows the same channels, though.)

As you can see, these channels give you access to a range of interesting Web sites, and all you do to see what they have to offer is click the channel button and, in some cases, *subscribe* to one that interests you. (Subscriptions are free, by the way, and require little more than a mouse click or two, so they're a no-risk kind of deal for you.) Rather than read about channels, however, take a look at what they have to offer. First let them tell you about themselves:

1. If the channel bar is on your desktop, click the button marked *channel guide*. If the bar is not on your desktop, click the View Channels button (marked with a small satellite dish) to the right of the Start button in the quick launch portion of the taskbar. When you do, this introductory tour should appear:

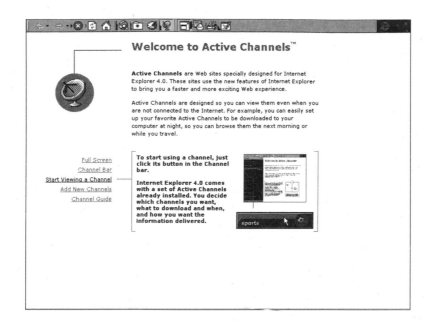

If this tour does not appear, don't despair. Click the Learn button near the upper left corner. You'll see this instead:

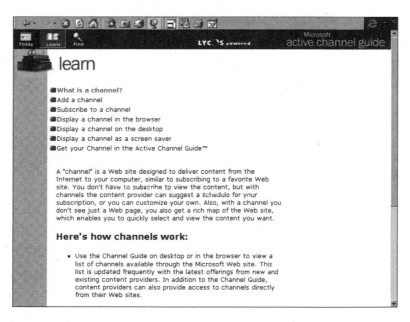

2. Whichever tour you see, take a few minutes to read up on the feature. These pages include links, so to see more, all you have to do is run the mouse over the text and click a link when the pointer turns into a hand.

3. When you've seen enough, close the window.

Now that you know what channels are and what they can do for you, take a final turn with the lesson CD.

Try It

There's a lesson on the CD that walks you through some hands-on with the Active Desktop and with channels. To try it out:

1. Restore the lesson window by clicking the PCs For Beginners button on your taskbar, and click the Lessons button. If the window is not minimized, start the CD by inserting it in your CD-ROM drive or by clicking the shortcut on your desktop, and then click your way to the Windows Overview lesson list.

2. Click the lesson titled "Exploring the Active Desktop."

3. When you finish the lesson, click the lesson window's Close button.

As you can tell by the buttons on the channel bar, there's a lot more to be seen in this area. If you like the idea of having information delivered to you instead of having to go out, find it, and fetch it, channels just might turn out to be just your cup of tea.

Choosing Your Browser (and Yes, You Do Have a Choice)

It's a fact that one person's delight might be another person's dislike. You've been using—and hopefully liking—Internet Explorer throughout this book. But a browser choice is ultimately a personal one, comparable to deciding whether you prefer Levis to Wranglers, or pizza to hamburgers. Because Internet Explorer and Netscape Navigator are both so well known, it could be that you also want to try Navigator. In addition, since some sites are better viewed with one, and other sites are better viewed with the other, you might want to be able to install both and choose between the two. Both options are fine and perfectly doable.

Netscape Navigator

Since IE is already installed on your computer, all you'll need is access to Navigator's setup program in order to install it, too. Installation is easy, so if you have a Navigator icon on your desktop, click it and follow directions from there. If a Navigator icon is not already on your desktop, ask your friends or your local computer store where you can get the browser. Once you have both browsers installed, just click the icon for the one you want to use each time you connect to the Internet. Answer Yes or No (your choice) if a dialog box appears and asks whether you want to make the program your main (default) browser.

Internet Explorer, Minus Active Desktop

On the other hand, if you want to keep Internet Explorer, either as your only browser or in addition to Navigator, but you prefer not to keep Active Desktop or Web View, that's easy too. Just remember that disabling both Active Desktop and Web View eliminates your ability to keep Active Channels on the desktop and to rely on the convenience of single-clicking your way through life. (Where you've been using a single click to open an icon, you'll be double-clicking instead.)

As you saw in the previous lesson, turning Web View on and off is a 1-2-3 proposition:

1. Right-click a blank part of the desktop.
2. Highlight Active Desktop on the pop-up menu.
3. Click View As Web Page to toggle it on or off.

And, although both Web View and Active Desktop make working with a computer more intuitive than the older Windows classic look, it could be that you still prefer Windows classic—perhaps because you use it on another computer or because that's still the way most people are doing it.

Again, the choice is yours, and it's one you can switch to and from as the mood takes you:

1. Open My Computer, click the View menu, and then click the Folder Options command.

2. On the General tab of the Folder Options dialog box that appears, click the work style you prefer. Single-clicking, as you've learned to do here, is Web style. To switch to Classic style, click that option. Or—if you're confident now—click Custom, click Settings, choose the exact settings you want, and click OK. Click OK to close the dialog box.

3. If you don't like working with your new settings, come back to the General tab and try something new. That's the Windows way, and it's a nice one.

Well, that's it. You've worked your way through a fairly long book and you've covered a lot of ground in the process, especially if you started out a little nervous or a little fearful. Here's hoping you can now sit back, smile, and say, "I came, I saw, and boy, I *conquered!*"

Salud.

Special Characters

A

B

N

O

P

Z

About the Author

JoAnne Woodcock is the author of several popular computer books, including *Understanding Groupware in the Enterprise, The Ultimate Microsoft Windows 95 Book,* and *The Ultimate MS-DOS Book,* all published by Microsoft Press. She is also a contributor to the *Microsoft Press Computer Dictionary.*

The manuscript for this book was prepared and submitted to Microsoft Press in electronic form. Text files were prepared using Microsoft Word 97 for Windows 95. Pages were composed by Microsoft Press using Adobe PageMaker 6.52 for Windows, with text in Melior and display type in Frutiger Condensed. Composed pages were delivered to the printer as electronic prepress files.

Cover Designer
Thomas Draper

Cover Illustrator
Thomas Draper

Interior Graphic Designer
Kim Eggleston

Interior Graphic Artist
Joel Panchot

Principal Compositor
Peggy Herman

Principal Proofreader/Copy Editor
Cheryl Penner

Indexer
Patty Schiendelman

Things are looking up!

Here's the remarkable, *visual* way to quickly find answers about Microsoft applications and operating systems. Microsoft Press® *At a Glance* books let you focus on particular tasks and show you with clear, numbered steps the easiest way to get them done right now.

Microsoft® Excel 97 At a Glance
Perspection, Inc.
U.S.A. **$16.95** ($22.95 Canada)
ISBN 1-57231-367-6

Microsoft® Word 97 At a Glance
Jerry Joyce and Marianne Moon
U.S.A. **$16.95** ($22.95 Canada)
ISBN 1-57231-366-8

Microsoft® PowerPoint® 97 At a Glance
Perspection, Inc.
U.S.A. **$16.95** ($22.95 Canada)
ISBN 1-57231-368-4

Microsoft® Access 97 At a Glance
Perspection, Inc.
U.S.A. **$16.95** ($22.95 Canada)
ISBN 1-57231-369-2

Microsoft® Office 97 At a Glance
Perspection, Inc.
U.S.A. **$16.95** ($22.95 Canada)
ISBN 1-57231-365-X

Microsoft® Windows® 95 At a Glance
Jerry Joyce and Marianne Moon
U.S.A. **$16.95** ($22.95 Canada)
ISBN 1-57231-370-6

Microsoft Press® products are available worldwide wherever quality computer books are sold. For more information, contact your book or computer retailer, software reseller, or local Microsoft Sales Office, or visit our Web site at mspress.microsoft.com. To locate your nearest source for Microsoft Press products, or to order directly, call 1-800-MSPRESS in the U.S. (in Canada, call 1-800-268-2222).

Prices and availability dates are subject to change.

Microsoft® Press

Get quick, easy answers— anywhere!

Microsoft® Excel 97 Field Guide
Stephen L. Nelson
U.S.A. $9.95   ($12.95 Canada)
ISBN 1-57231-326-9

Microsoft® Word 97 Field Guide
Stephen L. Nelson
U.S.A. $9.95   ($12.95 Canada)
ISBN 1-57231-325-0

Microsoft® PowerPoint® 97 Field Guide
Stephen L. Nelson
U.S.A. $9.95   ($12.95 Canada)
ISBN 1-57231-327-7

Microsoft® Outlook™ 97 Field Guide
Stephen L. Nelson
U.S.A. $9.99   ($12.99 Canada)
ISBN 1-57231-383-8

Microsoft® Access 97 Field Guide
Stephen L. Nelson
U.S.A. $9.95   ($12.95 Canada)
ISBN 1-57231-328-5

Microsoft Press® Field Guides are a quick, accurate source of information about Microsoft Office 97 applications. In no time, you'll have the lay of the land, identify toolbar buttons and commands, stay safely out of danger, and have all the tools you need for survival!

Microsoft Press® products are available worldwide wherever quality computer books are sold. For more information, contact your book or computer retailer, software reseller, or local Microsoft Sales Office, or visit our Web site at mspress.microsoft.com. To locate your nearest source for Microsoft Press products, or to order directly, call 1-800-MSPRESS in the U.S. (in Canada, call 1-800-268-2222).

Prices and availability dates are subject to change.

Microsoft®Press

Quick Course®

books—first-class training at economy prices!

"...perfect to help groups of new users become productive quickly."

—PC Magazine

Perfect for educators and trainers, Quick Course® books offer streamlined instruction for the new user in the form of no-nonsense, to-the-point tutorials and learning exercises. The core of each book is a logical sequence of straightforward, easy-to-follow instructions for building useful business documents—the same documents people create and use on the job.

U.S.A.	**$24.99**
U.K.	£22.99
Canada	$34.99
ISBN 1-57231-726-4	

U.S.A.	**$14.99**
U.K.	£13.99
Canada	$20.99
ISBN 1-57231-727-2	

U.S.A.	**$14.99**
U.K.	£13.99
Canada	$20.99
ISBN 1-57231-725-6	

U.S.A.	**$14.99**
U.K.	£13.99
Canada	$20.99
ISBN 1-57231-723-X	

U.S.A.	**$14.99**
U.K.	£13.99
Canada	$20.99
ISBN 1-57231-722-1	

U.S.A.	**$14.99**
U.K.	£13.99
Canada	$20.99
ISBN 1-57231-724-8	

Microsoft Press® products are available worldwide wherever quality computer books are sold. For more information, contact your book or computer retailer, software reseller, or local Microsoft Sales Office, or visit our Web site at mspress.microsoft.com. To locate your nearest source for Microsoft Press products, or to order directly, call 1-800-MSPRESS in the U.S. (in Canada, call 1-800-268-2222).

Prices and availability dates are subject to change.

***Microsoft*Press**

Take productivity in stride.

Microsoft Press® *Step by Step* books provide quick and easy self-paced training that will help you learn to use the powerful word processor, spreadsheet, database, desktop information manager, and presentation applications of Microsoft Office 97, both individually and together. Prepared by the professional trainers at Catapult, Inc., and Perspection, Inc., these books present easy-to-follow lessons with clear objectives, real-world business examples, and numerous screen shots and illustrations. Each book contains approximately eight hours of instruction. Put Microsoft's Office 97 applications to work today, *Step by Step*.

Microsoft® Excel 97 Step by Step
U.S.A. $29.95   ($39.95 Canada)
ISBN 1-57231-314-5

Microsoft® Word 97 Step by Step
U.S.A. $29.95   ($39.95 Canada)
ISBN 1-57231-313-7

**Microsoft® PowerPoint® 97
 Step by Step**
U.S.A. $29.95   ($39.95 Canada)
ISBN 1-57231-315-3

Microsoft® Outlook™ 97 Step by Step
U.S.A. $29.99   ($39.99 Canada)
ISBN 1-57231-382-X

Microsoft® Access 97 Step by Step
U.S.A. $29.95   ($39.95 Canada)
ISBN 1-57231-316-1

**Microsoft® Office 97 Integration
 Step by Step**
U.S.A. $29.95   ($39.95 Canada)
ISBN 1-57231-317-X

Microsoft Press® products are available worldwide wherever quality computer books are sold. For more information, contact your book or computer retailer, software reseller, or local Microsoft Sales Office, or visit our Web site at mspress.microsoft.com. To locate your nearest source for Microsoft Press products, or to order directly, call 1-800-MSPRESS in the U.S. (in Canada, call 1-800-268-2222).

Prices and availability dates are subject to change.

Microsoft Press

IMPORTANT—READ CAREFULLY BEFORE OPENING SOFTWARE PACKET(S). By opening the sealed packet(s) containing the software, you indicate your acceptance of the following Microsoft License Agreement.

MICROSOFT LICENSE AGREEMENT

(Book Companion CD)

This is a legal agreement between you (either an individual or an entity) and Microsoft Corporation. By opening the sealed software packet(s) you are agreeing to be bound by the terms of this agreement. If you do not agree to the terms of this agreement, promptly return the unopened software packet(s) and any accompanying written materials to the place you obtained them for a full refund.

MICROSOFT SOFTWARE LICENSE

1. GRANT OF LICENSE. Microsoft grants to you the right to use one copy of the Microsoft software program included with this book (the "SOFTWARE") on a single terminal connected to a single computer. The SOFTWARE is in "use" on a computer when it is loaded into the temporary memory (i.e., RAM) or installed into the permanent memory (e.g., hard disk, CD-ROM, or other storage device) of that computer. You may not network the SOFTWARE or otherwise use it on more than one computer or computer terminal at the same time.

2. COPYRIGHT. The SOFTWARE is owned by Microsoft or its suppliers and is protected by United States copyright laws and international treaty provisions. Therefore, you must treat the SOFTWARE like any other copyrighted material (e.g., a book or musical recording) except that you may either (a) make one copy of the SOFTWARE solely for backup or archival purposes, or (b) transfer the SOFTWARE to a single hard disk provided you keep the original solely for backup or archival purposes. You may not copy the written materials accompanying the SOFTWARE.

3. OTHER RESTRICTIONS. You may not rent or lease the SOFTWARE, but you may transfer the SOFTWARE and accompanying written materials on a permanent basis provided you retain no copies and the recipient agrees to the terms of this Agreement. You may not reverse engineer, decompile, or disassemble the SOFTWARE. If the SOFTWARE is an update or has been updated, any transfer must include the most recent update and all prior versions.

4. DUAL MEDIA SOFTWARE. If the SOFTWARE package contains more than one kind of disk (3.5", 5.25", and CD-ROM), then you may use only the disks appropriate for your single-user computer. You may not use the other disks on another computer or loan, rent, lease, or transfer them to another user except as part of the permanent transfer (as provided above) of all SOFTWARE and written materials.

5. SAMPLE CODE. If the SOFTWARE includes Sample Code, then Microsoft grants you a royalty-free right to reproduce and distribute the sample code of the SOFTWARE provided that you: (a) distribute the sample code only in conjunction with and as a part of your software product; (b) do not use Microsoft's or its authors' names, logos, or trademarks to market your software product; (c) include the copyright notice that appears on the SOFTWARE on your product label and as a part of the sign-on message for your software product; and (d) agree to indemnify, hold harmless, and defend Microsoft and its authors from and against any claims or lawsuits, including attorneys' fees, that arise or result from the use or distribution of your software product.

DISCLAIMER OF WARRANTY

The SOFTWARE (including instructions for its use) is provided "AS IS" WITHOUT WARRANTY OF ANY KIND. MICROSOFT FURTHER DISCLAIMS ALL IMPLIED WARRANTIES INCLUDING WITHOUT LIMITATION ANY IMPLIED WARRANTIES OF MERCHANTABILITY OR OF FITNESS FOR A PARTICULAR PURPOSE. THE ENTIRE RISK ARISING OUT OF THE USE OR PERFORMANCE OF THE SOFTWARE AND DOCUMENTATION REMAINS WITH YOU.

IN NO EVENT SHALL MICROSOFT, ITS AUTHORS, OR ANYONE ELSE INVOLVED IN THE CREATION, PRODUCTION, OR DELIVERY OF THE SOFTWARE BE LIABLE FOR ANY DAMAGES WHATSOEVER (INCLUDING, WITHOUT LIMITA-TION, DAMAGES FOR LOSS OF BUSINESS PROFITS, BUSINESS INTERRUPTION, LOSS OF BUSINESS INFORMATION, OR OTHER PECUNIARY LOSS) ARISING OUT OF THE USE OF OR INABILITY TO USE THE SOFTWARE OR DOCUMENTA-TION, EVEN IF MICROSOFT HAS BEEN ADVISED OF THE POSSIBILITY OF SUCH DAMAGES. BECAUSE SOME STATES/ COUNTRIES DO NOT ALLOW THE EXCLUSION OR LIMITATION OF LIABILITY FOR CONSEQUENTIAL OR INCIDEN-TAL DAMAGES, THE ABOVE LIMITATION MAY NOT APPLY TO YOU.

U.S. GOVERNMENT RESTRICTED RIGHTS

The SOFTWARE and documentation are provided with RESTRICTED RIGHTS. Use, duplication, or disclosure by the Government is subject to restrictions as set forth in subparagraph (c)(1)(ii) of The Rights in Technical Data and Computer Software clause at DFARS 252.227-7013 or subparagraphs (c)(1) and (2) of the Commercial Computer Software — Restricted Rights 48 CFR 52.227-19, as applicable. Manufacturer is Microsoft Corporation, One Microsoft Way, Redmond, WA 98052-6399.

If you acquired this product in the United States, this Agreement is governed by the laws of the State of Washington.

Should you have any questions concerning this Agreement, or if you desire to contact Microsoft Press for any reason, please write: Microsoft Press, One Microsoft Way, Redmond, WA 98052-6399.

System Requirements

- Multimedia PC with a Pentium 75 MHz or higher microprocessor
- Pre-installed Microsoft® Windows® 95 (8 MB RAM)
- 15 MB of available hard disk space (88 MB is required if you need to load Microsoft Internet Explorer 4)
- Double-speed or better CD-ROM drive
- Super VGA display with 256 colors or better
- Microsoft Mouse or compatible pointing device
- Windows-compatible sound board and headphones or speakers

System Requirements for Trial Version of Microsoft Money 98

- Personal Computer with a 486 50 MHz or higher microprocessor (Pentium 90 MHz or higher recommended)
- Microsoft Windows 95 operating system or Microsoft Windows NT® Workstation 4.0 or higher (will not run on earlier versions of Windows)
- 12 MB of memory (RAM) on Windows 95; 16 MB of RAM on Windows NT (16 MB on Windows 95 and 24 MB on Windows NT recommended)
- 25–55 MB of available hard disk space (55 MB required if Microsoft Internet Explorer 3.02 or higher and the ActiveMovie™ API are not already installed; both are required and contained on the enclosed CD)
- CD-ROM drive
- VGA graphics card or compatible video graphics adapter and 256-color monitor
- Microsoft Mouse or compatible pointing device
- 9600 baud or faster modem (28,800 baud or faster recommended) to use online features
- Audio board and speakers or headphones required for audio

NOTE: **The Microsoft Money 98 Financial Suite trial version included is intended for U.S. use only.** Due to differences in currency formats, data entered into this trial version is not compatible with international versions of Money 98.

Note also that Internet functionality requires an Internet service provider (ISP). Connect time charges may apply. All software required is included in Microsoft Money 98. Compatible with all Windows-compatible ISPs. Online Banking/Brokerage options vary by financial institution; some require Internet access while others offer direct dial up. Contact your financial institution for program details. To use Online Bill Payment, you need a checking account with any financial institution in the US.